THE POWER OF COMPETENCY-BASED TEACHER EDUCATION

Report of the Committee on National Program

Priorities in Teacher Education

Benjamin Rosner
Chairman

Final Report
Project No. 1-0475
Grant No. OOEG-0-71-2849

This work has developed under a contract with/or
grant from the U.S. Office of Education, Department
of Health, Education and Welfare. However, the content
does not necessarily reflect the position or policy
of that Agency, and no official endorsement of these
materials should be inferred."

THE POWER OF COMPETENCY-BASED TEACHER EDUCATION

Report of the Committee on National Program
   Priorities in Teacher Education

Benjamin Rosner, Chairman
 City University of New York

Saul B. Cohen
 Clark University

M. Vere DeVault
 University of Wisconsin

H. Del Schalock
 Oregon State System of Higher Education

Charles E. Stewart
 Detroit Public Schools

Richard L. Turner
 Indiana University

Carol K. Tittle, Research Associate
 City University of New York

CONTENTS

PREFACE

The Committee on National Program Priorities in Teacher
Education was formed during March and April, 1971. The
Committee included persons knowledgeable about the programs
under consideration, as well as representatives from a large
city school system and an urban teacher education institution.[1]

The procedures followed by the Committee included preparation and discussion of papers by Committee members, meetings to discuss papers with Task Force '72 and Bureau of
Educational Personnel Development personnel, and the circulation of abstracts of Committee papers to external critics and
individuals within the Office of Education. In addition,
papers on special topics were commissioned for Committee
consideration.

One of the Committee's first tasks was the clarification of definitions of protocol materials, training materials,
training complexes, performance-based certification, and the
Models for Elementary Teacher Education. Although major
papers had been prepared for BEPD and USOE on each of these

---

[1] M. Vere DeVault and H. Del Schalock, the Models for
Elementary Teacher Education; Richard L. Turner, Protocol
and Training Materials; Saul B. Cohen, Training Complexes;
Charles Stewart, Detroit Public Schools; and Benjamin Rosner,
City University of New York.

five programs,[2] the Committee prepared brief working descriptions which are presented in Appendix A.

In an effort to define possible relationships among the five programs, and to present an integrated program for development in teacher education, Committee members prepared papers which were discussed at a series of meetings (March 23-24; April 15; April 26-27; and June 1-2). Revisions and additions were made by the authors based on Committee discussions. These papers appear as Chapters 3 through 8.

Critical comments were solicited from a number of individuals knowledgeable about and concerned with the problems of teacher education. This group of critics was assembled from names suggested by Committee members, as well as by BEPD staff. The individuals who commented on abstracts of the papers represented community groups, school administrators and teachers, critics of teacher education, associations for professional groups in education, and university faculty and administrators--both in education and the liberal arts. These comments were used to guide individual members of the Committee in revising their proposals, and to provide a context within which to evaluate the recommendations of the Committee as a whole. The abstracts and a summary of the comments received are presented in Appendix D.

---

[2]
Training Complexes: Ad Hoc National Advisory Committee on Training Complexes, Final Report. Clark University: Training Complex Administrative Center, July 1, 1970.
Protocol and Training Materials: Smith, B. Othanel. Teachers for the Real World. Washington, D.C.: AACTE, 1969.
Models for Elementary Teacher Education: Burdin, J., and Lanzillotti, K. (Eds.) A Reader's Guide to the Comprehensive Models for Preparing Elementary Teachers. ERIC: EDRS--ED 034 076, 1969, 353 pp.
Performance-Based Certification and Teacher Education: Massanari, K. "Performance-Based Teacher Education: An Annotated Bibliography." Inquiries to Dr. Karl Massanari, AACTE Associate Director, Suite 610, One Dupont Circle, Washington, D.C. 20036.

The special papers commissioned by the Committee are presented in Appendices B and C. These papers dealt with the idea of educational specialty boards (Myron Lieberman) and the role of the disciplines in the training of teachers (Alan C. Purves).

The initial planning of the Committee's activities provided for the development of a cost analysis; however, time did not permit the anticipated analysis and, as a result, individual authors prepared some cost data. The main recommendations in the body of the report are accompanied by tentative cost estimates.

The Committee wishes to express its appreciation for the assistance and encouragement given by William L. Smith, Acting Associate Commissioner of the Bureau of Educational Personnel Development; and to Don Davies, Acting Deputy Commissioner for Development; who initiated Task Force '72 within BEPD and whose interest was critical to the establishment of the Committee and definition of its purpose.

The helpful criticism of B. Othanel Smith and Donald Orlosky is also appreciated, as well as the comments received from the many individuals who read and reviewed the Committee program proposals.

The Committee also wishes to acknowledge the services of staff members of Educational Testing Service who assisted the Committee by ensuring the competent administration of the project: Mrs. Peggy Bates, who initially coordinated the project; Mrs. Charlotte Farley, who was responsible for contract negotiation; and Mrs. Carol McKnight, who was responsible for exercising fiscal control for the project and who served as liason between ETS and the Committee.

The Power of Competency-Based Teacher Education

CHAPTER 1

RATIONALE FOR COMPETENCY-BASED
TEACHER EDUCATION AND CERTIFICATION

This section of the report presents a number of questions on the design of teacher education programs which arose during the course of Committee discussions. The answers to the questions provide a rationale for competency-based teacher education leading to the recommendations presented in the final section.

1. What criteria can be used to assess the effectiveness of teacher education programs?

One of the most complex problems confronting teacher education is the identification of criteria by which to assess the effectiveness of trainees and teacher training programs. This complexity derives in part from philosophic considerations about the appropriateness of specific criteria for objectives of the teacher education program, and in part from technical issues bearing on the feasibility of collecting analyzing, and interpreting data pertinent to criteria of program effectiveness.

LEVELS OF CRITERIA

Richard L. Turner

The levels of criteria presented here are intended to make clear the points at which feedback to teacher education programs could be generated and the points at which performance-based certification could occur. These levels are applicable to all teacher education programs which are performance and data based, such as the Elementary Models, as well as those which are oriented toward pupil outcomes.

3

Criterion Level 1

At the highest level, the criterion against which teachers (or teaching) might be appraised consists of two parts. The first part is observation of the acts or behaviors in which the teacher engages in the classroom. The observations must be conducted with a set of instruments which permit classification of teacher behaviors in both the cognitive and affective domains. The second part is systematic analysis of the level of outcomes achieved by the teacher with the pupils he teaches. Outcomes in both the cognitive and affective domains must be included. Because of variation in the entry behaviors of students and variations in teaching contexts, the residual outcomes in pupil behavior (the terminal behaviors corrected for entry behaviors and moderating variables) should be used as the criterion measures. To be placed at Criterion Level 1, the above two-part appraisal of teacher performance must be conducted over a relatively long period of time, probably at least two years (on a time sampling basis), with both the observational and residual pupil behavior components assessed during each of the years. The reason for the two-year period is that both teacher and pupil behavior are open to some random fluctuation and care must be taken to obtain a sufficient sample of behavior from both sources to assure fair conclusions.

There are two principal uses to be made of the data obtained at Criterion Level 1. First, if the data are obtained during the teacher's first three years of teaching experience, they might be used to certify that the performance of the teacher is at a level to warrant relatively permanent certification. How permanent the certification might be depends on whether a cyclical pattern of certification (e.g., recertification once every ten years) becomes a socially acceptable policy, or whether life certification remains as the socially acceptable policy. Second, if observational data on teachers as well as pupil performance data are included in the criterion, the relationships between the observed behavior of teachers and pupil performances can be utilized as general feedback to teacher education programs. These relationships will indicate which types of teacher behavior are most likely to be influential in bringing about particular changes in pupil behavior. Teacher education programs would thus be able to increase the amount of confidence they have in intermediate performance criteria which involve only the actions of the teacher.

4

Criterion Level 2

This criterion level is identical to Criterion Level
1 except that a shorter performance period is involved.
Some current thinking about performance-based certification, such as that in the Comfield Model,[1] appears to
assume a teacher performance period of one year or less,
after which initial certification might be awarded.
Although a performance criterion involving the latter
period of time is at a high criterial level, it is sufficiently open to error attributable to fluctuations in
teacher behavior, pupil behavior, and the teaching context that it inspires considerably less confidence than
does criterion performance based on wider sampling over
a longer period of time.

Criterion Level 3

This criterion level differs from Criterion Levels
1 and 2 in that pupil performance data are eliminated
from the criterion. Judgments about competence or proficiency are thus based on the observable behaviors of
the teacher rather than on the pupil outcomes associated
with these behaviors. Nonetheless, this criterion level
is still performance based in the sense that the teacher
actually does engage in teaching and is gauged on the
quality of his professional actions. How "good" or
valid this criterion level is depends almost wholly on
whether empirical relationships between teacher actions
and pupil performance have been established through research or through data obtained by use of Criterion
Levels 1 and 2.

The degree of confidence in Criterion Level 3 lies
in the upper intermediate range. This criterion seems
to yield sufficient confidence to be useful in the provisional certification of teachers. It is also highly
useful in teacher education programs since one may
observe teachers to determine explicitly whether they
evidence the behaviors which a particular teacher preparatory program claims to be producing. Observation
data at this criterion level provide evidence about the
efficacy of the teacher education program.

---

[1]Schalock, H. D. and Hale, R. Jr. (Eds.) A Competency Based, Field Centered Systems Approach to Elementary
Teacher Education, Vol. II. Final Report for Project No.
89022, Bureau of Research, Office of Education, U.S.
Department of Health, Education, and Welfare, 1968.

Criterion Level 4

This criterion level differs from Criterion Level 3 in that both the teaching context and the range of teacher behavior observed are restricted. The context might be a typical micro-teaching context involving a few pupils or even peers acting as students. The teacher behavior observed would be restricted to a few categories in the cognitive or in the affective domain.

This criterion lies in the intermediate range, but it inspires very modest confidence and cannot be construed as an adequate basis for performance-based certification. Rather, its utility lies in providing feedback about the efficacy of particular segments of the teacher education program and in providing diagnostic feedback to students about their own progress. It tells whether a student has acquired certain behaviors or skills and whether he can integrate these skills under specially arranged teaching conditions.

Criterion Level 5

This criterion level differs from Criterion Level 4 in that the teacher need not perform before live students (simulated students would be satisfactory). He must, however, be able to produce or show in his behavior at least one teaching skill, e.g., probing.

This criterion inspires virtually no confidence as a criterion for performance-based certification, but it is very useful for providing information about the efficacy of training materials or subcomponents of instructional modules or of courses. Its "goodness" as a criterion depends in substantial part on the extent to which the skill being assessed can be shown to be a skill associated with pupil performance outcomes as established either by research or by use of data obtained in using the higher order criteria noted above.

Criterion Level 6

This level differs from Criterion Level 5 in that the teacher need not engage in producing a performance, but rather, only show that he understands some behavior, concept, or principle germane to teaching. Within this criterion several levels of "understanding" can undoubtedly be identified. These levels of understanding can be operationalized by varying the kinds of problems the teacher is asked to respond to in accord with some

6

type of taxonomy, such as Bloom's.[2] Like Criterion Level 5, the utility of this criterion is primarily to provide data about the efficacy of particular program components within teacher education. Similarly, its "goodness" as a criterion level depends largely on the extent to which knowledge of particular behaviors, concepts, or principles may ultimately be shown to be useful in predicting attainment of one or more of the higher criterion levels.

Criterion Level 6 is concerned with the effects of a training program on improvements in teacher knowledges and understandings. Criterion Levels 5 and 4 are concerned with the effects of teacher training on improvement in pedagogic skills under laboratory or simplified training conditions. Criterion Level 3 addresses itself to the effects of training on a teacher's behavior under actual classroom conditions. The concept of pupil change as a criterion of teacher effectiveness is introduced at Criterion Levels 2 and 1. Criterion Level 2 is concerned with changes in pupil behavior that can be effected in a relatively short time period (one or two weeks) and under actual classroom conditions. Criterion Level 1 is concerned with the long range effects of teacher behavior on changes in pupil achievement and well-being.

There are fundamental differences between Criterion Levels 6 through 3, and Criterion Levels 2 and 1. Criterion Levels 6 through 3 focus directly on the impact of training on teacher behavior. Criterion Levels 2 and 1 are concerned with both the effects of training programs on teacher behavior and with the effects of teacher behavior on pupil performance.

Because teacher educators accept responsibility for the preparation of educational personnel whose performance under actual classroom conditions results in desired changes in pupil behavior, some teacher educators argue that Criterion Levels 1 and 2 are the most appropriate levels for assessing the effectiveness of training programs. (See, for example, Chapter 6 for a discussion by Schalock of the use of pupil change as the criterion for assessing the effectiveness of trainees and teacher training programs.) The emphasis on pupil change in criterion Levels 1 and 2, therefore, equates accountability in teacher education with school accountability. Teacher education, however, does not address itself

---

[2]Bloom, B. S. (Ed.) Taxonomy of Educational Objectives. Handbook I: Cognitive Domain. New York: David McKay Company, 1956.

7

directly to the modification of pupil behavior. It is uncertain, therefore, whether measures of school accountability are appropriate measures of the effectiveness of teacher education programs. On the other hand, teacher education does accept responsibility for the modification of teacher behavior. Training programs should, therefore, be held accountable for changing teacher behavior.

The most appropriate criterion level for accountability in teacher education is Criterion Level 3, i.e., demonstrations of change in teacher competency under actual classroom conditions. Moreover, the evaluation of individual trainees at Criterion Level 3 provides the evidence for competency-based certification at the entry and permanent certification levels.[3] The use of Criterion Level 3 to evaluate the effectiveness of teacher education programs and to evaluate the competencies of individual trainees for certification integrates the objectives of the teacher education programs with the requirements for professional service in the classroom. It is important, therefore, that teacher education introduce evaluation procedures at Criterion Level 3 to measure the degree of mastery attained by personnel in the program. Unfortunately, few inservice or preservice programs have carefully articulated the competencies to be acquired, nor does teacher education possess the necessary instruments to measure change in specific competencies. For these reasons, evaluations of the effectiveness of programs have relied almost exclusively upon subjective appraisals of quality by students (teachers) participating in the programs. Clearly, teacher education must adopt a more rigorous approach to the definition and evaluation of its training curricula.

Although Criterion Level 3 carries the major weight in competency-based teacher education and certification, Criterion Level 1 is the major criterion for assessing the validity of the competencies which comprise the teacher education curriculum. Assessing the validity of the curriculum is a research function. In this sense, the research criterion (Criterion Level 1) monitoring the selection of teacher competencies is distinct from the accountability criterion (Criterion Level 3) monitoring the effectiveness of the training program.

See also DeVault in Chapter 4, for a statement identifying three competency levels for certification and Turner, Chapter 8, for an extension of performance-based certification to master-supervisory teachers.

2. What steps must be taken to assure the validity of teacher education curricula?

A valid teacher education curriculum provides for the acquisition of teacher competencies with demonstrated capacity to effect changes in pupil behavior. The validity of the teacher education curriculum can only be established through research which relates teacher behavior to pupil behavior.

Three conditions must be present before the content of a teacher education curriculum can be validated: a) the training program must provide evidence of teacher growth in specified competencies; b) the school system must provide evidence of pupil progress in the attainment of specific educational objectives; and c) a research design must be developed to study the relationship between the two sets of measures. If either set of measures is missing, it is impossible to carry out the research essential to establish the validity of the teacher education curriculum.

At the present time the lack of specificity about the competencies included in the teacher education curriculum and the lack of measures to establish degrees of teacher competency preclude consideration of the relationship between the effects of teacher training and change in pupil behavior. It is essential, therefore, that teacher educators concentrate on the development of measures of teacher competency and contribute to the development of measures of school effectiveness. Unless such measures are developed, the validity of teacher education curricula will remain unknown.

3. In the absence of studies relating teacher behavior to school effectiveness, how are the competencies that comprise teacher education curricula to be identified?

Although the number of studies examining the relationship between teacher behavior and school effectiveness is small, some studies have been conducted and these offer a useful starting point.[4] In addition, specific concepts and skills may be identified by examining the research and theory of the behavioral and social sciences, by examining the content and skill emphases of specific school curricula, and by conducting inquiries of master teachers and teacher trainers.

---

[4]See, for example, Rosenshine, B. and Furst, N. "Research on Teacher Performance Criteria," in Smith, B. O. (Ed.) Research in Teacher Education. Englewood Cliffs, N.J.: Prentice-Hall, 1971.

The important point here is that the knowledges and skills
identified must be made explicit. In addition, mastery of the
curriculum to a specified level of expertise must also be made
explicit and confirmed with appropriate instruments.

4. Assuming the identification of a competency-based teacher
   education curriculum, what conditions are necessary in
   order to facilitate its mastery?

Four conditions must be met in order to facilitate the
acquisition of specified teacher competencies: a) the development of measures to ascertain the degree of mastery acquired; b) the development of instructional or training materials
to guide the study and practice of particular competencies;
c) the development of opportunities to study and practice with
little delay in the evaluation of performance; and d) the
development of incentives to motivate the acquisition of knowledges and skills. Each of these conditions is discussed
below.

a. Measures of Competency

The significance of measures of competency in the evaluation of teacher education programs has already been discussed. In addition, the role of measures of teacher behavior
in studies relating teacher competencies to pupil performance
has also been discussed. It is important to note here that
measures of specific competencies must establish degrees of
expertise in order to serve as standards of attainment for
teachers in the program. These standards would enable both
teachers and teacher trainers to determine the need for additional study or practice in order to attain specified levels
of mastery. By establishing levels of expertise, measures
of competency tend to motivate higher levels of performance.
As incentives, as yardsticks for training, and as tools for
research, measures of teacher competency are indispensable
elements of the teacher education program.

b. Instructional Materials

The efficiency with which specific knowledges and skills
can be acquired is a function of the effective integration of
both human and material instructional resources. Teacher
trainers are handicapped without instructional materials.
Instructional materials can give concepts concrete meanings,
they can display skills in different settings at various
levels of expertise, they may be independent of the level of
knowledge or level of skill of the teacher trainer, and they
can be field tested to assure their utility. The development
of instructional materials to facilitate the acquisition of

10

teacher competencies is essential to an effective program of
teacher education.

c. Opportunities for Practice

A third condition for the development of competencies is
provision for study and practice under supervision. In this
regard the teacher trainer has a number of critical functions:
1) to participate with other teacher trainers in designing
the teacher education curriculum; 2) to acquire and maintain
an adequate supply of instructional or training materials;
3) to acquire and maintain instructional equipment, e.g.,
audio-visual equipment; 4) to direct trainees to appropriate
materials and equipment for the study or practice of specific
knowledges and skills; 5) to provide a model for behavior;
6) to administer measures of competency in order to determine
the need for additional study or practice; 7) to report to the
trainee the results of systematic assessment in order to recommend additional study and practice or to recommend the
acquisition of new knowledges or skills; and 8) to participate in the evaluation of teacher education programs and the
field testing of instructional materials or equipment.

The various roles of the teacher trainer clearly establish the need for a highly trained clinical instructor. Although each of the roles is important, the training and evaluation functions implied by items 4, 6, and 7 are probably
the most critical for effective instruction. The need to
maintain instructional materials and equipment suggests the
desirability of a teacher education laboratory. In addition,
opportunities to practice at Criterion Level 3 will require
access to live pupils. Obviously the teacher training program
will need to develop organizational structures and facilities
to coordinate trainers, materials, equipment, pupils, and
trainees. It seems reasonable to suggest that these organizational structures and facilities will have to take into
account the opportunities and limitations unique to each
local situation.

d. Incentives for Learning

The major difference in the design of training programs
for inservice and preservice teachers is the matter of incentives. Preservice teachers are motivated by the need to
acquire certification in order to seek employment. Inservice
teachers are employed, although large numbers of inservice
teachers are motivated by the need to obtain continuing or
permanent certification in order to maintain their positions.
The problem of motivating staff development is most acute
for the majority of the nation's two million experienced
teachers who require no further certification to hold their

jobs. An effort must be made, therefore, to develop incentive systems for experienced educational personnel. Unless these incentive systems are developed, it is unlikely that fully certified teachers will seriously engage themselves in programs of inservice training.

5. If certification requirements are the major incentives for preservice and relatively inexperienced inservice personnel, is it possible to introduce additional certification requirements for more experienced personnel?

It is doubtful whether additional certification requirements can be introduced for senior educational personnel. Teacher unions are unlikely to agree to the introduction of additional certification procedures which would threaten the job security of the majority of their members. It is possible, however, to introduce certification which would not affect job security but which would have direct impact on senior educational personnel. Such certification would need to identify the bearer with a special expertise and entitle him to special salary increments. If experienced personnel can acquire new status and additional income through special certification as "master-level teachers" or teacher trainers, such certification would be an effective incentive for staff development.

For several reasons, new certification for master-level teachers or teacher trainers is best introduced on a national scale outside the legal framework of state certification. First, establishing special certification on a national level could be initiated immediately without modification in each state's legal certification procedures. Second, special "extra-legal" status permits experimentation with competency-based certification without tampering with legal certification procedures. Finally, special national certification could assure uniform standards of excellence by establishing Educational Specialty Boards to govern the certification process. These boards would consist of distinguished scholars, educators, school board members, representatives of professional teacher associations, representatives of civil rights organizations, and other prominent citizens. The development of Educational Specialty Boards would exercise great influence on the establishment of high standards of teacher competence in the public interest.[5]

---

[5]For additional discussion of Educational Specialty Boards, see M. Lieberman, Appendix B; and also The Future of Public Education. Chicago: University of Chicago Press, 1960

6. What other incentives might be introduced?

Other incentives are clearly necessary for certified personnel who are not at the "master-level teacher" or teacher trainer level. Some effective incentives for fully certified personnel include: a) staff development programs to meet immediate teacher needs; b) released time for inservice training; c) elimination or reduction of other direct training costs; d) salary increments associated with post-certification training; and e) the introduction of group "profit sharing" for efficient or highly effective school performance, that is, "performance contracting" with inservice personnel. The elimination of pay raises, threatened salary reduction, or threatened job loss are unlikely to prove useful incentives. In periods of teacher shortage such threats are idle; in periods of teacher surplus such threats invite union protest and defensive action, weaken staff morale, and create tense school-community management-labor relationships.

7. Are incentives the only factor differentiating in-service from preservice teacher education?

Although the need to introduce incentives for fully certified personnel appears to be the major factor differentiating inservice from preservice teacher education, it is not the only factor. In a given period of time, only a specified level of expertise in a limited range of knowledge and skill can be developed. The objective of inservice education is to build upon existing knowledges and skills and to encourage the development of new knowledges and skills. Inservice education, therefore, differs from preservice education in the range of knowledges and skills encompassed by the training program and in the levels of mastery anticipated. Accordingly, the scope of instructional materials and measures of competency will also differ.

8. What program development priorities are impiled by the preceding discussion?

The major need of preservice and inservice teacher education is the identification of teacher competencies associated with the attainment of educational goals. Unless teacher education can determine which teacher competencies are related to which instructional objectives (and under what conditions), investment in teacher training is speculative. It is imperative, therefore, that a major research effort be undertaken to identify the competencies associated with criteria of school effectiveness.

Although teacher education cannot be postponed until the requisite research has been conducted, new program development in teacher education should emphasize procedures and products that are compatible with research needs. The primary requirement for both training and research is the definition of teacher competencies. Accordingly, program development in teacher education must be directed towards the operational definition of the training curriculum.

Operationally, teacher education curricula are defined by measuring instruments and instructional materials. Despite their limitations, tests and textbooks--measurements and materials--have traditionally served to make concrete the objectives and procedures of educational programs. Teacher education is no exception. The development of instruments to identify beginning, experienced, and master levels of teacher competency, and the development of compatible instructional materials to define the elements of teacher education curricula are the highest priorities for teacher education training and research.

In addition to rigorous operational definition of the teacher education program, inservice teacher education must develop incentives for experienced teachers who no longer require certification to maintain their jobs. The development of special competency-based certification for master-level teachers or teacher trainers is, therefore, a high priority for inservice teacher education. Such "extra-legal" competency-based certification for master-level teachers not only establishes career incentives for teacher training, but also serves the instrumentation needs of teacher behavior research at superior levels of knowledge and skill.

An additional need for both preservice and inservice training is the provision of opportunities to practice under supervision, with little delay in the evaluation of performance. Opportunities to practice will require access to instructional materials and, frequently, pupils. The evaluation of performance would be facilitated by audio and video-tape recordings. A training laboratory to house instructional materials and equipment would seem desirable.

As noted earlier, there are several criterion levels to guide observation of the trainee's performance. During training, assessments of performance could be made under simulated conditions (Criterion Levels 5 and 4). At the conclusion of a training period, assessment of competencies should be made in actual classroom settings (Criterion Level 3). The location of the laboratory in a university setting would be compatible with the observational requirements of Criterion Levels 5 and 4, but would not easily accommodate the need for assessment at Criterion Level 3. (Universities would need to make additional provision for the observation and recording of student

14

performance in the actual classroom setting.) Conversely,
the location of an observational facility in a school setting would easily accommodate Criterion Level 3, but the cost
of the laboratory facility would have to be justified in
terms of the number of students under observation at Criterion
Levels 5 and 4.

The decision to locate a laboratory in a university or
school, therefore, needs to take into account at least two
factors: maximizing the number of preservice and inservice
students having access to the facility, thereby reducing laboratory costs per trainee; and maximizing opportunities for
practice under actual conditions, thereby minimizing the dis-
continuity between performance assessed at Criterion Level 4
and performance assessed at Criterion Level 3. It would be
useful to encourage schools and universities to develop prototypes for laboratory installations to reflect a number of
solutions to this cost/effectiveness problem.

9. In what ways can the elements of an effective competency-
    based teacher education program be organized to reflect
    the strengths of local settings?

The major elements of a competency-based teacher education program include trainers, trainees, pupils, instructional
materials, measures of competency, and evaluation procedures.
Specifically, the training program will need to provide for:

   1) installation of audiotape and videotape facilities
       to record demonstrations of pedagogic skills under
       simulated and real instruction settings (a training
       laboratory);

   2) use of materials for training teachers in the diag-
       nosis and interpretation of pupil behavior;

   3) use of materials for skill training;

   4) access to, and involvement of, teacher trainers
       skilled in observing and evaluating teacher competen-
       cies;

   5) access to school pupils;

   6) access to advanced work in subject or specialized
       fields;

   7) development of evaluation procedures, relating assess-
       ments of laboratory-based knowledges and skills to
       measures of competency in the classroom (Criterion
       Level 3);

8) access to and use of instruments and devices for competency-based certification at Criterion Level 3.

The organization of these elements must reflect the opportunities and constraints--the strengths and limitations of the local situation. Accordingly, the particular structure or facility for "housing" the essential elements of the teacher education program should be left to local discretion. This is not to suggest the desirability or expectation of hundreds of variations in structure nor is it to suggest that federally-funded programs ignore Federal guidelines.[6] It is, rather, to suggest that administrative or organizational structures must be valid for the setting and population served. In this sense, organizational structures should be "contextually valid." In addition, laboratory facilities for training must be justified by the development of competent educational personnel as defined by Criterion Levels 5, 4, and 3. The location and installation of laboratory facilities, therefore, must be cost/effective.

In all likelihood several major organizational structures will emerge to reflect the strengths of local organizations and satisfy cost/effectiveness criteria. These structures will draw upon the personnel and material resources of state education departments, universities, school systems, community agencies, and industrial organizations in local areas. In addition, the structures will necessarily take into account the number of trainees to be served, trainee costs associated with access to the program, and institutional costs associated with program maintenance.

Four types of organizations which seem sensitive to considerations of cost/effectiveness and local resources are identified below.[7] The first three are described in greater detail in Committee papers.

---

[6]Federal guidelines, however, might be written to encourage the pooling of Federal resources in order to facilitate program development more responsive to local needs. This issue is discussed in more detail by C. Stewart in Chapter 7.

[7]Additional descriptions of organizational structures are contained in the Models for Elementary Teacher Education. See, for example, Florida State University's portal school; Michigan State University's clinical school network; Syracuse University's teaching centers, located in the public schools; Teachers College's inquiry school; University of Pittsburgh's clinical settings; University of Toledo's multi-unit elementary school; in Burdin, J. and Lanzillotti, K., op. cit.

Organization 1. State-wide Consortium of Centers. This type of organization has been described in detail by Schalock (Chapter 6). It is characterized by a central coordinating agency, typically a state department of education or agency of the state department. The agency coordinates a number of regional centers, involving public schools and one or more universities, supported on a cost sharing basis. Under this type of organization, instruction and certification procedures would occur in regional centers, while support services would be coordinated by the central agency. A substantial strength of the organizational scheme is that the state department, the certifying agency, plays an intrinsic and important role. By assuming a state-wide focus, the model both recognizes the state as the primary political entity in the financing, preparation, and certification of teachers and attempts to deal directly and realistically at a state and individual program level with matters such as program development and implementation, coordination, certification, and resource management. Although the structure is applicable to all states, it is probably best suited to states in predominantly rural regions which have universities located around the state in small urban areas. In any circumstances, a strong, active state department is required.

Of special significance in the proposed plan is the commitment to level 2 criteria for purposes of initial certification (demonstrated ability to bring about desired short-term learning outcomes in children under regular teaching conditions) and level 1 criteria for permanent certification (demonstrated ability to bring about desired long-term learning outcomes in children under regular teaching conditions). In addition, the model strongly emphasizes the need to establish teacher education on a sound empirical base. The model also attempts to incorporate the ideals of a program that is student oriented, personalized, and open to input from a broad, representational decision making base.

Organization 2. The University Center. This type of center has been described by DeVault (Chapter 4). It is characterized by the presence of a university which coalesces with a number of school systems. Although the center resulting from this coalition is not necessarily based directly in the university, the university is the dominant agency and would be expected to play the key leadership role in the development and support of the center. This organization is best suited to universities which have by tradition held a strong service orientation to the state and to their locales, e.g., the mixed urban-rural areas of the Midwest.

DeVault describes the Competency-Based Program Center as a context for the implementation of teacher education in both the university and the public schools. The coordination of interinstitutional cooperation is the responsibility of an administrative unit called a Training Complex. The development, coordination, and implementation of instructional aspects of the teacher education program is a function of the university.

The heart of the university-based center is the organizational structure of an Elementary Teacher Education Model. This structure is hypothesized to serve equally well for secondary and elementary education programs. The structure requires the broad support of interinstitutional cooperation. The model is predicated on the feasibility of a heavily mediated instructional program and requires staff in both the university and the public schools willing to explore and implement new roles.

DeVault refers to the need for coordination of material development through a systems approach. This approach emphasizes a careful study of needs and development strategies, including cost/effectiveness and cost/benefit data, and careful attention to assessment of the continued effectiveness of materials within the Competency-Based Program and Centers.

Organization 3. The School Training Center. This type of organization has been described by Rosner (Chapter 5). It is characterized by a set of exemplary public schools, each of which has extended capability for training personnel and conducting inservice programs. In this organizational framework the schools are committed to a training function and share with the university responsibility for the preservice and inservice education program.

The governance of the program is the responsibility of a parity board including representatives of the university, the schools, professional teacher association, and community agencies.[8] The location of laboratory training centers in both the school and the university facilitates the acquisition of teacher competencies at Criterion Level 3.[9]

───────────

[8]See S. Cohen, Chapter 3,,for a discussion of the governance of a Training Complex.

[9]See also R. Turner, Chapter 8, for a discussion of university and field based laboratories in preservice and inservice programs.

The emphasis on developing schools with exemplary curricula is intended to relate the resources of teacher training institutions to the instructional needs of pupils in inner-city schools. This organization is probably best suited to major urban areas in which there are many large schools easily accessible to both preservice and inservice teachers.

Organization 4. The Technology-Based Individual Study Center. This type of organization has not been described in Committee papers. The Committee has discussed the key features of such centers and believes that the technological capability to support them exists. There would be a need for a special study and planning group involving personnel from the electronics and communications industries as well as school and university personnel to further develop the technology center idea.

The technology-based center should serve two functions. First, it should make quality training programs available to individual teachers and small groups in areas with remote schools, such as the Mountain States and the Great Plains. Second, it should serve as an important shared resource for other types of centers in more heavily populated areas. Although each such center would be expected to vary somewhat, several key features would appear in each with greater or lesser emphasis according to circumstances.

A. A telecommunications network. The network would consist of a closed circuit or microwave television system together with telephone connections so that both transmission and feedback could occur. Such a network would probably work best as a shared resource of several centers so that each could transmit or receive special instructional programs according to its own resources. As a device to aid in the instruction of individual teachers, the network would probably focus on transmission with limited telephone feedback since the cost of line rentals for extended sender-receiver interactions may be prohibitive.

B. Instruction by correspondence. The use of correspondence for instructional purposes is probably far below full potential in teacher education programs. A major advantage of appropriately developed and packaged instructional materials is that they can form the core of a program for individual teachers through correspondence. Correspondence study coupled with television transmission capabilities from the center may enhance the potential of each type of medium while preserving relatively low costs. In most instances, the costs of television receiving equipment and the video tape recording and playback equipment required for training are within the capabilities of individual school systems and, indeed, already exist in many.

19

C. Shared time computer assisted instruction. The feasibility of CAI for instruction and training teachers depends on individual schools and systems being able to use terminals regularly with pupils as well as with teachers. For example, the capability of the Plato system at the University of Illinois extends both to teachers and to pupils. By participating in a larger system on a shared time basis, a technological training center would be responsible primarily for assuring the presence on the computer of needed instructional materials and for managing communications and instructional costs. The cost of capital investment in computer hardware could be largely avoided by the center, which would rent the hardware on a shared time basis.

D. On-line, real-time computer monitoring of instruction. A forthcoming development in computer utilization lies in the use of small, inexpensive real-time computers which are connected on-line to classrooms. One method of using this type of system is to code the behavior of the teacher in the classroom as it occurs, transmit it to the computer for virtually instant analysis, and transmit the analyzed behavior back to the teacher so that he or she has continuous feedback about his own instruction. A second method is to transmit the events in the classroom by television or by telephone (audio only) to the center, where they are coded and, after immediate computer analysis, returned to the teacher where they may be continuously displayed by oscilloscope. Either of these methods permits precise training of teachers since feedback can be delivered on an almost instantaneous basis. The second method has the advantage of being able to employ coders in a central location from which many classrooms can be observed on a time-sampling basis.

The central advantage to a system of this type is that it has the capability to eliminate the direct supervision of teachers in training and replace it with a more effective method of changing teacher classroom behavior at Criterion Level 3. Its disadvantage is that the classrooms in which supervision is to occur must be properly equipped for transmitting behavior data and transmission lines to these rooms must be rented.[10]

---

[10]Although the over-all costs of establishing a technology-based individual study center cannot be determined without a special planning study, the cost data developed in conjunction with the Wisconsin Elementary Teacher Education Project suggests that the development and maintenance of a single center might require between $1M and $2M per year over a five year period. See Wisconsin Elementary Teacher Education Project Feasibility Study: Pricing and Economic Analysis, Vol. VI. Madison, Wisconsin: University of Wisconsin, January, 1970.

10. In what ways do the program development priorities identified above relate to the purpose of Task Force '72 and
CNPPTE?

As indicated in the introductory section, the Committee
and Task Force '72 were asked to make recommendations concerning the future development of protocol and training materials, training complexes, performance-based certification,
and the Elementary Models. The program development priorities discussed above include instrument development, instructional materials development, contextually valid organizational structures, cost/effective laboratory facilities for
training, and incentives for inservice personnel. The discussion also notes that program development for training must
be compatible with requirements for research. Accordingly,
the priority assigned to instrument development at Criterion
Level 3 is compatible with competency-based certification.
Similarly, the emphasis on instructional materials is congruent with the development of protocol and training materials.
The requirement that program development for instructional
materials be consistent with instrument development establishes the necessary articulation between competency-based teacher
education and competency-based teacher certification. Establishing incentives for experienced inservice personnel is an
operational extension of competency-based certification to
emphasize the highest levels of knowledge and skill available to the field.

Although the Committee's emphasis on instruments, materials, and incentives is completely compatible with the concept of the performance base and protocol and training materials, the Committee regards the "training complex" as a generic term for a contextually valid organizational structure
with cost/effective laboratory facilities for competency-
based teacher education and certification. Accordingly, the
Committee tends to deemphasize the concept of "neutral ground"
and emphasizes instead the concept of "contextual validity"--
organizational structure to reflect the opportunities and
strengths of the local setting. Finally, the emphasis in the
Elementary Models on modular instructional units, evaluation
of student performance against specific mastery criteria, and
the systematic integration of training and research for continuous curriculum renewal is reflected in the Committee's
stress on teacher behavior research, the emphasis on program
development to facilitate both training and research, and the
priority accorded operational definitions of teacher competencies for training and certification. The Elementary Models
also provide descriptions of organizational structures which
may be "contextually valid" for teacher training.

21

11. <u>What program development sequence is implied by these priorities</u>?

It is clear from the preceding discussion that the immediate needs of both training and research are served best by the development of instruments and instructional materials. Because competency-based certification is completely dependent upon instruments to assess knowledges and skills at both the preservice and inservice levels, instrument development for certification purposes must be initiated immediately. Moreover, because the development of Educational Specialty Boards for highly skilled and experienced teachers or teacher trainers offers an essential incentive for inservice teacher education, instrument development for competency-based certification at the highest level of knowledge and skill should also be initiated immediately.

As much as competency-based certification is dependent upon instruments, competency-based training is dependent upon instructional materials. Efficient and effective training cannot be instituted until the knowledges and skills that comprise the training program are defined. It is essential, therefore, that the protocol and training materials programs already underway be maintained. However, instructional materials development must be closely related to the development of instruments. They should, in fact, be developed simultaneously or at least derive from the same set of knowledge and skill specifications. In this manner training and certification reinforce and support one another.

The development of a modest supply of field tested instructional materials will probably require a period of two to three years. For this reason the installation of training laboratories should proceed slowly, with more time allotted to planning and development than is usually available. The immediate need in establishing training laboratories is not for full-scale training operations but for the design of cost/effective laboratory prototypes and the development of a variety of contextually valid organizational structures. These laboratory prototypes and structures would serve as models for other institutions in similar settings. In addition, they would serve as field testing centers for materials and instrument development, for pilot projects in competency-based certification, and for development as examining centers for the Educational Specialty Boards.

12. <u>In what ways do the program development priorities relate to priorities established in the Office of Education and the Bureau of Educational Personnel Development</u>?

The program priorities established by the Office of Education for the Bureau of Educational Personnel Development include: a) the improvement of the quality of educational personnel available to children and youth from low-income, racially and culturally isolated populations; b) the improvement of educational personnel serving the needs of handicapped children; and c) the improvement of educational personnel serving the needs of children between the ages of three and nine.

In addition to these general program priorities, specific BEPD program objectives include: a) the development of a career ladder in teaching which includes paraprofessional personnel; b) the introduction of an undergraduate teacher preparation program with emphasis on the integration of the liberal arts and professional education; c) the improvement of inservice education through the establishment of teacher centers; and d) the development of alternative training programs with the emphasis on innovation.

CNPPTE program development priorities appear to be compatible with the program objectives and priorities of the Office of Education and BEPD. CNPPTE strongly advocates program development to establish the conditions essential to competency-based teacher education and certification. The development of instruments, instructional materials, laboratory facilities for training, and incentives for inservice teachers offers an opportunity for a major test of the hypothesis that competency-based teacher education and certification will improve the preparation of educational personnel at the paraprofessional, preservice, and inservice levels. Further, within the framework of the general program development strategy, specific program development priorities are established addressed to the needs of low income, racially and culturally isolated preschool, elementary, and secondary school pupils. These priorities include establishing laboratory training facilities in depressed areas, proposing instrument and material development for bilingual teachers, and encouraging the location of master-level teachers or teacher trainers in ghetto schools by salary incentives for Board certified personnel. Other instances of compatibility with OE and BEPD priorities are included in the five year program development plan presented in the next section.

CHAPTER 2

RECOMMENDATIONS FOR COMPETENCY-BASED
TEACHER EDUCATION AND CERTIFICATION

The Committee on National Program Priorities in Teacher
Education recommends a major test of the power of competency-
based teacher education to improve the performance of educational personnel in the nation's schools. To implement this
recommendation, an integrated program development effort must
be undertaken. The elements of this program include:

a) a committee for program planning and coordination;

b) training laboratories for educational personnel;

c) instructional materials for concept and skill attainment;

d) instruments to define competencies in actual classroom settings; and

e) career development for master-level teachers and
   teacher trainers.

The elements of the program are described in greater
detail in the following sections. Tables 1-5 present costs
associated with the five year development plan. [1]

Program Planning

The creation of a committee on program planning and coor-

---

[1]The Committee wishes to be on record as recommending a
full-scale research effort to investigate the relationships
between teacher competencies and the attainment of school
objectives. The recommendations contained in this report provide essential elements for this research program and under-
score the interdependence of training and research. No attempt
has been made, however, to define the scope of research or
to estimate the research budget.

dination is essential to the development and maintenance of general program integrity. The Committee believes that competency-based teacher education and certification are critical to the revitalization of educational personnel development and strongly advocates a coordinated program development strategy to test the power inherent in the concept. As indicated in Table 1, the planning and coordination committee could design an evaluative research study to test the competency-based program on a broad scale; would recommend or carry out special studies; and would disseminate information and, in general, assist BEPD to establish the conditions vital to the program's success. The Committee recommends the allocation of $.3M per year for five years, or $1.5M for program planning and coordination.

Table 1.   FIVE YEAR PROGRAM DEVELOPMENT PLAN: COMPETENCY-BASED TEACHER EDUCATION AND CERTIFICATION*

Year	Program Planning and Coordination	Training Laboratories	Instructional Materials	Instruments	Career Development	Total
1	.3**	4.5	1.0	.75	.3	6.85
2	.3	23.0	2.0	1.00	1.3	27.60
3	.3	22.5	4.5	1.00	1.6	29.90
4	.3	14.5	5.5	2.00	3.3	25.60
5	.3	10.5	6.0	.75	6.5	24.05
Total	1.5	75.0	19.0	5.50	13.0	114.00

To establish a program planning and coordination committee to assure the unification of the competency-based teacher education program development effort (provides for special studies and reports--e.g., in Year 1 a survey of existing laboratory designs and development of specifications/cost estimates for alternative designs; recommends funding for special projects; disseminates information on the program; etc.)

* The budget estimates included in Tables 1-5 do not reflect a rigorous cost analysis and should be regarded as general guidelines. In particular, it should be noted that the estimates do not provide for indirect costs.

** Dollars in millions

To establish 100 training laboratories with minimal training
capacity of 20,000 educational personnel per year

To develop, field test, package, and distribute 1000 units of
instructional material for concept and skill attainment

To develop approximately 250 school-based criterion measures
leading to competency-based certification at the paraprofessional, provisional, and permanent certification levels

To develop a career line in teaching by establishing Educational Specialty Boards offering professional competency-
based certification to master-level teachers and teacher trainers

Training Laboratories

A fundamental component of competency-based teacher education and certification is the development of training laboratories to facilitate practice under real and simulated
instructional conditions. These laboratories would be part
of an organizational structure for teacher education and would
contain the equipment and materials for the evaluation of
trainee performance. In addition, the training laboratories
would collect and transmit data pertinent to competency-based
certification, would participate in the field testing of instructional materials, would evaluate the success of preservice
and inservice training against the criteria of classroom performance, and would participate as examination centers for
the Educational Specialty Boards.

The Committee recommends the establishment of one hundred
(100) training laboratories (TLs) with a training capacity of
at least 20,000 educational personnel per year at an average
cost of $.75M per laboratory. The distribution of training
laboratories should be flexible. Individual laboratories
might be located in universities or schools; school-university
consortia might make application for the installation of TLs
in both schools and universities; and state or city education
agencies might plan for the distribution of clusters of TLs
on a state-wide or city-wide basis. It is anticipated that
a number of these TLs would be distributed across the four
organizational structures described on pages 17-20. This distribution should provide for several replications of each of
the state, university, school, and technology-based organizational structures. Accordingly, the support base for each
organizational prototype would be obtained by multiplying the
per laboratory cost by the number of laboratory units required
to establish the organizational structure.

The development of 100 TLs would occur over a five-year
period.

as indicated in Table 2. During Year 1, for example fiscal
1973, up to 100 school-university or school-university-state
department consortia would be funded for planning "contextually
valid" organizational structures, including the location of
TLs on a cost/effective basis. Approximately $4.5M would be
required to support the planning activities.

During the second year, consortia would complete TL
specifications and install equipment. Approximately $23M would
be required to install 100 TLs during Year 2, fiscal 1974.
Year 3, fiscal 1975, has been allocated to staff development,
pilot projects, and field testing. The Committee estimates
$22.5M as necessary for these functions. Finally, during
Years 4 and 5, fiscal 1976 and 1977, the TLs would be approa-
ching optimal operating efficiency; that is, training at
least 200 educational personnel each, engaging in recording
and reporting services for certification, evaluating the training program, and examining master-level teachers and teacher
trainers for Board certification. Approximately $25M has been
allocated to TL operations during the fourth and fifth years.

Table 2. TRAINING LABORATORIES FOR EDUCATIONAL PERSONNEL

Year	Planning	Installation Field Testing Materials Maintenance	Staff Develop- ment	Records Reports	Evalu- ation	Total
1	2.5*	--	--	1.0	1.0	4.5
2	--	20.0	--	2.0	1.0	23.0
3	--	10.0	7.5	3.0	2.0	22.5
4	--	5.0	2.5	4.0	3.0	14.5
5	--	2.5	--	5.0	3.0	10.5
Total	2.5	37.5	10.0	15.0	10.0	75.0

Purpose: To establish approximately 100 training laboratories
with a minimal training capacity of 20,000 educational
personnel per year

Functions: Training, certification (Criterion Level 3), field
testing of materials and instruments, evaluation,
and record keeping

*Dollars in millions

27

Individual laboratory development and operations

Year 1 Plan, coordinate school-university operations, design
        preliminary specifications for laboratory facili-
        ties--$25,000
Year 2 Complete specifications and install laboratory--$200,
        000
Year 3 Train staff, conduct pilot projects, participate in
        field testing of materials and instruments--$175,000
Year 4 Operate laboratory and continue field testing acti-
        vities--$75,000
Year 5 Maintain equipment and materials and continue field
        testing activities--$25,000

Evaluation ($100,000): includes staffing, planning, com-
    puter programming and analysis, and program evaluation at
    Criterion Level 3
Records and Reports ($150,000): includes collecting and
    summarizing data for competency profiles and reporting for
    certification

Overall, $75M appears to be the minimal level of funding
essential to the development of 100 training laboratories for
competency-based teacher education and certification over a
five-year period. It should also be noted that the program
development schedule outlined above takes cognizance of the
two to three years lead time required for the preparation of
instructional materials and instruments. If competency-based
teacher education and certification is to succeed, BEPD cannot anticipate full competency-based operational services until the requisite materials and criterion measures have been
developed.

Instructional Materials

The rationale for competency-based teacher education and
certification has clearly underscored the importance of developing instructional materials for concept and skill attainment.
The Committee recommends that $20M be allocated for the devel-
opment, field testing, packaging, and distribution of approximately 1000 units of instructional material over a five-year
period. The Committee further recommends that the development
of these instructional materials be guided by committees of
school and college personnel responsible for the development
of competency-based teacher education in the training laboratories. The formation of these committees will serve to sensitize school and college faculty to their use and prepare
them for the necessary field testing operations. Finally, the
Committee recommends that priorities for material development
take into account the training needs of paraprofessionals,

28

the needs of elementary school teachers in the teaching of
reading and mathematics, and the needs of bilingual teachers
working with children who speak English as a second language.

Table 3 suggests a materials development program which
provides approximately 200 units of instructional material
for field testing, packaging, and distribution to 100 TLs
during the third year of development--a schedule compatible
with the field testing capability of TLs during their third
year of developmental operations--and approximately 700-750
field tested units for distribution to TLs during full competency-based operations. By the termination of the five-
year materials development program, 1000 units will have been
in use in competency-based teacher education programs across
the country. Regardless of the number of TLs installed, the
availability of 1000 units to facilitate the development of
understandings and skills will have a marked impact on the
design of teacher education programs throughout the nation
and may stimulate the private sector to develop additional
instructional materials. The development of instructional
materials by private sector is particularly important,
given the need for periodic revision of materials.

Table 3. INSTRUCTIONAL MATERIALS DEVELOPMENT

Year	Develop & Field Test	Package & Distribute	Total
1	1.0*	--	1.0
2	2.0	--	2.0
3	4.0	.5	4.5
4	4.0	1.5	5.5
5	4.0	2.0	6.0
Total	15.0	4.0	19.0

Purpose: To develop, field test, package, and distribute
approximately 1000 units of instructional material
for concept and skill attainment

Budget provides for field testing and distribution of materials to approximately 100 training laboratories.

*Dollars in millions

29

Instrument Development

No factor is more crucial to the success of competency-based teacher education than the method of assessing the mastery of concepts and skills. The preparation of instruments to define performance criteria is the sine qua non of competency-based certification. The Committee cannot emphasize too strongly the needed development of measures of teacher performance in the classroom.[2] If BEPD had to support a single effort to establish competency-based teacher education, it should invest in the development of instruments to assess teacher competencies.

Table 4 presents an instrument development schedule to prepare approximately 250 competency measures over a five-year period. All the measures are to be developed for use in actual classroom situations; i.e., assessments of teacher competency are to be made in the presence of pupils, at Criterion Level 3. The cost of instrument development at Criterion Level 3 is estimated as $5.5M.[3] No other investment in teacher education would yield the same dollar benefit.

During the five-year period, the development of approximately 250 instruments might be distributed among certification levels as follows: paraprofessional personnel (30); provisionally certified personnel (160); and permanently certified personnel (60). Areas of competency to be assessed would probably include; general elementary (reading, mathematics, etc.); early childhood; bilingual; and high school English and mathematics. The specific allocation of instruments across levels of certification and areas of competency would be made by committees of teacher educators--both school and university personnel--who would also participate in the identification of classroom instructional skills. (It should be noted that the design of the instrument blueprint should closely follow the design of the instructional materials blueprint, or vice versa. There is little point in generating instructional materials and standards of attainment that do not address the same set of competencies.)

------

[2] For futher discussion of school-based measures of teacher competency, see B. Rosner, Chapter 5.

[3] This budget does not provide for instrument development appropriate for Criterion Levels 6, 5, and 4. An additional $10M could be projected to assess knowledges and skills at these levels.

Table 4. INSTRUMENT DEVELOPMENT

Year	Project Adminis- tration	Plan- ning	Develop- ment	Train- ing and Dissem- ination	Installa- tion and Utiliza- tion	Total
1	.2*	.5	--	.05	--	.75
2	.25	--	.6	.15	--	1
3	.25	--	.6	.15	--	1
4	.25	--	1	.5	.25	2
5	.25	--	--	--	.5	.75
Total	1.2	.5	2.2	.85	.75	5.5

Purpose: To develop approximately 250 school-based criterion measures leading to competency-based certification at the paraprofessional, provisional, and permanent certification levels

*Dollars in millions

The preparation of instruments at the high school level, and the specific subject fields at the elementary level, would also involve university faculty from the liberal arts. The instrumentation part of the program thus offers the opportunity to involve the disciplines in the definition of competencies needed by teachers. The blueprint to develop the instruments would need to take into account a diversity of curricula in schools and universities and thus provide for the development of tasks representing various points of view of the competencies important for teachers. This would yield a set from which schools, universities, and state education agency consortia could select the instruments related to their objectives.

The need to coordinate all phases of instrument development--to assure the efficient allocation of resources, to maintain uniformly high standards of quality, and to facilitate liaison with training laboratories and BEPD--clearly underscores the importance of vesting responsibility for instrument development in the hands of a program planning and coordination committee empowered to subcontract with a consortium of instrument developers. Regardless of the form of project direction, the overall instrument development effort must be tightly controlled.

Career Development

The specific recommendations identified above establish the conditions essential to competency-based teacher education for personnel aspiring to provisional or permanent competency-based certification. In order to assure the impact of competency-based staff development for fully certified teachers, the Committee recommends the establishment of Educational Specialty Boards. The Educational Specialty Boards would offer a competency-based certificate to highly skilled master-level teachers or teacher trainers. These certificates would be awarded by the Board operating outside the legal framework for state certification. Individuals acquiring Board certificates would be recognized as among the most competent teachers or teacher trainers in the nation, and would be entitled to special salary increments. The status of Board certification and the right to special salary increments would offer experienced teachers considerable incentive for career development.

The Committee recommends, therefore, that BEPD allocate $13M over five years to establish the Educational Specialty Boards as indicated in Table 5. The program would provide for a national policy board consisting of approximately twenty distinguished educators, scholars, and lay-citizens to assure the establishment of Board certification at a high level and in the public interest.

Table 5. CAREER DEVELOPMENT
(EDUCATIONAL SPECIALTY BOARDS)

Year	National Board	Board Adminis-tration	Re-search & Devel-opment	Board Exami-nation	Federal Total	Dist-rict* Share
1	.10**	.20	--	--	.3	--
2	.10	.20	.50	.50	1.3	--
3	.10	.25	.75	.50	1.6	--
4	.10	.40	.80	2.00	3.3	(1.5)
5	.10	.50	.90	5.00	6.5	(3.75)
Total	.50	1.55	2.95	8.00	13.0	(5.25)

*Local district matching of salary increments for Board certification Salary increment estimated at $3000 per year
**Dollars in millions

Purpose: To develop a career line in teaching by establish-
          ing Educational Specialty Boards offering profes-
          sional competency-based certification to master-
          level teachers and teacher trainers

Provides for Board headquarters, National Commission (20 members) and administrative staff

Establishes 25 Board Examination Centers with capacity for
assessing 2500 candidates per year

Provides career development program in 12 master-level teacher
and teacher trainer specialty fields; e.g., General Elementary;
Early Childhood; Reading; Bilingual; Elementary Mathematics;
Special Education; High School Mathematics; High School English; High School Biology; and High School Social Studies

Provides salary increment of $1500 for 3500 Board certified
teachers for one year; assumes matching salary increment by
local districts

Provides Board Examination fee ($500) for 3000 candidates

     During the first year the Board, acting as a special com-
mission, would investigate the feasibility of developing
special certification for master-level teachers and teacher
trainers. The commission's studies would require consulta-
tion with school board associations, civil rights organizations, state education agencies, and other professional
specialty boards in order to determine the conditions under
which the Board certification procedures might be implemented.
In addition, the commission would request position papers on
a variety of issues affecting the public interest. Approximately $.3M is allocated for the commission during the first
year.

     Assuming the feasibility of the Educational Specialty
Board concept, the full program would establish 25 examination
centers with capacity for testing 2500 candidates per year.
Costs for establishing these centers would include a $500
examination fee for 3,000 candidates. It is anticipated that
individual candidates would bear the examination fee once the
Boards were instituted. In addition, the program would provide a salary incentive of $3,000 per year for 3,500 Board
certified personnel. The salary incentive of $3,000 would
consist of two parts--a $1,500 grant from the Office of Educa-
tion and a matching grant from a local school district or
state. In order to place large numbers of Board certified
personnel at the service of low income, racially or culturally isolated children and youth, OE-BEPD incentive grants
could be made available to school districts eligible for

33

Title I funds or in Model Cities communities. In effect, OE-BEPD salary incentives would be available to Board certified personnel upon their acceptance of assignment in schools located in legally designated poverty areas.

As Table 5 suggests, the program provides the developmental funds for 12 Board examinations at the early childhood, elementary, and secondary school levels. The development of instruments for Board certification at the secondary level will, once again, require the active participation of the most knowledgeable liberal arts faculty. In this manner, the Educational Specialty Boards may help to integrate the liberal arts with professional education at the highest levels of expertise in the field.

In summary, CNPPTE recommends the establishment of conditions necessary to test the power of competency-based teacher education to improve the performance of educational personnel in the nation's schools. The cost of the program is estimated at $114M. Investment in the program would require an allocation of approximately $7M the first year in order to carry out major planning activities and initiate preliminary development. Assessment of the results of the first year will help to determine needed changes in program development strategy for the second year. Assuming reasonable results during the first year, the program would require approximately $28M to install 100 training laboratories, engage in materials and instrument development, and initiate the development of the Educational Specialty Boards. During the third year, additional funding in the amount of $30M would maintain developmental operations at the training laboratories, contribute significantly to materials and instrument development, and introduce Board examination procedures. The fourth and fifth years, funded at $25M would maintain the program of competency-based teacher education at 100 training laboratories with a capacity to train at least 20,000 educational personnel annually.

The Committee is convinced that these recommendations should be implemented. The recommendations offer an integrated program development plan to introduce competency-based teacher education on a broad scale.

The concept of competency-based teacher education has great power. The power of the idea resides in the clear expression of the objectives of the teacher education program and the ability to assess teacher competencies. Both are critical to the introduction of accountability in teacher education.

SUMMARY

The Bureau of Educational Personnel Development established Task Force '72 in November, 1970, to study the utility
of five developmental programs in USOE: protocol materials,
training materials, training complexes, performance-based
certification, and the Models for Elementary Teacher Education.
In March, 1971, the Committee on National Program Priorities
in Teacher Education was formed to represent the non-Federal
sector of the teacher education community and to make recommendations for needed program development.

The procedures of the Committee included the preparation
and discussion of papers prepared by members, meetings with
Task Force '72 and BEPD personnel, circulation of abstracts
of the Committee papers to external critics, and commission-
ing of papers on special topics for Committee consideration.
As a result of these activities and deliberations, program
recommendations were developed. The rationale underlying the
program evolved during the course of discussions among Committee members, and as a result of the ideas presented in various papers prepared by and for the Committee.

The recommendations of the Committee are summarized in
the table for a five year program development plan (see below).
The program development effort has these objectives.

. To establish a program planning and coordination
   committee to assure the unification of the competency-based teacher education program development effort;

. To establish 100 training laboratories with a minimal training capacity of 20,000 educational personnel per year;

. To develop, field test, package, and distribute
   1000 units of instructional materials for concept
   and skill attainment;

. To develop approximately 250 school-based criterion measures leading to competency-based certification at the paraprofessional, provisional, and
   permanent certification levels; and

. To develop a career line in teaching by establishing Educational Specialty Boards offering professional competency-based certification to master-
   level teachers and teacher trainers.

The program development effort recommended by the Committee emphasizes specific activities which serve the function

of defining and making explicit the competencies required by
educational personnel within the career line of paraprofessional, provisional and permanently certified teachers, and
master-level teachers or teacher trainers. These activities
are intended to assist in the development and improvement of
training programs funded by BEPD through the development of
instructional materials, the construction of instruments to
assess competencies in the classroom, and the provision of
opportunities to practice specific skills with evaluation of
performance in the facilities provided in the training laboratories, and by extending careers for teachers through competency-based certification by Educational Specialty Boards
as master-level teachers or teacher trainers.

(Table 1.) FIVE YEAR PROGRAM DEVELOPMENT PLAN:
COMPETENCY-BASED TEACHER EDUCATION
AND CERTIFICATION*

Year	Program Planning and Coor- dination	Train- ing Labora- tories	Instruc- tional Materials	Instru- ments	Career Develop- ment	Total
1	.3**	4.5	1.0	.75	.3	6.85
2	.3	23.0	2.0	1.00	1.3	27.60
3	.3	22.5	4.5	1.00	1.6	29.90
4	.3	14.5	5.5	2.00	3.3	25.60
5	.3	10.5	6.0	.75	6.5	24.05
Total	1.5	75.0	19.0	5.50	13.0	114.00

*The budget estimates do not reflect a rigorous cost analysis
and should be regarded as general guidelines. In particular,
it should be noted that the estimates do not provide for
indirect costs.

**Dollars in millions

    The program recommended by the Committee on National
Program Priorities in Teacher Education represents an effort
to implement several major ideas which have developed during
the past decade. The idea of making explicit the competencies of educational personnel has power to become a major
force to improve teacher education. The clear expression of

the objectives of teacher education and the ability to assess teacher competencies are critical to the introduction of accountability in the preparation of educational personnel.

CHAPTER 3

A FIVE-YEAR GOAL FOR TRAINING COMPLEXES

Saul B. Cohen

The Training Complex is conceived as a new kind of mechanism within which teachers will be trained with the assistance of protocol and training materials. The guiding spirit
behind this mechanism is to provide the teacher with an experience which will sharpen his sense of professionalism and
which will put in the forefront performance-based criteria as
the indices for achieving and verifying long-range competence
in the field. The concept of a Training Complex has for its
objective at one and the same time development of an entity
sufficiently independent of existing institutions to take
responsibility for the training of the classroom teacher, and
establishment of a system that will interact and be interrelated with those institutions that are concerned with teacher preparation on a continuing, long-term basis. The training
regimen offered by the Training Complex follows the sequence
of teacher preparation in Higher Education, either undergraduate or the combination of undergraduate and graduate, and
precedes the inservice preparation that the schools continually provide the teacher upon entry into the system. "Neutral
ground," as a concept upon which the Training Complex is built,
therefore, does not mean isolation but rather inter-dependence.
"Neutral ground" is suggested as a functional technique for
involving both Higher Education and the Schools, and to a certain extent the Community and Industry, rather than as a means
of ignoring them or allowing them to disengage from the teacher training process. Perhaps the analogy of the medical
residency training process is stretching the point, but we see
the Training Complex as providing the prospective teacher with
an ingredient of professional training and on a saturation
basis, that neither college teacher preparation nor school inservice re-education can offer.

We see the Training Complex being operated by a consortium which would be built upon existing structures such as

universities and schools, and yet have an independent life of its own. This means not scrapping existing networks but gaining their support to create something new. To make the distinction sharper, the Training Complex would not try to displace existing institutions but rather undertake to do what such institutions currently are not doing. At no time in a prospective teacher's current training does the teacher serve as the focus. Instead, the teacher is either a student intern under the wing of a university supervisor who has many other duties to perform or a starting teacher in a school under the wing of a master teacher who is also preoccupied with day-to-day teaching. In the training Complex, responsibility would be solely to the trainee, providing both teaching and learning experiences and evaluation of those experiences in a clinical setting.

In addition to its linkage and dependence upon the aforementioned institution, we see the Complex serving as the core for another kind of an institutional framework, also linked to the existing educational and educationally-oriented institutions. This framework has been referred to in TEACHERS FOR THE REAL WORLD (ed. by Smith et. al., A.A.C.T.E., Washington, 1968), as the Educational Service District (p. 104). Such districts are conceived as bold and comprehensive agencies which would include the country's more than 20,000 public school districts and its over 3,000 higher educational institutions. These districts would serve as structured arrangements, linked to the schools, the universities, the community and industry. As systems they need not be organized in traditional geographical regions. They could, for example, cut across the county and state lines. Their cores, i.e., Higher Education institutions or key schools, might be located physically outside of the geographical area which contains the remaining elements of the system. Broadly speaking, these Educational Service Districts might number as many as 3,000 each including ten school systems, a college or university, an industry or groups of industry, and lay-community representation. Very large cities, on the other hand, might be subdivided into five to ten such educational service districts.

If the role of the Training Complex is to train teachers, then the role of the Districts in which they are located would include placement, paraprofessional recruitment and programming, diffusion of protocol and training materials, curriculum innovation, serving as a locus for community social action programs, and research services. Again, to stretch an analogy, the Educational Service District might be likened to the soil Conservation District, manned by a very small group of specialists whose operations serve a varied clientele. Educational Service officers would hold roles in the Districts similar to those of County Agents (or, for the United Kingdom, Her Majesty's Educational Inspectors). The Training Complex would, as has been suggested, serve as nucleus for the Education Service District.

Staffed by school teachers and college faculties (some part-time, and some on two-year leaves from their systems) and supplemented by part-time faculty from industry and from the community, the Training Complex would use as pupils youngsters from the schoolroom and school dropouts (after hours and summers), adults without schooling, and, for specialized purposes, other trainees. Starting with small groups, eventually, the trainee would take on full school classes, upon which his training needs would be further diagnosed. At the end of from half a year to a year in the Training Complex, the trainee would enter the school system as an intern, the internship to cover the first year as a teacher and under direct control of the School. The training milieu of the Complex would be the real world and teaching problems of the real world that teachers must face. This is why the students in the Training Complex with whom the teacher trainee would work would be "problem" people--the dropout, the handicapped, the adults without schooling, the bored suburban housewife. The prospective teacher should be sensitive to the individual needs of such individuals, and only through exposure to them in a clinical setup for a relatively long, intensive period can successful training be undertaken. The training period in the Complex is quite distinct from the period in which the starting teacher enters the school as an intern. During the internship period, the starting teacher could have experience with the typical middle-class student or the inner-city or rurally disadvantaged student depending upon the character of the school. The teacher would be sharpening the experiences gained in the Training Complex in a further extension of the real world.

College teacher preparation would abandon student internship and would concentrate on the theoretical aspects of learning, on subject matter specialization, and on career development. The Training Complex could perform a direct function in this preservice phase by conducting Career Interest Workshops for college students interested in teaching. These could take place during the academic year and in summers, first serving to identify those college students most interested in and suited to teaching careers, then, sequentially, exposing the student to the world of elementary education, secondary education, education of the handicapped, etc. These short-term workshops would be held at an early state (freshman and sophomore years). Then, during the junior and senior college years, Career Interest Workshops would be developed along specialized interest lines, and would include "reality" exposure (perhaps through work as teaching aides and tutors).

As the Training Complex focuses upon <u>training of teachers,</u> so college teacher preparation can focus upon teacher education in its broader context which is essentially a liberal arts-philosophical/psychological framework. It is possible to suggest that the best form of teacher preparation is a solid undergraduate, general educational--liberal arts foundation. From such a foundation, independent and sensitive teachers can emerge. The courses that would specifically be characterized as teacher education courses would deal with theoretical aspects of the learning process, an understanding of social systems, of personality and role, etc.

The number of individuals to be trained in a Training Complex would include the 225,000 beginning teachers who enter the school lists each year, half again as many teacher aides and other paraprofessionals (with perhaps two-to-three-month training periods), and about one-quarter as many inservice personnel who would go through the training process to become part of a rotating or part-time Complex staff, or who would take on supervision of the trainee's internship period. A total of approximately 400,000 individuals should be accommodated by the Training Complexes each year. Ideally, there would be 3,000 Training Complexes nested within 3,000 Educational Service Districts, each Complex handling between 100 and 175 trainees.

<u>The 400,000 trainees would be the target number to be handled by the Complexes.</u> Some of the larger Higher Educational Institutions and Big City Systems would have the capacity to be involved in several Training Complexes, but keeping the number of individuals at any one Complex to an average of about 150 would appear to represent the best way for individualizing the training needs. The rationale for having 3,000 Training Complexes is that nearly every Higher Educational Institution (and not merely the 1,000 institutions engaged in formal teacher preparation) could have some spearhead role in development of the Complexes (and the Districts). Aiming for 400,000 trainees would put the nation on a crash program for improving teacher education. All new personnel, and a significant number of key experienced personnel (60,000 per year, or over one-fourth of all experienced personnel in the schools over a ten-year period) would undergo the training It is significant to involve a critical mass of experienced personnel either through retraining or through operational tasks in the Training Complex so as to minimize the tensions between the prospective teachers who have gone through the Training Complex and existing school personnel.

Such a major effort, coming today, as part of a major effort to reshape the nation's economy to peace-time efforts would make economic as well as educational sense. To meet the crisis in the schools through an effort that provides a major boost to quaternary industry is not only necessary, but eminently practical.

To develop the networks of Training Complexes over a five-year period, we would opt for the following program:

1. First year - Total 100 Training Complexes, linked, essentially to the ten largest metropolitan areas which require almost one-fifth of all beginning teachers. By and large, these first Complexes would be built around large Higher Educational Institutions with strong teacher preparation capacities, and combinations of major big city and adjoining suburban systems.

2. Second year - Total rises to 400 Training Complexes, 300 in the ten largest metropolitan areas (to build about half the necessary networks there), and 100 Training Complexes, spread for pilot purposes, over rural, small and medium-sized city population areas.

3. Third year - Total rises to 900 Training Complexes including 600 in the ten largest metropolitan areas (completing the network there), and adding 200 more Training Complexes in rural, small and medium-sized population areas.

4. Fourth year - Total rises to 2,000 Training Complexes doubling the previous year's number.

5. Fifth year - Total rises to 3,000 Training Complexes, or adds approximately 1,000 more to complete the national network.

It is assumed that the cost of each Training Complex (150 trainees and 30 staff) would be $1,500,000 ($750,000 for the 30 instructional personnel, administration, materials, rents and $750,000 for the trainees @ $5,000). First year costs would therefore amount to $150 million. This would increase to $450 million for the second year, $1.35 billion for the third year, $3 billion for the fourth year, and $4.5 billion for the fifth year. Thus, with the program in full gear, annual costs for the Training Complexes would be $4.5 billion, exclusive of the $1.5 billion expended for the 3 to 4 year college preparation of the beginning teacher. The annual teacher "crop" (including paraprofessionals and inservice) emerging from the Training Complex would then represent a cumulative cost of $6 billion. Of this, approximately $3.5 billion would be spent on beginning teachers, as against the $1 billion that is currently spent on this group. As a percentage of the Gross National Defense Budget, $6 billion is a small price to pay for the

"professionalization" of the nation's teachers and for the
lifting of public education to a new plateau of achievement.
For if the schools are to be saved, they will be saved first
and foremost by the quality of the educational personnel who
must lead the educational process. Unless we're prepared to
invest in the professional training of the teacher, school
reform will continue to be a mirage.

To speak of jumping the number of Training Complexes
from 150 to 3,000 in a five-year period might appear wishful
and naive. But without a crash program, trainees would become isolated and lost. Our aim is to change the system, not
merely individuals. To do so, a mass impact must be made.
The numbers of instructional staff needed (at 30 per complex)
would be 3,000 for the first year; 12,000 for the second;
27,000 the third; 60,000 the fourth; and 90,000 the fifth.
Not all would be required on a full-time basis, but to start
with the first year, the 3,000 number seems attainable. Each
of the 100 Higher Educational Institutions directly involved
might be asked to contribute 4 faculty, and each of the Major
School Systems involved 4, for a total of 800. The remainder
would be recruited nationally through a program that eventually
(within 3 years) would draw one recruit from every Higher Educational Institution and one from every School District to
develop a national cadre that would then be available for the
National Network of Training Complexes.

Prior to the start of the five-year program, two years
would be necessary to recruit and do advanced training of instructional staff, to experiment with materials (an interim
measure while full-blown protocol and training materials are
being prepared at national centers), and to develop the organizational framework. During this period, a handful of Training Complexes, say twelve, would be established to experiment
with structure and with the functional aspects of the training. We would urge opening of such Complexes immediately, as
centers of experimentation and feedback. Aim of such centers
would include contact with all beginning teachers entering a
particular system (through summer workshops) prior to start
of employment, and on a part-time basis during the first year,
as a way of easing into the full-scale operation. Cost of
twelve such Complexes would be $12 million the first year and
$18 million the second.

Scope and cost of a Training Complex effort is not beyond
the capacities of this nation. What is required is an organizational effort of unprecedented proportions for educators,
parallel although hardly on the same scale, to what has been
done in industry and in the military. The educational bureaucracy, Federal and state especially, would be fully enlisted

in the effort. For perhaps the first time, this bureaucracy
would become a "field" bureaucracy bending most of its efforts
to helping the training process. For Federal government,
especially, this would be a challenging role. But if Federal
funding is to be used to spearhead the program, the bureaucracy must become directly and operationally involved in its
implementation. The problem is national and the initiative
for its solution should be national, regardless of whether the
Complex and Educational Service District funding mechanisms
operate directly or through the states. The current drive
for revenue sharing may make the funding of the Training Complexes as a combination Federal/state operation more feasible.

In considering the problems of developing the Training
Complex, the effect of such an institution upon a variety of
different groups, sometimes in conflict, must be assessed.
The following attempts to summarize in tabular form the positive and negative effects from both the short and long-term
perspectives.

Groups	Positive Effects		Negative Effects	
	Short-term	Long-term	Short-term	Long-term
Minority Groups	1. Recruitment of more talented teaching personnel. 2. Direct links to universities in operation of training complexes. 3. Retraining of Displaced Teachers.	1. Better teaching in the schools. 2. Improvement of Black Teacher Training Institutions through questioning of the current educational process. 3. Broadening of para-professional training opportunities.	Strengthening of position of teacher in community-controlled schools, vis-a-vis community control interests.	None
Colleges of Education Faculty	Recruitment of more talented preservice trainees at university.	Improvement of teacher education program, by differentiation from teacher training—more time at universities to emphasize the theoretical and to link with liberal arts.	Loss of inservice training links with schools.	Increase of gap between universities and schools.
Liberal Arts Faculty	1. Closer links with college educators, as latter have more time to emphasize the theoretical. 2. Opportunity to be involved in use of materials, especially curricular, at the teacher training level.	1. More competent teachers to disseminate content and knowledge in the schools. 2. Opportunity to be involved with master teachers in supervision school internships after training complex experience.	None	

Groups	Positive Effects		Negative Effects	
	Short-term	Long-term	Short-term	Long-term
Undergraduate Student	1. Excitement of a new mechanism. 2. Improved first-year inservice internship conditions. 3. More optimal job recruitment situation.	1. Sense of professionalization is heightened 2. Less turnover: better screening processes and greater success factor.	Increased length of preservice training.	Increased cost of professional training.
Professional Associations	More school personnel (especially paraprofessionals).	1. Stronger, more stable, more professional constituency. 2. Greater public fiscal support.	Harder to enter profession.	None
Boards of Education	Less personnel turnover.	Better teaching.	Less control over teacher training	Greater costs
School Administrators	1. Pre-screening of potential staff. 2. Involvement with university personnel in operating training complexes.	1. Better teaching 2. A more professional teacher.	Teacher as a more confident adversary, in day to day relationships.	None

CHAPTER 4

AN OPERATIONAL PLAN FOR
PROGRAM DEVELOPMENT IN TEACHER EDUCATION

M. Vere DeVault
Program Design

Mary Gollady
Economic Analysis

Abstract

Introduction and Rationale. The purpose of the Operational
Plan for Program Development in Teacher Education is to
create a climate and a context which will encourage change in
the nature of schools and schooling in this country. The creation of a corps of teachers and other school personnel competent to perform new roles is the first order of business if
schools are to change. Such reform requires the integrative
efforts of a wide variety of cooperating institutions. The
complexity of any undertaking designed to reform teacher education and the schools imposes a demand for maximum efficiency. It is hypothesized that systems designs provide the most
viable alternative presently available for the management of
this complexity. The presently emerging competency based
teacher education movement contains the essence of initial
steps in the reform which is to be given continuous direction
and encouragement through the Operational Plan. The Operational Plan is a context in which research can be generated
to provide a flow of information necessary to direct continuing reform of teacher education. Widespread reform will result from the Operational Plan through both product and process demonstration and dissemination. Existing Office of
Education programs provide the essential elements required to
give direction and impetus to the realization of the Operational Plan.

Teacher Education Program Requirements. Reform implied by the
Operational Plan clearly dictates that essential program re-

quirements will be set in new contexts facilitated by new relationships, and characterized by new instructional modes. Improved interinstitutional cooperation, new expectations of faculty roles, and adequate assessment and research facilities provide appropriate contexts for evolving teacher education programs. Management of facilities among and within institutions will create an even flow of human and material resources available to students from recruitment to certification and beyond. The new teacher education is predicated on the accessibility of new and varied learning modes made possible through the continuous generation of a wide variety of mediated materials.

Confirmatory Mechanisms of the Operational Plan. To identify specific objectives of the Operational Plan for Program Development is not enough. Mechanisms must exist to make it possible to assess the functioning of the Operational Plan. The Operational Plan -- a system of sub-systems -- accommodate to such mechanisms throughout its structure. Not only must we assess the success of the Operational Plan in reaching its objectives; we must be sure the Operational Plan does not become closed to innovation, persistent in error, or isolated from society's changing emphases. Multilevel confirmatory mechanisms represent the most reliable and accurate means of monitoring the Operational Plan and insuring its continous regeneration.

Resources for Realizing the Operational Plan. The effectiveness of the Operational Plan will be realized through the coordination of resources at the federal, state and local levels. Three specific activities must be continuously maintained if the Operational Plan is to function effectively. These include 1) policy and coordination, 2) implementation of operating instructional programs, and 3) the development and regeneration of protocols and training materials. As complementary elements in the Operational Plan, present programs underway in the Office of Education can maintain these requirements for reform in Teacher Education. The expectation that the Operational Plan for Program Development in Teacher Education can bring about needed next developments in American education carries a parallel expectation that adequate funding sources can be coordinated and directed toward essential elements charged with the responsibility to initiate and sustain the Operational Plan over a long-term period.

Benefit Analysis of the Operational Plan for Program Development. Benefits arising from the Operational Plan may be viewed as direct, interactive, and intertemporal. Direct benefits accrue immediately from specific components to specific audiences. Interactive benefits arise from the interaction of direct benefits from various components upon various audiences.

Intertemporal benefits flow from one point in time to another, from one set of receivers to another. We concentrate, in this analysis, primarily on direct benefits of the experimental models to various audiences within the university, the schools, the community, and the profession.

Cost Analysis for the Operational Plan. Policy decisions regarding the development of the Operational Plan must be based on a study of the relationships between the costs and the benefits of alternative development strategies. Estimates of the costs of one CBP Center provide the basis for determining costs of development strategies which vary the number of participating institutions and the variety of instructional programs. These estimates of alternatives, together with a discussion of their expected effects, illuminate the nature of the choices which must be made.

A Five Year Plan for the Development and Implementation of the Operational Plan. A five-year development strategy for the Operational Plan involves considering not only the nature and magnitude of the impact which the total program will have on teacher education, but also the interrelationships among aspects of the overall Operational Plan and their effect on development strategies over time.

Preface

The Operational Plan for Program Development in Teacher Education has evolved over a period of several months and has drawn on experience and discussions extending over a much greater period of time. Colleagues on campus at the University of Wisconsin, those working on the Committee on National Priorities in Teacher Education, others working in various capacities within the National Center for Educational Research and Development, and the Bureau of Educational Personnel Development, as well as the Directors of the Elementary Teacher Education Models have either directly or indirectly contributed significantly to the nature of the present paper.

We wish to mention specifically the thoughtful assistance provided at particular points by Michael Appel, Ted Czajkowski, and Ron Cohen at the University of Wisconsin. John M. Kean, co-director of the Wisconsin Elementary Teacher Education Project, provided continuous criticism of the manuscript as it progressed through a number of editions. Special appreciation is also expressed to Miss Dixie Carney whose editorial assistance made the completion of this assignment possible during heavily committed Spring and Summer months.

M.V.D.
M.A.G.

July 15, 1971

Introduction and Rationale

The purpose of the Operational Plan for Program Development in Teacher Education is to create a climate and a context
which will encourage change in the nature of schools and schooling in this country.

There is widespread agreement that the schools of this
country have improved substantially as a result of the educational revolution which has been underway during the past
fifteen years. Nonetheless, there is also widespread agreement that the gap continues to widen between what the schools
are and what they must be if they are to meet the changing
requirements of society. As the pace of change in society increases, schools and schooling must be able to adapt appropriately. The protests registered daily by students in colleges
and universities and by parents in the inner city are only
part of the evidence that attests to the need for creating
educational alternatives which more nearly meet the needs of
all youth.

The creation of a corps of teachers and other school
personnel competent to perform effectively in new roles is
the first order of business if schools are to function in a
climate of change.

The purpose of the Operational Plan for Program Development in Teacher Education is to create a heightened possibility of necessary change in schools through changes in the
nature of teachers and teaching. The model is designed not
to serve preconceived notions of what the schools should be
but to encourage, direct, and control evolutionary change.
Viable national alternatives evolving simultaneously may be
tested at the same time. A system which monitors progress by
providing knowledge about the nature of change and its impact
on learners delivers a continual flow of information useful
in determining the utility of various alternatives.

Major reform in teacher education requires the cooperative efforts of a wide variety of cooperating institutions.

If reform in teacher education is to result in changing
schools and in teachers who are competent in new roles, the
importance of contributions which can be made by each individual faculty member and by specific institutions cannot be
overestimated. The major hypothesis of the Operational Plan
is that these variable resources, faculty and institutions
can be organized to focus the uniqueness of each on the task
to which all are committed.

The complexity of any undertaking designed to reform

teacher education imposes a demand for maximum efficiency. It is hypothesized that systems designs provide a management alternative to assure the efficiency.

It is hypothesized that the uniqueness of the audiences to which the plan is addressed, the learners or would-be teachers and the schools they serve, can be served most effectively through an efficiently operating systems design. These diverse demands of persons and institutions coupled with the varied contributions which can be made by other persons and institutions pose both the threat to and the hope for improvement in teacher education. The hope stems from the rich potential of innovative thrusts in many directions; the threat stems from the danger of losing contact, understanding and control of innovation so that necessary resources can no longer be applied effectively at appropriate points.

The presently emerging competency based teacher education movement provides the initial essence of improvement which is to be given continuous direction and encouragement through the Operational Plan.

The competency-based teacher education movement has developed along with management by objectives and accountability emphases. Criteria of teacher competency have been identified at three levels. In the past and presently, certification has been based largely on knowledge demonstration. We have had substantial evidence that the certified teacher possessed given sets of knowledge. A second level requires assessment of the performance of the teacher. This is the focus of the Operational Plan. Certification, at this level, is based on assurances that the teacher can perform in stated and specified ways. The third level involves product criteria. Evidence is given that the teacher can, in whatever way, obtain specified results with learners in the classroom. The Operational Plan based primarily on performance criteria assumes that all three levels will be considered in establishing the evidence on which a given teacher can be certified although major emphasis will be at the performance level.

The Operational Plan is the context through which research can provide a flow of information necessary to direct continuing improvement in teacher education.

Through the operating systems design, the Operational Plan for Teacher Education serves as a major research instrumentality. Working with a set of hypotheses about what teaching is, what teaching should become, and how we can move in the directions indicated, the Operational Plan serves as a testing ground through the utilization of a wide variability of resources and responsiveness to the demands of variable audiences. These audiences include both prospective teachers and their respective employees. Needed is a plan which can respond to the desire of one student to prepare for teaching in a "free" school while at the same time responding to needs of other students who choose to prepare for any of several other patterns of schooling.

Three descending orders of phenomena are inherent in the research potential of the Operational Plan. The first of these is the concept of systems and its implications and applications in education. The first order of business for the educational research community in the Seventies may well be determining the viability of using systems designs for both management and instruction in education. At the second order the Plan provides a setting for research in a variety of related areas: systems designs and academic freedom; technological systems and human values; competency-based instructional systems; interinstitutional cooperation; economics and educational efficiency. Further, the Plan provides an opportunity to test a wide range of specific hypotheses related to instructional and management techniques with wide applicability throughout the educational community and special relevance within systems contexts.

Extensive improvement in teacher education will result from the Operational Plan through the dissemination of both its product and process.

Generalizability of findings within the context of the Operational Plan can be made both for product and for process. Many of the products developed, tested, and refined can be transferred to other institutions as parts of other programs or as collections of parts which make up a new system with special adaptive mechanisms appropriate to the setting. On the other hand, the processes (e.g., the use of systems management, procedures for faculty training) by which the plan has been developed and implemented can be shared with other institutions. Exchange of faculty members and other technical specialists would make it possible to duplicate a process which has resulted in the successful implementation of a program at one set of institutions for implementation at another.

The Operational Plan will ultimately be judged a success only if it demonstrates the capacity to respond to students with diverse needs, who can leave the program with diverse talents, and who serve effectively in diverse schools. In this context the Operational Plan is expected to lead to substantial diversity within the competency based movement through implementation in a large consortium of institutions, each testing hypotheses in a different model. There are common bases from which such models may be initiated and common patterns of organization which may be expected to generate the anticipated model program. To these common beginnings, the identification of essential tasks and the organizational patterns designed to facilitate the implementation of these tasks, we now turn our attention.

Existing Office of Education programs provide the essential elements required to give direction and impetus to the realization of the Operational Plan.

Teacher Education Program Requirements

The major functions of the Operational Plan for teacher education are 1) the preparation of educational personnel for the schools, and 2) research designed to contribute to reform in education. The central theme of the Operational Plan is the potential of systems in education. Because the use of systems is central to the Plan, the two functions are integral to each other. Models and modeling imply the generation of new knowledge even as the preparation of personnel is underway. The Operational Plan then, is concerned with the demonstration of an operating model, with basic and applied research endeavors, while continuously utilizing information to improve the model, either as a total entity or as an educational system meeting specific requirements for specific learners.

Teaching/Learning

The Operational Plan provides a teaching/learning facility which derives its focus from carefully defined and publicly displayed sets of performance criteria. The environment in which learning is to take place is carefully contrived so that learners may move efficiently to performing at criterion level. In its fullest operation the teaching/learning facility is extensive enough, both in quantity and in variety, to provide for a vast array of individual differences in goals (the kind of teacher I want to be), sequence (I'm really more interested right now in creativity, whatever the content area), instructional mode (I'm on an independent study kick right now), rate (political activities are taking much of my time this month) and personal involvement (I have this one instructor who helps me make sense of all this). Without this variety potential, a model is static and modeling is impossible. Only as students are able to design for themselves instructional programs which result in the competencies they deem essential may we expect the system to reflect the needs of individuals or the changing needs of schools. Within the Operational Plan the evolution of schools to new forms depends upon parallel evolution of educational personnel in preparation.

Management

Essential to the most fruitful use of the teaching/learn-
ing environment is the management of both students and resources. In the first instance, the problem is one of providing enough information about the student and about the potential teaching/learning opportunities for appropriate decisions.
In the second instance, it is essential that resources both
human and material are available when a learner needs them.

Monitoring student progress. From the student's entry
into the program, information is generated for an extensive
individual profile. Throughout the preparation program the
student's progress is closely monitored and information is
continuously made available to him and his counselor/instruc-
tor/advisors so that choices are made on the fullest possible
information. Although the student may have preferences for
a given instructional mode, abundant evidence may be available
indicating that some other mode for the learner is more efficient. On the basis of this information the student may or
may not wish to make a specific choice on the basis of an
earlier preference.

Managing resources. The most difficult and essential
resource to manage -- by making certain it is available when
required by the student -- is the human resource. Human resources include those who would provide instructional guidance
by helping the student interpret and understand data about
himself and the program opportunities, instructors who help
students through individual conferences or group seminars, or
other learners who are ready for common seminar or other small
group learning experiences.

Materials Development and Regeneration.

Both protocol and training materials are essential in-
gredients of the Operational Plan for teacher education. Although it is anticipated that for most students heavy emphasis in the program will center on experiences in the schools,
protocol materials are essential for at least two reasons.
In the first place, most students derive the greatest benefit
from classroom observation or participation when they have
been conceptually prepared for the experience. Protocol materials provide visual images of learner activities organized
as a base of experience for the development of psychological,
philosophical and sociological concepts. They prepare the
learner to organize what he sees and experiences in the classroom. The experience of interpreting in simulated settings
is expected to contribute much to the student's ability to
interpret in the live classroom setting.

Training materials of a wide variety are required of the
Operational Plan Materials of instruction, drawn from many
media including films, computerized instructional sequences,

and slidetapes, are all potential sources of effective units in the integrated instructional system.

By design, the use of both protocol and training materials has been anticipated in the Operational Plan and can be tested for effectiveness only in the crux of an operating system. Regeneration of materials is essential as data on effectiveness and use become increasingly available and concepts of the nature of schooling are altered. The Operational Plan has the potential for creating a context for continually changing schools. If the renewal of schools and school personnel is to be expected, then every element of the system must be viewed with this in mind: the potential to create must be held open and the response to the needs of all learners must be highly valued.

Faculty Training.

New programs in new schools require new teachers. Both at the university level and in the schools retraining is essential. The Operational Plan is designed on the assumption that teachers will play roles either in addition to or completely other than those which are presently exhibited in the lecture halls and classrooms throughout the country. No reform in teacher education will succeed without a comparable reform in the faculty member's concept of his own role. Much has been written about these roles; by and large these statements have been mildly reformational and have been received by the profession with little recognition of their significance. Not only must vigorous efforts be made to initiate the needed reform in faculty roles, both in the universities and in the schools; comparable study and effort must be made to assure that the nature of faculty roles for the future can be designed and redesigned as the nature of schooling takes on new dimensions reflecting the variety envisioned in earlier segments of this document.

Interinstitutional Cooperation

Education is the responsibility of all society. For too long the responsibility for the education of youth has been delegated. The failure of the schools so delegated is not so much in what they are, but rather in problems associated with their isolation from society, and from our demands which deny youth choice in the nature of their schooling. Interinstitutional cooperation as envisioned in the Operational Plan is but an opening wedge designed to make teacher education, the schools and schooling, responsive to and a part of a larger society. Teacher education in the universities has been separated too much from the schools it serves, and schools have been separated too much from the communities they serve. Interinstitution cooperation is required if the schools are to become a part of the whole again. Not only must schools

55

respond to institutions in society but those institutions must
soon come to serve the educational requirements of all youth.
Business, government, and the arts all have a stake in the
schools and a responsibility to become actively involved, not
only in helping schools, but in actually providing schooling
for youth everywhere.

The educational enterprise as it presently functions is
fragmented and frequently at odds with itself. Schools and
universities function on differing philosophies; state departments of public instruction too often are ineffective either
because they lack direction or because they move to institu-
tionalize a monolithic design for education throughout the
state; and the dichotomy between preservice and inservice education provides a watershed in the professional career of
each teacher. Initially progress must be made in clarifying
these enormously distracting discrepancies before we can move
on to the more essential cooperative efforts which lie outside the presently conceived educational establishment.

Student Recruitment and Placement

Recruitment and placement procedures which are integrated
with the total teacher preparation program are essential in-
gredients of the Operational Plan. If reform in teacher education and thus in schooling is to take place, mutable initiates are required. Although our definitions of education
typically imply that learners are mutable, we here imply that
initiates have potential to become the innovators now and in
the future. Of equal importance is the placement of these
initiates in mutable schools. There are few of these in exis-
tence today and those schools that are thought to be innovative are usually only mildly so. The Operational Plan must
make possible the recruitment and placement of teachers whose
qualities commend them to a philosophy of the changing nature
of schooling.

Certification

Perhaps in no facet of teacher education of the past
have we been more Procrustean than in our certification practices. The entire structure of certification needs careful
reexamination in the light of the essential demands of reform
in teacher education and education. If individual teacher
education programs are to be generated, and if extensive variety is to be fostered in the schools, new flexible concepts
of certification are essential. Through the Operational Plan
the option is presented to teachers in preparation, or at
points in midcareer, to identify the sets of criteria by which
their own performance is to be judged and ultimately certified
Schools then will be in a position to identify the kinds of
performance they want in the teacher they seek. Certification

is then a verification of the fact that the teacher can perform as indicated in the records available. With such a system, variability is possible in two dimensions. The first is the variability associated with the nature of the performance itself, and the second is variability in the extent (amount) of performance which can be verified at any given time. Thus, teacher aide, teacher, master teacher are not discrete entities but exist along a continuum on which a given teacher can be specifically placed on his own terms.

Assessment and Research

Although assessment and research are closely related concerns in the Operational Plan each serves a unique function. Assessment data, continually collected make possible the essential monitoring of student progress, provide feedback on the effectiveness of specific instructional activities, and suggest the appropriateness of a given teacher's associated personal goals, instructional program, and ultimate career expectations.

The Operational Plan as a research facility functions at a variety of levels. At the highest level, the Plan provides a facility for the investigation of the utility of systems in education. The Operational Plan is a system. It functions as an evolving system and its success is as a system open to change, creating teachers of diverse characteristics for service in schools of diverse nature.

At a second level, the Plan provides for research in a number of areas essential to the continued improvement of schooling in the decade ahead as the utility of systems in education is investigated in a variety of settings. Competency-based instructional systems, systems and academic freedom, systems and personalization, technology and human values, systems as means of implementing interinstitutional cooperation, and systems as vehicles to increase economical efficiency of education are some of the major areas needing research throughout the Seventies if we are to meet our educational obligations in the Eighties.

Finally, at a third level, research within the Operational Plan focuses on the relative effectiveness of various instructional modes; on the viability of specific modes for learners of identified characteristics; on the impact of specific faculty roles on college instruction; on the impact of learner choice in program plan and implementation; on the need for the amount of in-school experience which is required; on the effectiveness of protocol materials in the development of concepts about learning, learners, teachers, and schools; on the effectiveness of units of the interinstitutional cooperative; and on the impact of changing teacher education programs on changing concepts and practices in schooling.

Confirmatory Mechanisms of the Operational Plan

Each of the Elementary Models projects has emphasized the importance of feedback at points on a variety of levels. Throughout the development and implementation of those programs some kind of comfirmatory mechanism is the sine qua non of competency based education. To identify specific objectives is not enough without some mechanism to serve as a check on the extent to which those objectives have been achieved. In the Models projects many such mechanisms have been designed to ask and seek answers to questions relating to viability, consistency, or efficiency. Such mechanisms are integrated elements within the Operational plan; they are empowered not only to analyze, but to apply the resultant findings to future operations.

Integrating Confirmatory Mechanisms.

A generalized model of a confirmatory mechanism is shown in Figure 1.

Purpose:

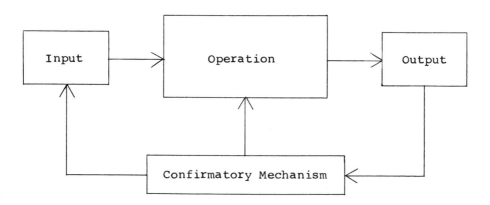

Confirmatory Mechanism

Figure 1

This model assumes the system has been designed to achieve a specific purpose, already clearly identified. In relation to that purpose, the system has an input, operation, and an output. Through the confirmatory mechanism, staff members consider the extent the output of the system is congruent with the stated purpose of the system. The review of the output may, indeed, indicate that the system fulfilled its objectives in any given instance. In this case, achievement of purpose is confirmed.

Often, however, an analysis of output will indicate the purpose has not be achieved. Now the disposition of the case is not quite so simple. It is not enough to indicate simply that the purpose is not confirmed. Essential to the continued operation and improvement of the system is some evidence as to why the purpose was not achieved; so the confirmatory mechanism seeks additional evidence. Failure to confirm achievement of purpose is usually, at first, cause for scrutiny of the operation. What was done within the operational component of the system has been inadequate or misdirected. Were the operation the only place for error to exist, the focus of confirmatory mechanisms would be relatively simple, but such is not the case. There are at least two other points at which the system may be at fault. One of these is the nature of the input. The operation may be appropriate for the purpose if, and only if, the input does adequately meet certain prerequisites. Perhaps those prerequisites have been improperly identified or emphasized. At still another point, the purpose itself may be inappropriate either in intent or in statement. The purpose may be impossible to achieve; it may be stated in such a way that it is difficult to determine which operation to use or what standards to apply to the output. Additional complications grow from the interaction of these components. These interactions exist in almost every system. The purpose may be right for some inputs but not for others. Perhaps the operation as in an instructional system, is appropriate for some inputs (learners) but not as appropriate for others. Perhaps the assessment devices used to measure the output or the prerequisites of the input (learners) may be inappropriate (not reliable, e.g., not culture free). These complexities indicate both the difficulties involved and how essential an effectively operating confirmatory mechanism is as an aspect of any system.

The Operational Plan for Program Development in Teacher Education is itself a system. As such, it contains confirmatory mechanisms at a number of points and throughout the interrelated network of system and subsystem. That network of system and subsystems ranges from the macro-level of the Operational Plan for Program Development to the smallest micro-level system which can be identified as a single learning experience. Macro-level systems include the Operational Plan as shown in Figure 2, the State Model (not diagrammed), and the Local Teacher Education Program Model depicted in Figure 3. At the micro-level I is the Program Element or interrelated Set of Modules; at micro-level II is the Instructional Module shown in Figure 4. Micro-level III, not shown, is the single instructional activity.

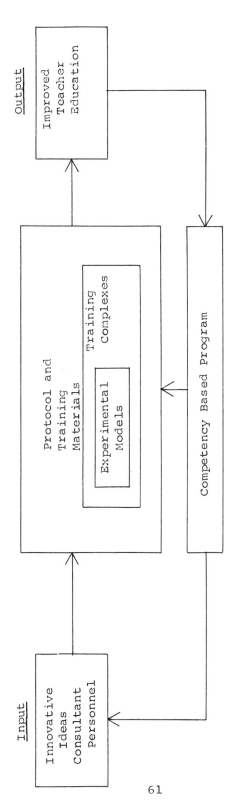

Purpose:

Input

Innovative
Ideas
Consultant
Personnel

Operation

Protocol and
Training
Materials

Training
Complexes

Experimental
Models

Competency Based Program

Output

Improved
Teacher
Education

Confirming Mechanism at Macro—level I:
Operational Plan

Figure 2

61

Purpose:

Input

Operation

Output

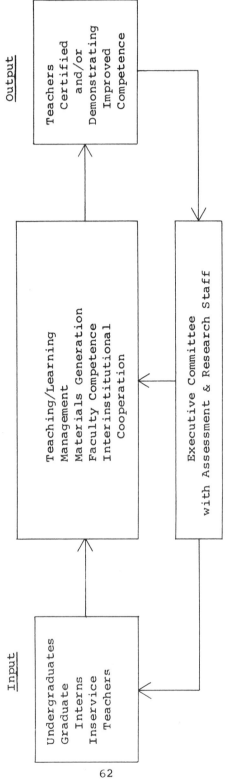

Undergraduates
Graduate
Interns
Inservice
Teachers

Teaching/Learning
Management
Materials Generation
Faculty Competence
Interinstitutional
Cooperation

Teachers
Certified
and/or
Demonstrating
Improved
Competence

Executive Committee
with Assessment & Research Staff

Confirming Mechanism at Micro-level III:
Local Teacher Education Program

Figure 3

Purpose:

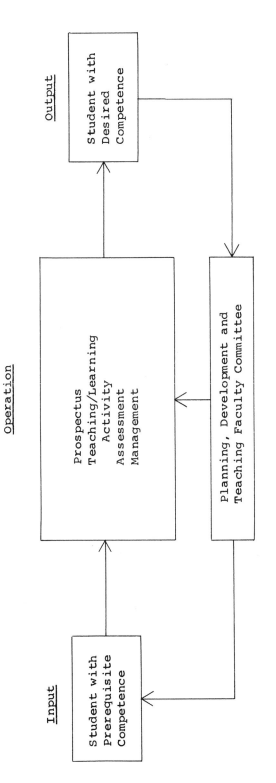

Confirmatory Mechanism at Micro-level II:
Instructional Module

Figure 4

All of these subsystems, those pictured, those mentioned, and perhaps others still to be identified or designed depend for their success on many things; none is more crucial than the confirming mechanism. Within each of these subsystems the confirming mechanism by design and function has much in common with the others. Each depends upon carefully identified and administered measuring devices which directly reflect the intent stated or implied in the purpose. These measuring devices provide a flow of data which must be processed. The processing provides a continuing analysis of the output of the system. If this analysis does not confirm the achievement of the purpose, a series of hypotheses must be made about where the fault lies. Methodical investigations must be made to determine at what specific point the system has failed. Ultimately corrections are made on the recommendation or at the direction of staff members responsible for the confirming mechanism. Data are continually collected again at the output to determine the nature of the improvement which has resulted from the change made in the system.

Because instructional systems are sensitive to a variety of changes outside themselves, one would not expect a satisfactorily operating system to remain so over time. Students who enter educational institutions each year differ from those who entered the year before. Materials which are effective one year may be quite ineffective later for any number of reasons. The impact of a McLuhanesque treatment five years ago would have resulted in different responses from those it would cause today. Martial music accompanying an instructional film would have a very different impact on many students today from that on their counterparts ten years ago. Even changes in clothes styles can at times alter student response to visual materials. We can readily see that a well adjusted, well balanced, and finely tuned instructional system serving our purposes today will not necessarily serve our purposes tomorrow. This is as true within our macro-level systems as within our micro-level systems. The importance of a continually functioning complement of interrelated confirmatory mechanisms cannot be over-stressed. Without their effective and continuous monitoring service no educational/instructional system can be expected to remain relevant both to its own purposes and society's demands.

Resources for Realizing the Operational Plan

Realization of the Operational Plan will require human and financial resources of considerable diversity. Only through the coordination of these resources at the federal, state and local levels can the Plan be effectively realized. The role of the federal government through the Office of Education will be that of initiating and coordinating a long-term well-planned change effort.

Present programs underway in the Office of Education can contribute significantly as complementary elements in the Operational Plan for Program Development in Teacher Education. Three specific kinds of activities are required if the Operational Plan is to function effectively. These include 1) policy making and coordination, 2) implementation of operating instructional programs, and 3) the development and regeneration of protocols and training materials.

The development and maintenance of policy which gives direction to the Operational Plan and is supported widely within the professional community is of utmost importance. It is recommended that policy leadership be provided through the Competency Based Program presently supported at the national level by the Office of Education. A strong national committee, not unlike that presently funded through AACTE, should assume the responsibility 1) to identify continuing national needs, 2) to monitor and disseminate information concerning the effectiveness of competency based programs as they evolve, 3) to coordinate through sub-committees, local level OE partially funded Competency Based Program (CBP) Centers, and 4) to make regular reports, including recommendations, to the Office of Education. In a sense, the Competency Based Program will serve as the feedback system serving the Operational Plan for Program Development in Teacher Education (Figure 5).

The operating instructional programs of the Operational Plan take place within the CBP Centers. These centers include the operating elements of both the Training Complex and the Experimental[1] Models Program. The Operational Plan function of each of several present OE programs are identified in Figure 6 which details the interdependence of these programs within the Competency Based Program Center at the local level. The experimental Models Program functions within the Training Complex in that the latter is responsible for the interinstitutional cooperation which gives major impetus to operating instructional programs. The Training Complex assumes certain

---

[1]The term Experimental rather than Elementary is used throughout this paper to imply the need for including both elementary and secondary education in the design and implementation of the Operational Plan for Program Development in Teacher Education.

management functions, faculty training within the schools, and final certification of teachers. On the other hand, within each CBP Center the Models Program assumes responsibility for teaching/learning activities, management of resources and learners, faculty training on campus, student recruitment and placement, and assessment and research activities.

Each of the CBP Centers is served by the National Program for Protocols and Training Materials. It is recommended that these instructional materials be developed with balance between the need for program variety among CBP Centers and the need to reduce to a minimum duplication of materials which could be equally effective for instructional programs in more than a single center.

The expectation that the Operational Plan for Program Development in Teacher Education will create the reform so necessary for next developments in American education carries a parallel expectation that funding sources must be coordinated and directed specifically to essential elements charged with the responsibility to initiate and to sustain the Operational Plan over a long-term period.

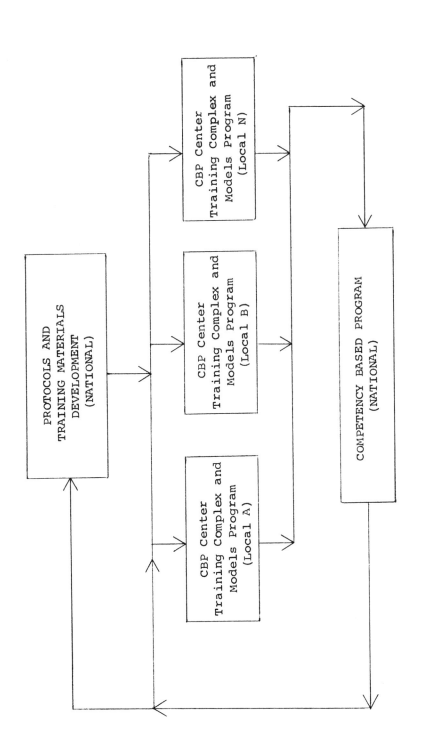

Relation of the Present BEPD Programs Within the
Operational Plan

Figure 5

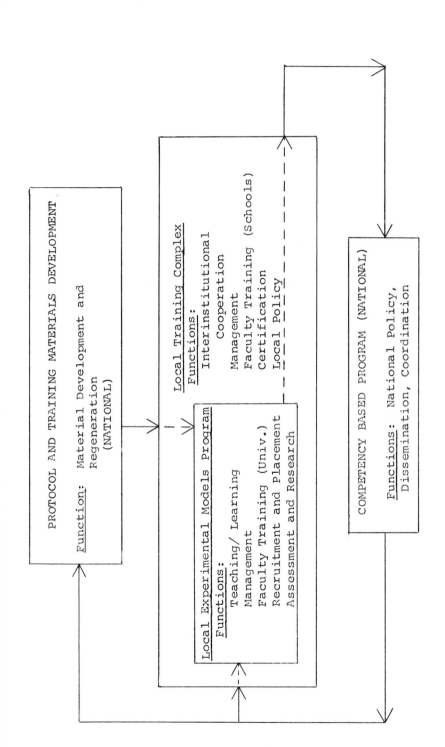

Functions of the Present BEPD Programs
Within a Competency Based Program Center

Figure 6

Benefit Analysis of the Operational Plan for Program Development

Any analysis of the benefits of educational innovation first must clarify the nature of these benefits. Benefits may be viewed as direct, interactive, and intertemporal. Direct benefits are those that accrue immediately to specific audiences. Since both audiences and innovations are multifaceted, a second class of benefits are interactive. That is, they arise from the inter-action of direct benefits of various innovations upon various audiences. Third, benefits flow from one point in time to another; from one set of receivers to another. In this sense, benefits of the experimental models accrue to students at the pre-certification level; in following years additional benefits accrue to their pupils; in turn these pupils return benefits to society. This flow of benefits from college students, to public school pupils, and to society is an example of intertemporal benefits.

Comprehensive benefit analysis, then, must deal with these three benefit streams: direct, interactive, and intertemporal. First, direct benefits will be considered for each of the major components of the Operational Plan. These will include the experimental models, the training complexes, protocol and train-ing materials, and the competency based program identified as the confirmatory mechanism. Although the training complexes, the protocol, and training materials, the competency based program, and the experimental models exist as an integrated system, in this analysis, the focus is primarily on the bene-fits resulting from the implementation of the experimental models. The models are emphasized for two reasons. First, they have been more extensively defined than other components; second, the authors have been closely associated with the experimental models program.

Benefits of the Experimental Models

Benefited audiences are easily identified by location. These we shall order to include the university, the schools, and the community.

The University

Audiences within the university to be considered here include precertification students, teacher education faculty, graduate students and faculty throughout the university.

Precertification students. The experimental models programs emphasize the individualization of instruction in four ways: rate, sequencing, mode, and goals.

An instructional program which allows each student to

progress at his own rate assures an optimum use of student
time only if students are capable of judging wisely; to do
this, they need information and counseling. The models' designs
encourage students' progress at individual rates while progress
data are made continuously available for student and instructional

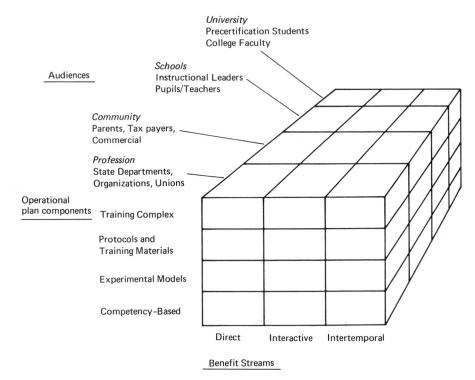

Benefit Analysis Framework: Components X Audiences X Benefit streams

Figure 7

staff review. This benefit (rate) makes it possible for students
to continue their teacher educational study twelve months of
the year or any segment of that twelve months. It is possible
for students to drop out of the program temporarily for whatever
reason and return again at their personal and professional
convenience. Students enjoy the benefit of moving easily to and
from their education and non-education work elsewhere on campus.
This same characteristic makes it possible for students to move

in and out of public school experience or other work experiences. Each student develops a rate of progression most efficient for himself.

In typical educational programs the class structures is such that sequence freedom is limited to two or three credit units. Usually there is an additional constraint: certain courses may be taken only after other prerequisite courses have been completed. The models, on the other hand, are designed to enable students to choose frequently among sequence alternatives. Minimal sequence requirements are established; beyond that, personal choice dictates the student's next topic for study. Not only can a student pursue topics of personal interest, he can delay other topics until he feels he is ready; or until he can pursue such a topic in close association with related topics; students enjoy the benefits of many possible variations. Of special benefit is the opportunity to study topics in association with immediate problems in the clinical setting. For instance, a student may find, in working with elementary children, that he is lacking in his understanding of language. This student can turn at that time to the study of linguistics; should he become interested in that topic, he can pursue it in depth. The student is able to put his program together according to his own sense of coherence.

Instructional mode choices as a function of individualization are of special significance in the experimental models program. Students do not learn equally well from instruction in any given mode. Choice of mode throughout the experimental models is of double benefit. First, the student is enabled increasingly to decide (both intuitively and from data feedback sources) which modes serve him best. Further, that he can make a choice is a substantial benefit; a student is a better motivated learner if he has helped choose his learning resources.

Within the experimental models, each learner has an opportunity to determine to a considerable extent the kind of teacher he wishes to become. His area of specialization, his level of competence (aide, teacher, master teacher) and the manner in which his professional program is related to his education in the arts and sciences are determined by the individual learner in cooperation with his advisors. We have recognized that no one learning theory describes all teaching or all teachers. The models permit individual students to determine the theory or theories they wish to use to design their teaching styles. This will result in teachers who differ substantially from each other but understand the bases on which they make their individual decisions.

Personalization is emphasized in each of the models. Two personalizing functions are significant in terms of student benefits. The first is that personalization derived from faculty/ student conferences and small group seminars; from peer group relations, both in advisory sessions and in planning and decision making in (simulated and actual) team teaching experiences. There seems to be an increasing evidence that individualization alone, through independent study, is not enough. Apparently, in the schools as well as higher education independent study must be associated with personal interaction. Through inter- action the social aspect of ideas developed through independent study is made clear to individual learners. Thus, learners are able to identify points of application for their new understanding of other learners and teaching.

Another important dimension of personalization designed as part of the models program is program negotiation. Negotia- tion between students and faculty advisors enables students to identify and develop programs appropriate both to their own interests and to the needs of the schools they will serve.

Finally, the benefits to precertification students are clear in relation to the competency based programs within the models. A crucial advantage to the learner is the knowledge of those competencies he must master to progress within his program; to meet the objectives he has set for himself; to understand fully the implications of his study for his image of himself as teacher.

The competency based nature of the program makes it poss- ible for the student to obtain continuous information on his progress in developing the desired competence. Specific and immediate information on results is a particularly strong motivational source; the models program, through its competency based nature, provides the student with such information.

We expect schools to move increasingly toward instruc- tional systems, behavioral objectives, and accountability. Many students will work during their precertification program in schools where such emphases exist. The competency based programs inherent in the models benefit the student by provid- ing him with experiences relevant to such concepts. Through such experiences the student not only sees examples of practices and attitudes comparable to those unfolding in many schools now, and through the Seventies; also, the student can become familiar with both the advantages and the problems he will typically confront in such an orientation.

Professional Education Faculty. The professional education faculty responsible for teacher education benefits from the implementation of the experimental models in a number of ways. Specifically, benefits can be classified as 1) resource support, 2) faculty retraining, 3) administration, and 4) scholarship.

Instructional staff associated with the models are recipients of continuous feedback data concerning their own
(and their students') effectiveness. This flow of data will
make it possible for faculty to improve the quality of their
own learning and instruction decisions. Just as the effectiveness of instructional mode and strategy varies with the
individual learner (ATI) it can be expected that something
like Instructor/Strategy Interaction (ISI) is also operating.
If ISI is to be understood, and if actions are to be based on
the realities of ISI, pertinent information to the instructor
is essential. The variety of mediated materials which will
be readily available to instructors will improve their effectiveness. The need for continuous updating of instructional
materials and strategies will keep instructors up-to-date.
The demand of the models for new faculty roles and increased
competence can be met through extensive in-service training
activities; such training can be continuously provided to
faculty, both prior to and throughout implementation of the
models operation.

The concept of the models can do much to benefit faculty
by keeping Schools of Education in the vanguard of education-
al/technological/humanistic integration. Presently we believe
there is a division among those who would individualize; this
division exists as a tendency to humanistic-technological
polarity. The free school movement and American technological
society at large both generally support the drive to find appropriate ways to individualize instruction at all levels.
The humanistic/technological polarity, therefore, reflects
disagreement on means, not ends. The challenge of the Seventies is to find ways of bringing together these divergent
views, projections and practices into a coherent approach to
humane education. Technological expertise will contribute to
our success in this venture. To be part of this unifying
vanguard throughout the Seventies and Eighties is the major
benefit we expect to accrue to involved faculty.

Faculty involvement in part-time administration of professional education programs consumes too much of the time of
a large proportion of the faculty. The systematic design
inherent in the models provides for administrative support
that is more specific and more clearly defined; it is separate
from the instructional responsibilities assumed by professional education faculty. The separation of these tasks and the
resulting efficiency (in the use of both time and energy) represents a major benefit in faculty. Administration, scholarship, and teaching -- each will benefit from the systematic
approach implementing the models will entail.

The benefits of the models to faculty scholarship appear
to be unlimited. The developing model represents the best
we can project concerning the future of education both in the
schools and in colleges and universities. Curriculum developments in the schools and in teacher education will be constant-
ly evolving under the direction of faculty and staff committed

to maximal quality in the teacher education programs. The research potential in the models program is extensive. The operating experimental model system is a major research vehicle; a wide range of variables can be independently manipulated and a continuous flow of data can be derived. These data may be expected in such quantity as to make present data sources for educational research seem miniscule in comparison. The faculty association with such an ongoing curriculum and research development facility will substantially benefit those faculty members who are primarily interested in research.

The service opportunities for faculty participation in an operational model have been suggested by the dissemination project resulting from the initial development of specification and feasibility studies. Many faculty members at each of the institutions involved have been widely used as consultants, locally and nationally. Operating models can serve as demonstration centers and as continuing sources of consulting assistance, as these initial efforts demonstrate.

Graduate Education Students. The character of the experimental models program, both in the development and implementation stages, assures that innovation and research activities are continually underway; that competent educational scholars and researchers will be continually required to assist professors and other development and technical staff in the model program. Opportunities to work at the theoretical stage of development will be continually available as data are collected which must be analyzed, and put into a theoretical framework. From such a framework implications for further refinement and development of the model can be drawn. Perhaps most important is the student's participation in an environment designed for the study and creation of change. The model is change -- guided, modified, explored. Today most of us read this word and accept it; few of us comprehend fully the extent to which the word change today can be used as a synonym for reality. The essence of society and of education is change. If we accept that, then the availability of a context of development and research where the first principle is change, is a primary benefit of the experimental models.

Benefits identified as available to faculty are also available to graduate students. Learning new instructional roles, and drawing on resources of a comprehensive system approach will aid students in decision making, hypothesis creation and testing, and projections for future programming.

Higher Education. The experimental models program, or

something similar, could have been envisioned in any number of areas and at almost any instructional level. The 1967 request from USOE for preliminary specifications, however, was directed to teacher education. It may be that a professional education program, either in teacher education, engineering, medicine, or law, is more appropriate for initial work than is general education: but that is not certain. The success or failure of the models program will have implications for higher education in all areas; we can expect to find our colleagues across the disciplines watching critically, cautiously, approvingly. Implementing the models, in some form, is a crucial benefit in providing examples of success (or failure) in this area of educational projection. Throughout higher education, but especially on a campus where a model is being implemented, a number of complementary applications may be expected to develop.

Problems for study in higher education are numerous. One of the first of these lies in the potential conflict between systems design and academic freedom. With the discussions currently underway and the trend toward Planning - Budgeting Systems in higher education, we must expect much attention to be focused on this phase of the models. Can faculty commit their efforts and energies to cooperative systematic participation in program implementation without surrendering some portion of their highly valued academic freedom? What problems will faculty be confronting? A major benefit of the model to higher education, then, is the opportunity it provides us to make a case study of this relation between systems designs and academic freedom.

Individualized-personalized education is an obvious need; diverse efforts are underway to create such programs. In many instances these efforts are of limited scope; the change required is minimal. Probably the results will be minimal. The experimental models program (in implementation) provides higher education the benefit of a comprehensive reorganization directed toward personalized education.

Accountability, competency based education, and behavioral objectives are all aspects of the program which will receive attention in higher education. Too much innovation at all levels is piecemeal; it is only too likely higher education innovation in the future will remain so. Needed are comprehensive, integrated thrusts such as those represented in the models. Accountability concepts of competency based programs cannot be tested in a minimal, limited fashion. They must be tested in inclusive, realistic contexts. The benefits to higher education derive mainly from the comprehensiveness of the models. Information derived from the models will be useful to those who plan for education in the arts and sciences, in other professional schools, in technical schools, and in junior and community colleges.

The polarity represented by technology and human values is of special import to a wide higher education audience. Ways must be found to utilize technology to enhance the humanness of our educational endeavors at all levels. The difficulty of reconciling these emphases is due, in part, to limitations in our technological know-how; in part, to our inability to be creative in our search for harmonious solutions. We expect that initially those working with the models will find it difficult, but not impossible, to resolve this polarity. Higher education will benefit through the demonstration of a working model's various efforts to resolve this polarity.

Higher education is undergoing special scrutiny at this time of difficult budget problems. The systems design concept utilized in the models provides a context for the student of economic efficiency in education. Such study will have broad implications throughout higher education. Any economic analysis of innovative practices begins with an analysis of costs and benefits of present programs. At present, these are too seldom available or too superficially done to be of substantial value in educational planning. Major steps have been taken within the past few years to move in appropriate directions on these problems; soon we may expect to understand more clearly the efficiency or lack of it in our current operating of institutions of higher education. The implementation of the models provides an analysis of present practice; but it also provides a continuous flow of cost data which is relevant to other evolving educational programs. Both the demonstrable system for the study of economic efficiency and the findings which emanate from the system will provide benefits to higher education.

If universities and colleges are to change significantly, they will do so as a result of changing faculty roles. New institutions where faculty members only lecture as they have in the past, can hardly be called new. Buildings may be new; scheduling procedures may be new; student and faculty lifestyles may be new; committee structures may be new; but none of this matters if the faculty member does not see himself in a new role. The experimental model provides the benefits of new staffing patterns and new roles for faculty. The nature of these roles and staffing patterns will evolve over time. Projections of their character can be made at present only tentatively. Needed now are illustrative environments; from these, accumulating evidence concerning the nature of needed innovations can be collected and disseminated.

The Schools

The benefit audiences in the schools include instructional leaders, teachers, and pupils.

Instructional Leaders. Those who assume responsibility for curriculum planning, development, and implementation in the schools benefit in a variety of ways through association with the experimental models. Through the close interaction of personnel in the universities and those in the schools. ideas evolve as each faculty draws on the experience and expertise of the other. The benefit to the schools is first: the university staff develops a better understanding of the schools philosophy and practice as it will be experienced by precertification students; and in the assistance cooperating faculty can render. The parallel nature of teacher education and the school curricular programs creates a set of common problems; faculty can seek solutions at both levels. As faculty move easily back and forth between schools and the university through the medium of the experimental model, tentative solutions can be formed through cooperative action.

Perhaps the major benefit of the experimental models to the instructional leadership in the schools is the nature of the students who are becoming teachers. Their competencies are known; their goals are clearly established. The result is an improved relationship between these students, their teachers, principals and others in leadership roles within the schools. Such understanding results in students who are not only better served by the schools as they learn; the students can be more appropriately directed for optimum effect on the students they will teach.

Teachers. The experimental models benefit teachers in the schools in a variety of ways. First, and most significant, are the advantages already identified for the precertification students. All of these advantages also accrue to the in-service teacher seeking improvement of her teaching skills or better understanding of her teaching role and her students. The experimental models include designs for in-service work. This in-service work extends the instructional mechanisms of the models beyond the precertification level. The benefits already identified for precertification students will not be repeated here. However, those benefits (of individualization, personalization, and competency based programs) accrue to in-service teachers as well.

Beyond these direct benefits accruing to teachers working directly within the models context, intertemporal benefits evolve as precertification students become teachers in schools everywhere. In that sense teachers in the schools experience a new set of benefits separate from those mentioned above. Teachers coming into the schools from the experimental models have a more comprehensive understanding of the schools, of learners in the schools, and of faculty roles and expectations.

But the most important benefit is their perception of themselves as teachers. They have identified and developed a set
of theories to guide their teaching practice, they understand
the competencies they possess, and they understand that schools
are changing as society changes. This appreciation of change
provides what may be the most crucial benefit in the two or
three decades ahead as graduates of today's universities help
create schools for the twenty-first century. The entire model
is essentially a confirmatory mechanism; the student learns
to use the continuous flow of data to make decisions relevant
to an ever-changing school.

    <u>Pupils</u>. Ultimately the benefits of the experimental model
are designed to enhance the quality of education for the individual pupil in the school. The flexibility of the model,
the individualization provided for the learning teacher, and
the teacher's resulting appreciation of the individuality of
learners is a direct benefit to pupils. For too long schools
have responded to pupils as though they were all of a kind.
Provision for pupils with diverse backgrounds has been rare
and continues to be rare in our schools. Pupils from minority groups -- ethnic, cultural, racial, religious -- have
often found their identity ignored in schools geared to homo-
geneity. The experimental models provide teachers who have
been dealt with as individuals and who have been helped to
view learning as a very individual matter. They have come to
appreciate the importance of varied learning environments to
provide individuals with ideas or experiences which are personally useful. It is in this context that the models contribute most significantly to the education of disadvantaged
youth.

    Teachers can be assigned according to their specific
competencies; pupils will have teachers who recognize and appreciate their differences. Pupils will experience more effective teaching. Learners will benefit as schools move increasingly to individualize and personalize programs; as they
come in contact with teachers who understand and can implement such programs.

The Community.

    Benefited audiences within the community are: parents,
tax payers, public educational services, foundations and commercial enterprises. All these derive benefits from the implementation of the experimental models program.

    All benefits to children (from the experimental models
program) are benefits to parents as well. More specifically,
however, parents derive a number of other benefits. Perhaps
most important is the opportunity parents will have of knowing
how their children are doing. Parents will rely less on a
teacher's opinion that tells them as much about the teacher
as it does about the child. Instead, parents will be given
assessments that specify the tasks to be learned and that

evaluate progress in terms of the achievement of these specific competencies. Parents will understand better what their
children are learning.

Since administrators will be able to select teachers
with the specific competencies needed for a particular school,
parents can be confident teachers have been selected on the
basis of better evidence than in the past.

A fully operating experimental models program with paral
lel development in the schools will provide parents with instructional models. These will make it possible for parents to
better plan educational experiences for their own children.
Certainly the school is not the only educating institution in
the community. For some children the school is the major educational institution; for others it is but one of several,
including the home, the church and a variety of community
organizations. Parents who better understand what the schools
are contributing will be in a better position to plan for the
use of other community resources in educating their children.

Finally, a major benefit of the competency based experimental models program for parents is that they will be able
to use its resources for their own development. Parents
wanting to know more about the mathematics program will be
able to undertake independent introductory studies of it.
The school can become a known educational quantity to everyone within its sphere of influence.

Tax payer benefits from the experimental models are difficult to analyze at this time for two reasons: development
and implementation costs are, as yet, unknown. Also, we cannot yet anticipate how widespread the effects of the program
will be. The level of sophistication required of delivery
systems for competency based programs is still unknown. Cost
is related to that level of sophistication. Likewise, we
need demonstration sites. These will provide evidence of the
most efficient way to disseminate competency based programs
to large numbers of learners. The main benefit to tax payers
at present arises from the implications of systems designs for
management and budgeting (of both development and implementation) of teacher education programs. This systematic approach
assures the tax payer of efficient use of available funding
and provides him with data concerning what the costs are; what
expected or actual benefits are; and how specific items are
related to budgetary allocations.

Each community supports a large number of educational
services. More often than not these services are totally un-
coordinated and minimally used in relation to school programs.
The experimental models will encourage coordination of these
services. First, the models provide a demonstration of effective and efficient management of a wide variety of learning
resources within the formal educational community. Indeed,
in many instances, these resources from the larger community
may be built into the school's more formal network of resources

through the activities of the training complex. Secondly, the specificity with which the school and the university define their responsibilities will make it possible for other educational institutions to review and re-define their own potential for supplementary contributions. The result is a community-wide consciousness of educational responsibilities. Schools can serve but a small proportion of them. The recognition and assumption of responsibility to coordinate this larger educational world for all citizens in the community is a major benefit that will result from several elements of the models program, implemented at the community level.

Foundations seek ways of supporting innovations to serve the common good. The foundations will benefit from the developing models program through the profusion of ideas generated by an evolving program. Foundations will find many of these ideas useful in their continuing search for useful educational alternatives.

Commercial enterprises including hardware, software, and service organizations will find many cooperative ways to work with and through the developing experimental models programs. While they will find many benefits from such a cooperative arrangement, they also will make substantial contributions in terms of packaging, marketing, and servicing instructional materials. Their expertise in these areas will assure wide dissemination of the process and products developed by the models programs; as a result the cost per learner/unit will be reduced over time. Thus, cooperation between the business and education communities can make the innovations resulting from the models program more economically feasible. It is expected that business dollar investments in education will be more economically sound than they have been in the past.

The Profession

Audiences within the profession include State Departments of Public Instruction, professional organizations, teachers unions, and certification agencies.

Several state departments are carefully investigating the potential of competency based certification. Such certification is nearly useless if it is not accompanied by competency based programs. Initial efforts to certify on such a basis may not be accompanied by competency based programs; if this happens, such efforts will fail. If we are to determine the validity of competency based certification, it must be accompanied by comparable programs. One of the benefits of the models is the provision of such program bases.

Professional organizations in education represent a wide range of philosophies. The Association for Supervision and Curriculum Development, The Association for Educational Communications and Technology, The National Council of Teachers of English, and the National Council of Teachers of Mathematics may each take different positions on the issue of competency based education programs. A major benefit of the fully implemented models program is that it will provide a testing ground for these positions. The models can provide an opportunity to demonstrate the potential problems of competency based education. A widely diverse professional community will have the opportunity to observe, discuss, and debate the merits of an evolving entity at all levels.

Teachers unions themselves, hesitant, but generally supportive of competency based education, will have an opportunity to study the nature of such programs through a series of fully operating programs. What new roles will be required of teachers; how teachers may be expected to prepare themselves for these roles; what impact cooperative group teaching procedures will have on the individual teacher; and the implications that recognized levels of teaching competency will have for the profession are all questions of substantial interest to teachers' bargaining agents. The use of the models context in which to make such a study is essential to the effective integration of a wide variety of views on these issues.

Certification agencies at both college and local school levels utilize sets of standards developed over time, often informally. The certification of competency based programs will require a new approach to the establishment of criteria. A fully operating model will provide bases for judgments on functional standards. Once certification by competencies becomes a major route into the profession, we expect the obvious benefits of such programs to encourage direct certification of the prospective teacher; current indirect methods will be unnecessary.

Benefits of Other Components of the Operational Plan for Program Development

Training complexes, protocols and training materials, and the Competency Based Program of the Operational Plan for Program Development in Teacher Education are viewed as essential to the facilitation of the instructional environments provided by the experimental models. While the benefit section of this has concentrated primarily on the experimental models, we have assumed the support of other components.

It is through the training complexes that we expect to achieve much of the essential coordination between universities and schools, between formal and informal educational institutions of the community, between the local educational establishment and the professional organizations, between schools and the community. The experimental models require the extensive use of protocols and training materials. Without them, the experimental models cannot exist. A plan would need to be developed to provide these materials if the protocol and training materials program has not been established. The confirmatory mechanisms inherent in the Compentency Based Program are essential to the effectiveness of the experimental models. The essence of the models is change. That change must be monitored and directed. It is through the confirmatory mechanism that the models are kept in contact with reality. Part of the confirmatory mechanism is within the models themselves; part is at the larger state and national levels where the Competency Based Program assumes the responsibility.

Although the major focus of this paper is on the benefits of the experimental models, all benefits are dependent upon the interaction of these several programs. Direct benefits of protocols and training materials accrue first to the experimental models; without both, neither functions. In the same way, the direct benefit of the training complex is the systematic coordination of all components of teacher education. Through this interaction -- training complex/protocols/training materials/models -- a fully operational, comprehensive teacher educational program comes into being.

The Competency Based Program provides benefits in two directions. First, it provides continuing assessment of the effectiveness of various components of the Operational Plan. Second, it provides reports to the profession generally, concerning the nature of the evolving teacher education programs exemplified in the Operational Plan for Program Development in Teacher Education.

Many of the various interactive benefits of the Operational Plan are also intertemporal. That is, benefits from the program generate other benefits later, as they are disseminated to other audiences. An illustration of an intertemporal benefit stream might be: protocol materials, as they provide direct benefits to the experimental models; in turn the experimental models provide benefits to precertification teachers; who, upon certification, provide benefits to their pupils.

Summary

Because it is difficult to separate benefits derived specifically from each of the four or five major components of the Operational Plan we have focused here on the experimental models. The experimental models seem to provide the interface between the Operational Plan and learners in the schools. Other components feed benefits into a functioning model; through it benefits flow to precertification teachers and ultimately to the children they teach. It would be possible to focus on other aspects of the Operational Plan; either on the training complex or on the Competency Based Program, for example. In such cases, the integration of these components with the functioning experimental model would have been assumed. The comprehensive nature of these thrusts

and the commitment to total reform in teacher education they
represent provide an extensive array of benefits; ultimately
these benefits can be expected to redirect teaching and learning in many segments of educational endeavor.

A Cost Analysis for the Operational Plan

Several alternative strategies may be employed to develop the Operational Plan. Each strategy offers differing benefits and has different costs. Policy choices must therefore be based on a study of the relationship of costs to benefits. This section develops cost estimates for the Operational Plan and then uses the estimates to formulate alternative development strategies. The presentation of strategies, with a discussion of their costs and expected impact, highlights the policy decisions which must be made regarding development of the Operational Plan.

While this cost analysis should be considered in relation to the statement of benefits provided by the Operational Plan, the analysis does not constitute a complete benefit-cost analysis. None of the benefits have been presented in quantified form. While the quantification of some direct benefits may be possible (for example; each CBP Center will have a direct impact upon 450 preservice and inservice teachers or their equivalents in part-time participants), the quantification of all interactive and intertemporal benefits is currently impossible. Too little is currently known about the exact impact of teachers on student behavior and student learning. In addition, the values in monetary terms which one might place on student learning, particularly at the elementary school level, would be arbitrary if not capricious. Nevertheless, the following presentation should assist in the intuitive evaluation of alternative development strategies.

Costs of a CBP Center

As a first step in determining costs of alternative development strategies, the costs of developing and implementing an CBP Center have been estimated. In preparing this initial estimate, program categories were selected which were consistent with the organization of the Operational Plan as five thrusts and with the interdependent functions which the thrusts would serve (Figure 2). The four categories employed here—Protocol and Training Materials, Training Complexes, Experimental Models, Confirmatory Mechanism—also permit the examination of alternative development strategies later in this section.

Two distinct costing categories arise in preparing a five year plan for the Operational Plan which will culminate in a functioning program: development and implementation. Development cost is defined as the cost of resources necessary to design, prepare and test a "master copy" of all materials required for the Operational Plan with one CBP Center. While some costs for development would obviously be devoted to pilot testing of materials with a group of students, development costs will depend principally upon the nature of the Model and not upon the size of the student body who will ultimately be participating in the program. Implementation costs is defined as the cost of resources required to install a fully developed CBP Center. It includes capital equipment and the reproduction of instructional materials. Implementation costs depend upon both the nature of the program and the size of the student population.

It will be observed in the following presentation of estimates that some of the program categories fall exclusively or predominantly into either development or implementation, while others have major components in each. Hence, the presentation of costs seems slightly artificial and redundant. The distinction between development and implementation has been made, however, to facilitate the presentation of alternative development strategies, where the number and size of participating institutions become important parameters.

The estimates of costs were derived from several sources, including Teachers for the Real World, various feasibility studies from instutions participating in the Models program, and USOE reports. The following discussion describes the categories used to present estimates and indicates the manner in which the estimates were obtained. Table 1 summarizes these estimates.

Development Costs
1. Protocols and Materials Development: preparation of mediated materials which are designed to develop cognitions or skills within teacher education students. This category includes both capital equipment for production and technical personnel. The estimate of $4,500,000 shown here represents the estimate of a commercial firm for the design and production of mediated presentations which comprises 80 percent of the activities in a teacher education program. This estimate does not reveal the

fact that costs of protocols and training materials would be on-going; revisions and additions to the set of materials would imply an on-going cost of a fraction of this total sum on an annual basis, once the Operational Plan was completely functioning. Depending upon the portion of the program selected for revision this year, this annual cost could range from 1/8 to 1/5 of the total development sum.

2. Training Complex: design of a system to coordinate the efforts of universities, schools, communities and industry and to conduct certification activities. This category also includes the development of clinical experiences for teachers. The costs of the various functions identified here are drawn from detailed cost analyses by the Universities of Massachusetts, Georgia, Toledo, and Wisconsin.

    a. Development of Interinstitutional System: the estimate of $360,000 reflects the assumption that the costs of developing an interinstitutional system over five years will be roughly comparable to that for developing an extensive management system for a complete teacher education program at a single institution.

    b. Development of Clinical Experiences Activities: the estimate of $256,000 represents development of the portion of the instructional program of the Experimental Models which includes activities in the schools. An arbitrary percentage was placed in the category on the basis of an examination of cost estimates.

3. Models: design of a professional education program to prepare teachers, culminating in a B.A. degree and at least a provisional teaching certificate. This category includes the design and development of a system to manage the instructional program and guide students through the program, as well as the costs associated with designing instructional materials. Cost estimates here are taken from a report summarizing costs of all models.

a. Development of Instructional Programs: the estimate of $6,144,000 includes professional and supportive personnel, supplies and space for five years to be used to identify, formulate, and develop materials to fulfill program objectives.

b. Design of Inservice Program: the estimate of $1,250,000 is an average of the estimated costs of developing three extensive inservice programs. The figures ranged from $.5 million to $2.0 million. In each case, the inservice program was independent of the undergraduate teacher education program.

c. Management and Information System Design: the estimate of $1,900,000 assumes the complete development of a system to manage instructional activities of participating students. It includes both software development and hardware time.

d. Development of Student Assessment: the estimate of $1,000,000 assumes design and testing of evaluative instruments to screen prospective students, assess students' progress, diagnose students' weaknesses and in some cases permit students to bypass instructional activities.

4. Confirmatory Mechanism: formulation of research strategies to test all aspects of the Operational Plan's effectiveness in relation to teacher performance and impact upon students. The total estimate of $1,400,000 used here is the cost of developing an extensive research program to complement the development of a model undergraduate program. The research would study all aspects of program effectiveness and impact upon teacher behavior and pupil change.
    a. Competency Based Program: the estimate of $300,000 represents that portion of the total research effort which would be directed to studying means of ultimately attaining teacher accountability for pupil performances.
    b. Research on Instructional Effectiveness: the estimate of $1,000,000 is for costs of developing an on-going system of research to complement the development, redevelopment, and pilot testing for the instructional program.

Implementation Costs

2. Training Complex: the estimate of $500,000 used here for implementation costs for a training complex represents an arbitrary estimate of $100,000 for annual operating expenses. This is the only category for which operating costs as such are included in implementation estimates. These funds might be from federal, state or local sources.
3. Models: the equipment to present and manage students' use of media in the instructional program.
    a. Media Presentation Equipment: the estimate of $1,033,000 shown here will serve the needs of 600 participating students for both A-V equipment and computer terminals in a highly mediated program. This estimate presumes extensive use of the Protocols and Training Materials. Approximately one-fourth of this figure is allocated to computer terminals.
    b. Media Management System (Dial Access): the estimate of $750,000 will provide an automated system which will enable students at terminals to request specific media presentation.
    c. Faculty Retraining: the estimate of $700,000 represents the costs of a program for university faculty to acquaint them with the new roles imposed by a highly individualized, mediated program and to assist them in adjusting to a less autonomous role than they presently have. This cost would be less if the Experimental Models assumed a more traditional stance.
4. Competency Based Programs: the implementation costs for competency based programs at a CBP Center are here considered to be the costs of maintaining the activities of an advisory board which will direct the research activities. The estimate of $150,000 represents estimated yearly costs of $30,000 throughout a five-year period. The annual costs are restricted to expenses for a twelve member board.

TABLE 1

CBP CENTER COST SUMMARY

Program Category		Five Year Estimated Cost
Development		
1.	Protocols and Materials Development	$4,500,000
2.	Training Complexes	
	a. Development of Interinstitutional Systems	360,000
	b. Development of Clinical Experiences Activities	256,000
3.	Models	
	a. Development of Instructional Programs	6,144,000
	b. Design of Inservice Programs	1,250,000
	c. Management and Information Systems Design	1,900,000
	d. Development of Student Assessment	1,000,000
4.	Confirmatory Mechanism	
	a. Competency Based Program	300,000
	b. Research on Instructional Effectiveness	1,100,000
Implementation		
2.	Training Complexes	500,000
3.	Models	
	a. Media Presentation Equipment	1,033,000
	b. Media Management System	750,000
	c. Faculty Retraining	700,000
4.	Confirmatory Mechanism	
	a. Competency Based Program	150,000
TOTAL		$19,943,000

Illustrative Development Strategies

Many alternative plans may be employed in developing a complete Operational Plan for Program Development in Teacher Education. Alternative development and implementation strategies may be designed by varying the number of schools participating in either development or implementation and the number and nature of the Training Complexes and Experimental Models which are being developed. These alternatives cannot be expected to be equivalent, in either their effect upon teacher education or in cost. This discussion considers both effects and costs, in presenting three alternatives to the basic pattern of a single CBP Center.

For purposes of discussion, three different development strategies are outlined here. The three choices have been made to display the possible range of alternatives as well as the manner in which additional alternatives may be designed and priced. The alternatives are:

1. Develop ten CBP Centers using three Experimental Models.
2. Develop eight CBP Centers, each with a different Experimental Model.
3. Develop fifteen CBP Centers, using instructional materials from two Experimental Models.

Before the effects of these alternatives are discussed, together with their costs, some general guidelines should be presented.

Development Effects. Alternative development strategies will substantially affect the type of benefits to be derived from any development activities. Three dimensions of the impact which will accompany a development strategy will be noted in the following discussion: the extent of the change which a strategy imposes on teacher education; the size of the population of teachers who are affected; and the characteristics of this population of teachers.

The range of effect which can be attached to each of these three dimensions is considerable. The extent of change imposed by activities may range from improvements in existing teacher education programs to a radical restructuring of teacher education. The size of the population which is affected could vary from future teachers at one institution to comparable groups at several hundred institutions. Characteristics of the population immediately affected are likely to reflect the nature of the institution they attend, its size and its resources.

Each of these dimensions must also be considered in relation to a time horizon; a maximization of the impact of one dimension may imply a time horizon different from that required for maximization of another dimension. Radical restructuring of teacher education on even a small number of campuses, for example, is not possible as rapidly as is the introduction of changes into existing programs.

Development Costs. The cost estimates for a complete CBP Center have been used to estimate the total costs of the three alternatives presented here. In some categories, estimated costs were extrapolated directly from the base estimates. In several cases, however, allowances were made for additional costs which would be incurred by any development strategy which involves many institutions. These additional costs are greatest when the development or implementation of a single program are shared. Activities such as program coordination, program piloting, preparation of materials, program conversion and faculty retraining, will be repeated for participating institutions.

Estimated costs for each of the proposed alternatives are shown in Table 2. Numbers in parentheses indicate the multiples used to convert the figures from Table 1.

Benefits and Costs of Alternative Strategies. Each one of the three alternative development and implementation strategies offers advantages which are not evident from a simple comparison of costs. This discussion examines the alternatives in terms of the three dimensions of effect: extent of change; size of affected population;and characteristics of the affected population. Additional comments suggest some advantages and disadvantages which may not be obvious from the discussion of effects.

1. Ten CBP Centers using three Experimental Models. $65,161,000.

The development of ten CBP Centers provides an opportunity to plan and carry out major changes in teacher education. Judicious selection of participating institutions, with attention to geographic and organizational diversity, will permit the introduction of changes in a variety of institutional settings, maximizing the demonstration effect of the program. The size and characteristics of the population which is immediately affected depends upon the nature of the participating institutions; obviously, considerable diversity is possible.

Comments

The channeling of resources from ten institutions into the development of three models would provide a strong base for development activity. While there may be occasional communication problems,the expanded resource base should make the multiple-institution development a greater advantage than disadvantage.

The implementation of three Experimental Models at ten CBP Centers will facilitate the examination of each model's effectiveness in a variety of settings. Multiple implementation of each model will also reduce the possibility of program failure for strictly institutional reasons.

2. Eight CBP Centers, each with a unique Experimental Model. $88,063,000.

The development of eight unique models should provide the maximum amount of change in teacher education in the long run, by insuring the availability on a demonstration basis, of a broad spectrum of programs. The size and characteristics of the student population which would be affected immediately would again be dependent upon the choice of participating institutions.

TABLE 2

OPERATIONAL PLAN FOR PROGRAM DEVELOPMENT IN TEACHER EDUCATION

Development and Implementation Alternatives

... Alternatives ...

Program Category	Ten CBP's, Three Models [1]	Eight Unique CBP's [2]	Fifteen CBP's Using 2 Models [3]
Development			
1. Protocols and Materials Development	(1) $4,500,000	(1.5) $6,750,000	(1.5) $6,750,000
2. Training Complex			
a. Interinstitutional Systems	(3) 1,080,000	(3) 1,080,000	(3.5) 1,800,000
b. Clinical Experiences Activities	(3) 768,000	(8) 2,048,000	(2) 516,000
3. Models			
a. Instructional Programs	(3) 18,432,000	(5) 30,720,000	(2) 12,289,000
b. Inservice Programs	(3) 3,750,000	(5) 6,250,000	(2) 2,500,000
c. Management and Information System	(1.5) 2,850,000	(5) 9,500,000	(1.5) 2,850,000
d. Student Assessment	(3) 3,000,000	(8) 8,000,000	(2) 2,000,000
4. Confirmatory Mechanism			
a. Competency Based Program	(10) 3,000,000	(8) 2,400,000	(15) 4,500,000
b. Instructional Effectiveness	(3) 3,300,000	(7) 2,100,000	(15) 3,000,000

. . . Alternatives . . .

Program Category	1 Ten CBP's, Three Models		2 Eight Unique CBP's		1 3 Fifteen CBP's Using 2 Models	
Implementation						
1. Protocol and materials [1]	(10)	$2,000,000	(8)	$1,600,000	(15)	$3,000,000
2. Training Complexes	(10)	5,000,000	(8)	4,000,000	(15)	7,500,000
3. Models[2]						
a. Media Presentation Equipment	(7)	7,231,000	(5)	5,165,000	(10)	10,330,000
b. Media Management System	(7)	5,250,000	(5)	3,750,000	(10)	7,500,000
c. Faculty Retraining	(5)	3,500,000	(5)	3,500,000	(10)	7,000,000
4. Confirmatory Mechanism						
a. Competency Based Program	(10)	1,500,000	(8)	1,200,000	(15)	2,250,000
		$65,161,000		$88,063,000		$73,785,000

Notes to TABLE 2

1. The arbitrary figure of $200,000 is meant to cover duplicating costs, to supply a single program center with a complete set of materials.

2. Anticipated scale economics or variations in needs for media presentation equipment are reflected in the multiples for the program category.

92

Comments

The implementation of each Experimental Model in only one CBP Center would reduce the tested generalizability of each model. However, with such a range of programs from which to choose, adopting institutions might be encouraged to be more eclectic in their choice of programs, drawing from each the features which would contribute most to their own model.

The development of eight unique models will impose very heavy manpower requirements on developing institutions; handling this comparatively short-run phenomenon without incurring surplus staff later will pose a problem for each institution.

The population which would be immediately affected would be smaller with this alternative than with the preceding alternative. A comparison of long range effects is not so easy; this alternative may have substantially greater impact by offering eight alternatives, not just three, to institutions interested in new approaches to teacher education.

3. Fifteen CBP Centers using Two Experimental Models. $73,785,000.

The development of two Experimental Models is not so likely to produce long-run major changes in teacher education as are the first two alternatives. The implementation of these models at fifteen centers would, however, provide considerable opportunity to view each model in a wide variety of settings. A large population of teachers would be affected immediately; their characteristics could be widely varied.

Comments

This alternative emphasizes one of the major policy decisions which must be made in choosing a development strategy: whether long-run, radical change or comparatively short-run, substantial improvement is preferred. The alternative provides the opportunity to work out many operational problems likely to arise with the CBP Centers, though it provides the Centers with less variety in the instructional program.

A Five Year Plan for the Development and Implementation of the Operational Plan

A five-year development strategy for the Operational Plan must consider not only the nature and magnitude of the impact which the total plan will have on teacher education, but also the interrelationships among aspects of the overall Operational Plan and their effect on development strategies over time.

The strategy outlined here presents costs for the development of five different Experimental Models and their implementation at fifteen CBP Centers. This alternative should both have considerable impact on the nature of teacher education and also affect large populations of students in the short run. The long-range, demonstration effects resulting from the development of five complete and unique models for teacher education will be highly significant. The implication of these models at fifteen CBP Centers should afford considerable opportunity to examine the effectiveness of each model in several environments and under a variety of institutional arrangements. This strategy may be compared with three other less costly alternatives which are presented and discussed in the preceding section.

The development strategy outlined here is designed to insure the development of prerequisite portions of the Operational Plan and to preserve maximum flexibility within the development plan. Thus, instructional materials are developed and tested before their integration into instructional systems and total implementation. Development activities are begun slowly to permit maximum "learning" related to operational considerations in the development period.

The program categories used in Table 3 to present the five year plan are those developed in the previous section of this paper; a description of each category and the activities it includes is presented there.

Several additional alternative development strategies could also be formulated on the basis of cost estimates presented in the previous section. Table 4 offers estimated totals for implementing one highly mediated Experimental Model at varying numbers of CBP Centers.

TABLE 3

OPERATIONAL PLAN FOR PROGRAM DEVELOPMENT IN TEACHER EDUCATION

Proposed Development and Implementation Strategy

Five Models, Fifteen CBP Centers

Program Category	Year					TOTAL
	1	2	3	4	5	
	2%	20%	40%	35%	3%	
1. Development						
1. Protocols and Materials Development	$135,000	$1,350,000	$2,700,000	$2,362,000	$202,500	$6,750,000
2. Training Complex						
a. Interinstitutional Systems	21,600	216,000	432,000	378,000	32,400	1,080,000
b. Clinical Experiences Activities	20,480	204,800	409,600	358,400	30,720	1,024,000
3. Models						
a. Instructional Programs	482,320	4,823,200	9,646,400	8,440,600	723,480	24,116,000
b. Inservice Programs	100,000	1,000,000	2,000,000	1,750,000	150,000	5,000,000
c. Management and Information System	152,120	1,521,200	3,042,400	2,732,100	158,180	7,606,000
d. Student Assessment	100,000	1,000,000	2,000,000	1,750,000	150,000	5,000,000
4. Confirmatory Mechanism						
a. Competency Based Program	20,000	200,000	400,000	350,000	30,000	1,000,000
b. Instructional Effectiveness	60,000	600,000	1,200,000	1,050,000	90,000	3,000,000

Year

Program Categories, Cont.	1	2	3	4	5	TOTAL
II Implementation	0%	2%	20%	40%	38%	
1. Protocols and Materials	0	60,000	600,000	1,200,000	1,140,000	3,000,000
2. Training Complex	1,500,000	1,500,000	1,500,000	1,500,000	1,500,000	7,500,000
3. Models						
a. Media Presentation Equipment	0	206,600	2,066,000	4,132,000	3,925,400	10,330,000
b. Media Management System	0	150,000	1,500,000	3,000,000	2,850,000	7,500,000
c. Faculty Retraining	140,000	1,400,000	2,800,000	2,450,000	210,000	7,000,000
4. Confirmatory Mechanism						
a. Competency Based Program	450,000	450,000	450,000	450,000	450,000	2,250,000
III Administration	520,000	520,000	520,000	520,000	520,000	2,600,000
TOTALS	$3,701,520	$15,201,800	$31,266,900	$32,423,100	$12,162,680	$94,756,000

TABLE 4

OPERATIONAL PLAN DEVELOPMENT ALTERNATIVES

One Model, Varying Number of CBP Centers

Number of CBP Centers	Development Cost	Implementation Cost	Total Cost
15	$21,660,000	$37,580,000	$59,240,000
30	21,660,000	75,160,000	96,820,000
60	21,660,000	150,320,000	171,980,000
120	21,660,000	300,640,000	322,300,000

CHAPTER 5

NOTES ON A SCHOOL-UNIVERSITY
CONSORTIUM FOR TEACHER EDUCATION

Benjamin Rosner

1.   Introduction

     The levers or mechanisms by which reform in teacher ed-
ucation can be attained come from five sources--the school,
the community, government agencies, the university, and
professional associations. The levers which are derived
from the operation of the schools reflect the school
curriculum and its organizational structures. The school
curriculum contributes to much of the content of the
teacher education program; the school organization
contributes to a definition of staffing patterns and roles
of specific educational personnel.

     Community here refers to the lay public. The levers
which the community provides are statements of educational
goals and financial support. Government agencies also
provide levers for change. The levers associated with local,
state, and Federal agencies are financial support, and
accreditation and certification of educational programs
and personnel.

     At the university level, a primary lever is associated
with the governance of the institution. In addition, levers
may be identified with admission practices, the reward
structure for the teaching, scholarship, research and public
service functions of the faculty, and degree requirements.
Finally, the activities of subject matter associations
influence the content emphases of school and college
curricula, while professional teacher associations have
marked impact on staff utilization, conditions of employment,
and compensation.

     Reform in teacher education must take into account the
distribution of power among all sources. Reform based solely
on the power inherent in any single source is inadequate.
identification of mechanisms which focus the power of all
sources on common objectives is essential for the
institutionalization of change in teacher education.

II. Levers for Change

Levers may be identified by examining the pertinent policies and practices of the school, the university, the community, government agencies, and professional associations. Such examination suggests that changes in teacher education must be accompanied by changes in policy formulation, university admissions, university teacher education curricula, personnel evaluation procedures, personnel certification procedures, school curricula, and school employment practices. More specifically, the levers may be defined as: parity (policy formulation), student recruitment practices (admissions), performance-based teacher education, exemplary school curricula, confirmatory mechanisms (evaluation), performance-based certification, and staff utilization. The systematic manipulation of these levers will yield modifications in teacher training. Each of the levers for change is discussed below.

A. Parity

Parity effects change in teacher education by including representatives from the lay public, school administration, teacher associations, university liberal arts and education faculties, and students in teacher education on an advisory board influencing the governance of teacher training programs. The board would assist in the development of policy governing both school and university based components of the teacher education program. This modification of policy formulating procedures tends to assure the responsiveness of teacher training to the publicly expressed objectives and priorities of the school and community.

B. Student Recruitment Practices

Recruitment serves as a lever by systematically manipulating the flow of human resources into teacher education. Such recruitment may be directed towards high school students entering colleges or universities, adults entering the schools at the paraprofessional level, and teachers aspiring to positions of educational leadership. Moreover, based on the assumption that many knowledges and skills are common to education and other professions, recruitment can be aimed at individuals with special experience and competencies to minimize the time and cost of training; e.g., some mathematics teachers may be recruited from engineering, and some school administrators may be recruited from government or business.

C. Performance-Based Teacher Education

Performance-based teacher education is a lever for change because it requires the explication of the specific knowledges and skills that comprise the teacher education program. Performance-based teacher education requires systematic assessment of the student's performance at various stages of the program. A graduate of such a program would have demonstrated mastery of the knowledges and skills included

99

with the training program to a specified level of competence. It is anticipated that performance-based teacher education would encourage modularization of the curriculum and personalization of the training process.

   D. Exemplary School Curricula

   An exemplary school curriculum has two functions: to educate children and to prepare educational personnel. In its first function, the curriculum serves the needs of children. In its second function, the curriculum provides students of teaching with opportunities for practice within the framework of an internally consistent education-al program. In this manner, the capacity of a school to serve the needs of children is prerequisite to its capacity to serve as a teacher training institution. The British Infant School and the Montessori School are two examples of exemplary curricula.

   Schools vary in the quality of their educational programs and in their willingness to serve as teacher train-ing facilities. If a school can be identified by a parity board as possessing an exemplary program and if the school is willing to serve as a teacher training institution, the objectives of the school-university teacher training pro-gram are mutually supportive. If a school is willing to become a training facility, but does not provide an exemplary curriculum, the school curriculum would need to undergo transformation under the auspices of a parity board so that the school offers an effective environment for teacher education.

   E. Confirmatory System

   The confirmatory system provides evidence of the effectiveness of each element of a training program, and for the program as a whole. The confirmatory system may operate at six criterion levels. At the highest level, the confirmatory mechanism assesses the degree to which teachers possessing specific knowledges and skills utilize them in actual classroom situations, and whether these competencies produce changes in pupil performance. At this level, the confirmatory system operates as an accountability system for school personnel.

   At the lowest level the confirmatory system offers evidence about whether trainees have acquired specific knowledges and understandings of concepts relevant to the interpretation and modification of pupil classroom behavior. At the middle level, the confirmatory mechanism speaks to the effectiveness with which trainees have acquired specific pedagogic skills and requires the development of specific school based measures of teacher competence.

   F. Certification

   Both legal and "extra-legal" certification are levers for reform. Legal certification establishes minimum standards of competence as a condition for seeking and retaining employment in the schools. Extra-legal certification, functioning outside the direct control of state agencies, may establish standards of performance reflecting the highest levels of teacher competence.

The form of legal and extra-legal certification manipulates the form of training. If certification is based on profiles of specific competencies, teacher education programs will provide training addressed to these competencies. In addition, extra-legal certification can facilitate experimentation with new modes of certification, establish a career line in teaching, and encourage the integration of the disciplines in the program of teacher education.

G.   Personnel Employment Practices

Employment is a lever because it institutionalizes the roles and competencies of educational personnel. The creation of a new position, or the modification of existing positions, frequently requires personnel with new competencies. The demand for different skills establishes the need for new or modified training programs. For example, the introduction of teacher training positions in the schools would require some school personnel to assume new roles and acquire additional competencies. The need for competency as a teacher trainer would create the demand for new teacher education programs.

The ideas mentioned above identify points at which leverage can be applied to effect reform in teacher education. The parity board and the exemplary school are powerful levers to reconnect teacher education with the schools and the community. Performance-based teacher education and certification make public the knowledge and skills expected of educational personnel. As a consequence teacher education needs to establish itself within the framework of a strong confirmatory system. The development of this confirmatory system is a major priority for teacher education.

III.   A Parity-Based Teacher Education Program

The levers identified above may be manipulated in a variety of teacher training contexts. The model proposed here begins with a school-university-community consortium. The consortium is represented by a parity board which advises on the formulation of policy governing the full range of teacher training. The training program calls upon the resources of a university or college as well as the resources of special schools identified as school training centers.

Undergraduate students enter the teacher education program through the university and gradually move to the school. Paraprofessionals enter the program through the schools and gradually move to the university. Both the university and the school provide routes for entry into the profession--the school based training center route for paraprofessionals and the university route for general undergraduate students.

The college or university must provide each student with opportunities to become familiar with a variety of human service careers, including teaching. For those students electing education as a profession, the university is held accountable for their general education, their competency in one or more academic disciplines, and their mastery of concepts relevant to the diagnosis and treatment of human behavior in formal or informal learning situations. In addition, the university is responsible for assisting pre-service students to acquire a degree of mastery in a number of critical pedagogic skills. Concepts and "entry-level" skills can be acquired in a laboratory setting using a variety of audio-visual materials, including protocol and training materials, and micro-teaching procedures. A student would be held responsible for the acquisition of specified levels of pedagogic skill prior to his entry into the school training center for further skill development.

School training centers offer the real-world context for practicing and assimilating the skills acquired in the university laboratory. Opportunities for practice are offered by trained cooperating teachers (teacher trainers) under the supervision of a school-based director of training and his staff. A school serves as a training facility when it has installed an exemplary curriculum and its staff has been trained to use the school as a laboratory for the pre-paration of education personnel. Typically, a college would work with a cluster of four to six school training centers so that students would have practice opportunities within two or more exemplary schools. In this manner preservice (or inservice) teachers would become knowledgeable about several school curriculum and organizational patterns and avoid ideological indoctrination by exposure to a single point of view.

The university education faculty would divide their time between the schools and the campus. Some of the faculty would be housed primarily at the university (more than 50 percent of work-load) and assume responsibility for the foundations of education (concept development), the installation and maintenance of the university-based confirmatory system and research relevant to teaching and learning. Others on the faculty would be principally housed in school training centers (more than 50 percent of workload) and would be concerned with development of the exemplary curriculum and skill development.

The goals of the school-based faculty are:

1. the establishment of the exemplary curriculum;
2. the preparation of cooperating teachers for the training of preservice teachers, paraprofessionals, and new teachers;
3. the development and installation of school training programs; and

4.   acquisition of a new role as change agent and
     disseminator of innovative instructional practices
     and materials.

One of the major responsibilities of the education
faculty is the design, installation, and maintenance of an
exemplary curriculum. The faculty must work closely with
community and school personnel to assist in the formulation
of school objectives, the design of the school program, the
selection of curriculum materials and resources, and the
training of school personnel to implement the program. Responsibility for the maintenance of the exemplary curriculum
preserves the school-university-community relationship and
establishes the college faculty as change agents.

A second goal of field-oriented faculty is the preparation of the school staff for responsibility as teacher
trainers. The faculty must sensitize school staff to their
roles as teacher trainers in order that preservice teachers
are assured sufficient practice for the acquisition of
pedagogic skills. In addition, school staff must be trained
to administer the School Based Tasks (see Confirmatory
System). One criterion that can be employed to determine
whether or not a school staff has attained the competencies
essential to their roles as teacher trainers is their
ability to obtain "extra-legal" certification as teacher
trainers. Teacher trainers would be expected to take over
the training responsibilities of the school training center
within two or three years.

The training of cooperating teachers is but one aspect
of the establishment of a center. The education faculty
must assist in selecting and training key administrative
personnel, establish a closed-circuit TV facility to observe
practice sessions and the administration of School Based
Tasks, and develop a professional library and a curriculum
materials center.

Upon the installation of the exemplary curriculum, the
training of cooperating teachers, and the development and
installation of the administrative and training components
of the school training center, the education faculty would
be assigned to a new school. It is anticipated that the
transformation of education faculty from trainers to change
agents will significantly reduce the lag between R and D
and implementation. In addition, the process of systematically rotating college faculty to transform schools into
training centers is viewed as a fundamental strategy for
educational reform.

Figure 1 summarizes the school and university components of the teacher education program. Although the
design is primarily for the elementary school, it can be
extended to the secondary school where individual departments assume the curricular and training responsibilities
of a training center.

IV.   The School Training Center

103

The selection of a school for conversion into a school training center is the responsibility of a parity board. The parity board needs to negotiate with local school boards, school administrators, professional teacher association and the community at large in order that the training responsibilities of the institution and staff are thoroughly understood by all parties.

Figure 1.   Parity Based Teacher Education Program

Parity Board

University		School Training Center

General Education | Professional | |University faculty→Cooperating
                | Component | | Teachers
                | | | (Teacher

Career Orienta- | Laboratory | | Trainers)
tion | Based | |

Liberal Arts and | Concept | |Program
Science Speciali- | Attainment | |Exemplary Curriculum
zation | | |Preprofessional Teacher
                          | | |Training
                          | Pedagogic | |New Teacher Training
                          | Skill | |Paraprofessional Training

Initially centers might be selected from among schools with exemplary programs whose staffs express a strong commitment to teacher training and a willingness to prepare for the responsibility. Alternatively, centers may be selected from non-exemplary schools on the condition that the schools are willing to undertake curriculum transformation and staff development. Parity boards may also offer incentives to exemplary schools which are unwilling to use their resources for teacher training. Such incentives might include the creation of district teacher-trainer positions with additional financial remuneration for the completion of training and acquisition of appropriate certification, adjunct faculty status, sabbatical leave with pay for preparation as teacher trainers, and payment of examination fees for teachers who are candidates for Board certification as teacher trainers. [1]

A school training center has two major responsibilities: the maintenance of an exemplary program for service to children and the maintenance of a training program for preservice, paraprofessional, and beginning teachers. A third function of selected centers is to serve the examination needs of

---

[1] See the discussion of Educational Specialty Boards in Lieberman, M. The Future of Public Education. Chicago: University of Chicago Press, 1960.

Educational Specialty Boards. In addition, centers can
serve the performance-based certification needs of state
agencies. Finally, centers can serve as sites for the
field testing of new curriculum materials.

The staff of a center includes personnel with major
responsibility for the exemplary curriculum and a small unit
with major responsibility for the training and examination
program. The training and examining unit would include a
director, several trainer-examiners, audio-visual technicians and secretarial personnel.

The director of training would report to the principal
of the school training center and hold the rank of assistant
principal. The director would be responsible for assigning
trainees to teacher trainers; supervising training sessions;
supervising the administration of School Based Tasks; maintaining liaison with the university, state certification
agencies, and Educational Specialty Boards; maintaining the
video facility, the professional library and the curriculum
resources center; and participating in the field testing of
new training and examination materials and procedures. The
director would be assisted by trainer-examiners who would
share responsibility for specific aspects of the center's
operations. Under the supervision of the director, audio-
visual technicians would maintain the center's closed
circuit video facility.

Centers would be established in schools with 25 to 50
teacher trainers (cooperating teachers). Accordingly,
each center could train between 50 and 100 preservice
teachers annually. In addition, a center could accommodate 50 to 100 paraprofessionals. If a center does not
offer training opportunities for paraprofessionals, the
center could accommodate 100 to 200 preservice teachers.
The maximum number of preservice and paraprofessional
personnel to be trained in a center would depend on the
center's size and the staffing pattern appropriate to its
exemplary curriculum.

Although school training centers are principally de-
dicated to the training of preservice and paraprofessional
personnel, centers may also serve as examining agencies for
legal and extra-legal performance-based certification. Under
the assumption that performance-based certification would
require evidence of a teacher's knowledge and skills, the
center's training unit and its closed-circuit video facility
could arrange for an monitor the examination process.

V.   The Confirmatory System

Teacher education programs, performance-based or otherwise, need to operate within the context of a confirmatory
system. A confirmatory system is defined as the use of
evaluation procedures to measure the effectiveness of each
component of the program and the competencies of its
graduates. Such an evaluation program is both formative and

summative, since both the procedures and products of the
training program must be continually assessed. In the present model, both the university and the school based components are subject to the confirmatory system. Figure 2
suggests the confirmatory system operating in the service of

Figure 2. Confirmatory System

Parity Board

University			School Training Center	
General Educa- tion	Professional Education	Subject Special- ization	Training Program	Exemplary curriculum
	KNOWLEDGE SKILLS		1. Paraprofessional 2. Preservice[a] 3. Inservice[b] 4. Teacher Trainer[c]	
Criterion Level: 6 5 4 (Accountability	6 5 4	Criterion Level: SBT 1-4	3	Criterion Level: 1, 2 (Account- ability)

← ——————————— CONFIRMATORY SYSTEM —————————— →

[a]should contribute to decisions regarding provisional certification
[b]should contribute to decisions regarding continuing certification (permanent)
[c]should contribute to decisions regarding extra-legal certification

a parity based teacher education program. The criterion
levels indicated are described in Appendix A of the final
report.

Examination of Figure 2 shows the confirmatory system to
be operating at both the university and school training center
locations. At the university the confirmatory system operates
at Criterion Levels 4-6 to assess the program's effectiveness
in the knowledge domain (Criterion Level 6) and in the development of specific skills under simulated and micro-teaching
situations (Criterion Levels 5 and 4, respectively).
Criterion Levels 4-6 comprise the accountability program for
the university-based components of teacher education.

The training responsibilities of the center require the
installation of the confirmatory system at Criterion Level 3.
Criterion Level 3 confirms the attainment of competency in the
classroom setting. It is recommended that these competencies
be assessed through the administration of a series of

standardized exercises, or School Board Tasks.

It is suggested that four sets of School Based Tasks (SBT) be developed. The first set of SBT would define the competencies of paragrofessionals, would contribute to a definition of paraprofessional job responsibilities and would assist in defining the nature of the training program. The development of SBT (1) would have to take into account the varying responsibilities of paraprofessionals in different exemplary programs.

SBT (2) would be developed for preservice teachers. These tasks would probably include a number of tasks from SBT (1) but would require demonstration of a higher order of skill. In addition, SBT (2) would include tasks unique to the role of professional teachers in various exemplary schools. Just as SBT (1) would serve to clarify the competencies required of paraprofessionals, SBT (2) would assist in defining the skills of entry-level teachers. Obviously, SBT (2) would also help to shape the nature of the preservice training program.

A third set of tasks would need to be developed for teachers preparing for continuing or permanent certification, that is, teachers with one to three years of teaching experience. Again, it is likely that SBT (3) would include many tasks from SBT (2), but with expectations of greater skill mastery. It is also likely that SBT (3) would contain some tasks defining the unique responsibilities of more experienced teachers.

Finally, a fourth set of tasks would be developed for teacher trainers. SBT (4) would not only define the skills expected of teacher trainers, but would also contribute to a sharper definition of the training program.

Although the four sets of School Based Tasks might be developed by individual school-university teams, it is recommended that the development of SBT (1-3) be coordinated by a single agency in order to assure compliance with a common set of technical specifications and to minimize duplication of effort and cost. In addition, a national program of SBT (1-3) development would provide a set of standardized exercises to facilitate research on teacher education. Lastly, sets of School Based Tasks (1-3) would encourage experimentation with performance-based certification at the paraprofessional, provisional, and permanent levels.

It is also recommended that the development of SBT (4) be the responsibility of the extra-legal Educational Specialty Boards. SBT (4) would function at the level of teacher trainers. If Educational Specialty Boards develop examinations to reflect the highest levels of competence in the field, recipients of extra-legal certification should be qualified as teacher trainers. The competencies required of teacher trainers should, therefore, be built into the specialty boards for each field.

The confirmatory system operating at Criterion Levels 3-6 is concerned exclusively with the assessment of knowledges and skills. At Criterion Levels 1 and 2, the confirmatory system is concerned with the effectiveness of the exemplary curriculum. Criterion Levels 1 and 2 introduce an accountability program for the school. In turn, Criterion Levels 1 and 2 provide a yardstick by which to measure the effectiveness of skills associated with Criterion Level 3. Similarly, School Based Tasks at Criterion Level 3 offer a criterion against which to measure the effectiveness of the university components of the training program. In general, the confirmatory system assists both the university and the school training center to review and revise each component of the parity-based school-university teacher education program.

CHAPTER 6

BEPD, NCERD, AND TEACHER EDUCATION
THAT MAKES A DEMONSTRABLE DIFFERENCE

H. Del Schalock

INTRODUCTION AND OVERVIEW

The Bureau of Educational Personnel Development, U.S. Office of Education, has established within the past two years a number of program development thrusts that have come to be thought of as basic or foundational to other BEPD program efforts. These include the Protocol Materials Development program, the Training Materials Development program, the Training Complex program, and the Performance Based Certification program.[1] In addition, BEPD has assumed responsibility for the Elementary Teacher Education Models program, a developmental effort of the National Center for Educational Research and Decelopment, U.S. Office of Education, that was taken by NCERD through its design and feasibility testing stages.

In September of 1970, Dr. Don Davies, Associate Commissioner of Education and then Director of BEPD, established a task force internal to BEPD--Task Force '72--to study the implication of the five foundational thrusts for the structure and operation of the Bureau. The primary responsibility of the Task Force, headed by Dr. Allen Schmieder, is to submit alternative recommendations relative to the development of the five program thrusts outlined above, plans for implementing the alternative recommendations, projected costs associated with each plan, and the implications of each plan for other BEPD programs.

To help in the execution of its work, Task Force '72 has

_____
[1]For a definition of Protocol Materials, **Training** Materials, Training Complexes and other related terms see the GLOSSARY that is attached.

established an external working committee that is to generate
a primary set of inputs for Task Force consideration. These
inputs are to take the form of position papers prepared by a
number of persons familiar with one or more of the thrusts
being considered by the task force. The present paper is one
of that set.

The direct charge to those preparing position papers
was fourfold:

1. Present one or more proposals as to the "mix" of
    the five thrusts being considered by Task Force
    '72 that will optimize their impact, either
    individually or collectively, upon American ed-
    ucation particularly;
2. Spell out the implications of the mix (es) proposed
    for the operation of schools, for children within
    schools, for educational personnel development pro-
    grams, for state-wide certification procedures, for
    the Bureau of Educational Personnel Development and
    for OE generally;
3. Set out a plan of procedure, including tasks and
    timelines, for implementing the proposals made;
    and
4. Project cost estimates for carrying out the im-
    plementation plan.

While straightforward enough on the surface a number of
assumptions underlie the charge, and a number of issues
emerge from it. Two basic assumptions are (and these seem
to underlie all of the efforts of BEPD and Task Force '72)
(a) that American education is in need of reform; and (b)
that educational personnel development programs provide a
primary vehicle by which to effect such reform. Some of the
issues that arise are (a) Do the five thrusts under consideration provide the necessary and sufficient conditions
for the design of educational personnel development programs
that have the leverage to reform American education? (b)
If they do constitute such conditions how are they to be
organized into operational preparatory programs? (c) If they
do not constitute the necessary and sufficient conditions to
effect reform in American education through more effective
preparatory programs, what conditions would? (d) If educational personnel development programs could be developed
that effect the kinds of change in elementary and secondary
education desired, what would be needed to effect such changes
across the nation? A public stance in relation to such
matters would seem to be an additional charge that those
preparing position papers must meet.

The plan of the paper is relatively straightforward. As
a point of departure, and as a backdrop to the proposals made

in the paper, a position is presented with respect to the assumption and issues outlined above. Within the context of this position a "preferred" proposal relative to the mix of the five thrusts with which the paper is to deal is presented. Implications of the proposal are then traced, in cost-benefit terms, for staff and students, in a preparatory program so designed, for school personnel, for state departments of education, for children and the adult members of a community, and for several Bureaus within the U.S. Office of Education.

The rationale for and organization of the paper rests upon a careful definition of the five thrusts with which the proposal deals. These definitions are presented in an attached Glossary, and the reader is encouraged to study them carefully.

BACKGROUND NOTES

The Bureau of Education Personnel Development (BEPD) has responsibility by law, for providing assistance in and leadership to the preparation of educational personnel in the nation. It is constrained by law from the execution of research--and perhaps evaluation and development as well--yet it is committed intellectually to the necessity of these activities for the effective discharge of its legal responsibilities.

As it is currently organized BEPD has a number of "targeted population" programs, e.g., Rural-Urban and TTT; a number of "non-targeted" programs, e.g., Teacher Corp and COP; some experimental or demonstration programs, e.g., the Site Concentration and Performance Based Certification efforts; and some foundational or basic programs, e.g., Protocol Materials, Training Materials and Training Complexes. It also has inherited the Elementary Models program.

To an outsider looking in it is not clear how these various efforts relate to one another. The purpose of Task Force '72 is to make recommendations in this regard, particularly as to how the basic or foundation thrusts relate to one another and to other programs within the Bureau.

The National Center for Educational Research and Development (NCERD) has responsibility for providing assistance in and leadership to all aspects and levels of education in the nation through the application of research and development activities. Although it currently sponsors training programs in the areas of educational research, development, evaluation and diffusion, it is not generally responsible for the training function.

As one of its developmental activities NCERD sponsored
the design of new models for elementary teacher education.
Upon completion of their design and feasibility testing
they were transferred to BEPD for development and implementation. NCERD interest in the models remains,
however, partly because of interest in seeing that its
initial investment bears fruit and partly because the
models have build into them a strong R & D component.
As such, model based teacher education programs represent
extremely promising contexts for the pursuit of education R & D activities that have recognized significance.

A remarkable research finding has just been reported: experienced teachers in the areas of social science, auto
mechanics and electronics were unable to bring about greater learning gains in high school pupils in those subject areas--as measured by "performance items" of a paper
and pencil variety--than were college students studying
social science or tradesmen working as mechanics or
electronic equipment repairmen.[2]

PART I: A POINT OF VIEW

In this section of the paper a point of view is developed with respect to the assumptions and issues that underlie BEPD operations generally and the task of Task Force '72
specifically. Since it seems inescapable that the position
one takes with regard to these assumptions and issues will influence the position one takes as to the most desirable mix or
mixes of the five thrusts being dealt with, it would seem important that the reader of the paper be provided information
as to where the writer stands on these matters. It also seems
essential that this be done if the proposals with respect to
the structure, function, content and interaction of the five
thrusts which follow are to be fully understood.

Is Elementary and Secondary Education in the United States in Need of Reform?

In spite of the curriculum development and classroom reorganization efforts of the late 1950's and early 1960's, the
desegregation of the schools, the rather dramatic increase in
literacy in the nation, the increased emphasis upon the individualization of personalization of instruction, and the increasing emphasis upon accountability, there is general agreement across the land that genuine reform in elementary and
secondary education is sorely needed.[3] The severe problems

---

[2] Popham, James W. Performance Tests of Teaching Proficiency:
Rationale, Development and Validation. Amer. Educ. Res. J.,
1971, vol. 8, No. 1, pp. 105-117.

[3] See, for example, Charles Silberman's book Crisis in the
Classroom: The Remaking of American Education. New York, Random
House, 1970.

which persist in the area of reading, the inadequacy of occupational preparation and planning, the perceived "irrelevance"
of much that is offered as education by its consumers speak to
the need for fundamental reform at the elementary and secondary
level. So too does the political unrest within the schools,
the revolt of the tax-payers at the ballot box, and the increasing concern on the part of legislators, the congress and
the federal administration with the governance of education.
Silberman's concept of the "mindlessness" of American education captures as well as any other the characteristics of the
total system that cry for its reform.

In addition to such general concerns there are a number
of specific concerns that are increasingly in demand of attention: (a) the lack of clarity as to the goals and the indicators acceptable as evidence of the realization of those goals
for education generally or for the various populations of
learners for which a particular school is responsible (which,
contributes of course, in a major way to Silberman's concept
of mindlessness); (b) the apparent narrowness of the goals
that are operating within the schools either implicitly or
explicitly--in relation to the needs of children and youth in
today's world; (c) the failure of the schools to provide
systematic evidence on the relationship of program costs to
program benefits; (d) the failure thus far to fully implement
the ideal of individualized or personalized education; (e)
the relative lack of community participation in the entire enterprise. All of these aspects of elementary and secondary
education seem appropriate targets for change, and in this
sense the basic assumption of BEPD as to the need for educational reform would seem to be justifiable.

Can Educational Personnel Development Programs be Effective Tools for Educational Reform?

This is a more difficult question to answer than the
first, and it would seem that an honest response would be "it
depends." If educational personnel programs are designed to
perpetuate what IS instead of create what OUGHT TO BE, or poor
models are provided as to what ought to be, then it is hard to
see how educational reform can be effected through them. If,
on the other hand, there is some degree of clarity as to what
education in the future ought to be, and there is clarity as
to the role and task responsibilities of personnel within that
context--and there is a commitment to and a methodology for
insuring that personnel can in fact assume such roles and perform such tasks--it then seems reasonable to believe that preparatory programs could in fact effect reform in the larger
educational arena. Such a stance assumes, of course, that the
goals of education for various populations of learners are
clear, that the indicators acceptable as evidence of the realization of those goals have been made explicit, and that both

113

have been agreed to by all participating in the educational
enterprise.

<u>What Characteristics must Educational Personnel Development</u>
<u>Programs Assume if They are to Become Effective Instruments</u>
<u>of Educational Reform?</u>

In addition to being clear about the purpose of education
and the nature of the schools needed to bring those purposes
about, educational personnel development programs must assume
a number of additional characteristics if they are to effect
change in the broader educational picture. Some of these are
discussed in the paragraphs which follow. While not exhaustive they do provide guidelines for the development of preparatory programs that are likely to make a difference.

1. A SHIFT FROM AN EXPERIENCE-BASED TO A PERFORMANCE-BASED MODE OF OPERATION

Two broad strategies for the design and operation of
teacher education programs are currently in competition:
that which can be called an <u>experience based</u> strategy and that
which is being called a <u>performance based</u> strategy. Most
teacher education programs in operation today can be considered to be experience based, for by and large they involve a
specified number of courses or course hours in specified
areas of study. They are "performance based" in so far as
the requirement of a particular grade point average in
courses taken can be considered a performance measure, but
they do not specify in precise terms what it is that is to
be taken from such experiences. They do not specify what
prospective teachers need to know or be able to do or be able
to accomplish in order to become certified.[4]

Performance based programs differ from those that are
experience based in that the outcomes expected to derive from
them are specified. Operationally this means that the
knowledge, skills, attitudes, sensitivities, competencies,
etc. that prospective teachers are expected to have upon

---

[4] In spite of some performance language, a large share of
the recommendations appearing within the 1970 Standards and
Practices statement are still largely experiential in nature.
Specifically course work in the area of general studies,
content of teaching specialty, humanistic and behavioral
studies, teaching and learning theory with laboratory and
clinical experience, and a "practicum" experience are recommended. For details see <u>Recommended Standards for Teacher</u>
<u>Education</u>. The American Association for Colleges of Teacher
Education, One Dupont Circle, Washington, D.C., March, 1970.

completion of a teacher education program, and the indicators
acceptable as evidence of the realization of those outcomes,
are specified and made public. Performance based programs
do not deny the significance of experience, but they openly
recognize and treat experience as a means rather than an end.
They treat experience as a variable to be manipulated in the
realization of given ends, rather than as an end in itself.
By so doing, performance based programs are open to continuous
change on the basis of feedback as to the success they are
having in realizing the ends that they are committed to accomplish. By clearly specifying the ends for which they are
to be held responsible performance based programs meet the
requirements of "an accountability model" in the fullest sense
of the term. By and large experienced based programs do not.

Even further from a performance based or an accountability model is the historic concern with institutional
resources as a basis for accreditation, for example, concern
that a certain proportion of a faculty hold a PhD degree,
concern over the scholarly performance of faculty, concern
over the "quality" of students admitted to a program,
library facilities, etc. (see pp. 7-12 of the 1970 Standards
for Teacher Education). While there is some logic to such
an approach, that is, in order to provide the experiences
needed to bring about the outcomes desired a sound resource
base must exist, the problem with it is that the provision
of such a base in no way assures the realization of the
outcomes desired. As a consequence, while performance based
programs must be deeply concerned with the resources that
they can bring to the task they face, assessing the resource
base of a performance based program becomes critical only
when the outcomes expected from that program are not being met.

In terms of their relationship to an accountability model
resource based, experience based and performance based strategies in teacher education can be conceptualized as follows:

Resource Based	Experience Based	Performance Based

public accountability

———————————————————————————————————>

2. A SHIFT FROM A PRIMARY FOCUS UPON KNOWLEDGE AND
      SKILL MASTERY TO A PRIMARY FOCUS UPON
                    OUTPUT

Assuming the desirability of moving to a performance

based model of operation within teacher education, the designers of such programs must decide upon the focus they wish to give them. In broad terms performance based programs can assume any one, or any combination, of three foci: the mastery of knowledge, the mastery of skill, or the demonstrated ability to apply the knowledges and skills mastered to effectively carry out the tasks that need to be performed within a particular school setting. As used here the completion of tasks involves the production of tangible outputs, that is, the completion of instructional tasks results in specified learning outcomes in children and the completion of instructional support tasks results in outputs such as a "unit" of instruction, an examination, a curriculum guide, a course evaluation plan.

Historically, teacher education programs have focused heavily upon knowledge as the primary basis for certification. As a consequence courses within the discipline that constitutes one's teaching speciality. In the liberal arts, in teaching methods, and in human learning and child development have become standard requirements throughout teacher education. Often they represent the only requirements for certification, save a one term or one semester student teaching experience. The basic assumption underlying such an approach is that knowledge of subject matter, teaching methods, childrens' learning, etc. as measured by course grades or more refined performance measures--coupled with a brief testing of the ability to apply what is known in a student teaching situation and a subjective judgment as to the acceptability of a particular student to the teaching profession-- is a functional basis for predicting the success of a prospective teacher. The reverse assumption is also applied: there is no need to systematically gather evidence as to the ability of a prospective teacher to behave in specified ways, or of his ability to carry out the functions for which he will be responsible within a school once he is certified. Schematically, such an assumption can be illustrated as follows:

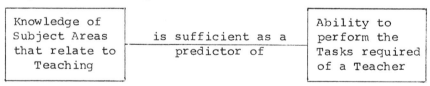

| Knowledge of Subject Areas that relate to Teaching | is sufficient as a predictor of | Ability to perform the Tasks required of a Teacher |

While such an assumption is becoming less and less acceptable to many in the profession, it is still acceptable to some. Accordingly some teacher education programs can be considered to be performance based but focus only at the knowledge level--providing of course that the desired knowledge outcomes are specified and the indicators to be used as evidence of the realization of those outcomes are made public.

<u>The criterion level set for performance has nothing to do with</u>
<u>a program being or not being performance based!</u>

As indicated above, an increasing number of persons in
the profession are unwilling to accept the assumption that
because one knows something he can necessarily apply it.
Or, put in other terms, an increasing number of persons in
the profession are becoming uncomfortable with the magnitude
of inference between knowing and doing, and are asking for
evidence that prospective teachers can do that which is expected of them as well as know that which has been specified
for them. The move to focus upon what a prospective teacher
can do as well as what he knows rests on four interrelated
assumptions:

knowing, and the ability to apply what is known, are
two different matters, and the certification of
teachers should focus as much upon what a prospective
teacher is able to do as it does upon what he knows;

the criteria for assessing that which a prospective
teacher can do should be as stringent, as systematically derived, and as explicitly stated as the
criteria for assessing that which he knows;

the assessment of both that which is known and that
which can be done must be carried out and described
systematically; and,

when a prospective teacher has demonstrated that he
knows and can do that which is expected of him, and
only then, will he be granted certification.

Accepting the reasonableness of such assumptions there
is still the problem of deciding what is meant operationally
by a prospective teacher "being able to do." As interpreted
by most teacher education programs that have moved beyond
knowledge as a basis for certification <u>being able to do has</u>
<u>meant being able to perform specified teaching behaviors</u>.
Such a focus parallels closely the emergence of the study
of teaching behavior as a subject for research,[5] and with
it the translation of the categories of behavior used in
research into training systems to be mastered by preservice
or inservice teachers, or to be used by supervising teachers.
The arguments for adopting teaching behaviors as a basis for
certification are roughly as follows:

the reasonableness of logic of focusing upon what a

---

[5] Cf Simon, Anita and Boyer, E.G. (Eds.) <u>Mirrors for</u>
<u>Behavior, An Anthology of Observation Instruments</u>. Vols. I-
XIV. Philadelphia, Pa., Research for Better Schools, Inc. 1970.

teacher does instead of what he knows, believes, or
feels, since what he does is a reflection of what he
knows or believes or feels;

since it is a teacher's behavior that is the primary
determinant of teacher influence, it is important that
prospective teachers be able to behave in ways that are
desirable;

the research that has been done on teacher behavior has
laid out categories of behavior that are observable,
measurable, and relatively easily mastered; and, because such a focus has a good deal of common sense
about it, and because it permits systematic measurement, it provides one means for meeting the requirement of "accountability" in teacher education.

The assumption outlined in the paragraph above can be
illustrated as follows:

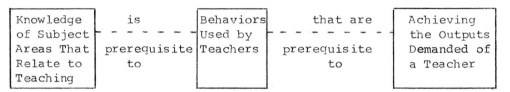

A program derived from such assumptions will have two foci:
knowledge and teaching behavior. If it is to qualify as a
performance based program it will have to make explicit the
knowledge and teaching behaviors that prospective teachers
will have to demonstrate, and the indicators acceptable as
evidence of their realization.

While a teacher education program that incorporates
both a knowledge and a teaching behavior focus satisfies
most persons in the profession at this point in time, there
are some who hold that such a program still involves too
much inference making. Those who take such a point of view
argue that simply because a prospective teacher is able to
behave in certain ways is no assurance that he will be able
to effect the outcomes for which he will be responsible in
an ongoing educational setting. They further argue that
teacher education programs should, therefore, adopt still
another focus, namely, the requirement that prospective
teachers demonstrate that they can bring about such outcomes as a basis for certification. The rationale underlying this argument is simply that if a teacher is to be
accountable for bringing about specified classes of learner
outcomes or non-instructional outcomes subsequent to
certification, it would seem reasonable to require that they

demonstrate that they can bring about such outcomes prior
to certification. While such a point of view does not take
all inference making from the relationship between performance
prior to certification and performance subsequent to it, it
does reduce it significantly.

There are a number of advantages to such a position:

It represents a logically defensible criterion of
teaching effectiveness, program effectiveness, and
teacher and program accountability;

While doing so, it accommodates individual differences
in teaching performance or style in that it allows for
wide variation in the means of achieving the outcomes
for which teachers will be held responsible once they
take a job;

It allows for the fact that at this point in time we
are not at all clear about the specific teaching
behaviors that bring about specified outcomes in
pupils, or the specific behaviors that bring about
selected non-instructional outcomes, but it does
require that effective behaviors and/or instructional
programs be developed and utilized (which is precisely
the circumstance of teachers);

it forces the entire educational system, as well as
teacher education, to be clear about the goals or
objectives of education, and to become clear about
the means for the realization of those objectives;

it takes much of the guesswork out of hiring new
teachers, for each teacher would have a portfolio
which summarizes in detail what he can or cannot do
at the time he is certified.

If pressed to defend the position on the basis of education
not being clear about its goals or objectives, or not being
clear about how the means by which the objectives that it
is clear about are to be realized, the answer is simply
"then that's a task that education must get on with, and
a teacher education program so designed will contribute
to that task." The relationship between program
characteristics, performance criteria and identifying
labels is summarized below.

119

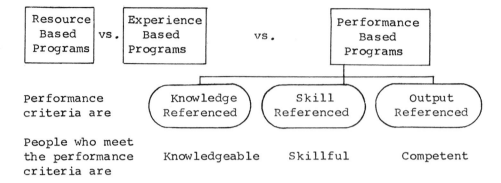

	Knowledge Referenced	Skill Referenced	Output Referenced
Performance criteria are	Knowledge Referenced	Skill Referenced	Output Referenced
People who meet the performance criteria are	Knowledgeable	Skillful	Competent

A number of problems are inherent in implementing an output referenced personnel development program. The most obvious one has already been alluded to, namely, the necessity of being clear about the educational outcomes that we want from our schools, the difficulty in measuring such outcomes, and the fact that the discipline is not at all clear as to the factors that contribute to the development of particular learning outcomes in particular kinds of children. Without clarity about such matters it obviously will be difficult to implement such a program. On the other hand, it is precisely these matters that education must be clear about. Adopting a stance in teacher education that forces the discipline and the profession to confront its weaknesses in this regard would seem to be a reasonably good strategy for eliciting movement within the profession as a whole. It goes without saying that the teacher education programs so designed would be at best a bit "rickety" until the conceptual, methodological and empirical base needed to support them has been established, but is there any reason to believe that as rickety as they might be they would be any less productive than the programs that are currently maintained?

Three additional problems need to be considered briefly: (a) the inability to attribute in any absolute sense success or failure in pupil learning to a teacher's performance in a school setting, (b) the apparent denial by an output referenced approach of the utility of a prediction model in training, and (c) the whole issue of the economic feasibility of such an approach.

The problem of linging classroom learning to teacher-performance for purposes of certification is obviously troublesome, but no more so than it is for the schools as they attempt to assess the effectiveness of staff performance for purposes of rank or salary or tenure considerations. As a consequence, there would seem to be little justification for ducking the issue at the teacher education level. But what conditions must exist if teacher influence is to be linked to learning outcomes? At least three would appear to be necessary:

(1) be clear about the nature of learning outcomes that can be expected to be influenced in a demonstrable way by what occurs in the school, and those which cannot be expected to be so influenced--especially on a reasonably short time basis;

(2) construe the matter of influence to be a function of teacher-materials-context and system interaction rather than a matter of teacher influence alone; and

(3) adopt a sensible position with respect to what is meant by success. Operationally success as a teacher will probably have to be defined in terms of the frequency with which a given proportion of students achieve particular kinds of outcomes, with kinds of students working towards kinds of outcomes under kinds of conditions being systematically varied. It will also require sensible measures of student learning, for example, individual patterns of growth in reading skill across time rather than average grade level scores for a first or second or third grade. Such assessments will obviously require a great deal of sophistication in both their conceptualization and in the sampling of contexts within which they are to be taken. In the writer's judgment, however, the sophistication needed is available if and when teacher educators wish to draw upon it.[6]

The apparent problem of inefficiency in an output referenced program is especially bothersome to the scientific community. Their argument, which is essentially the argument that has been dominant in teacher education since the writer can remember, is the logical one that says in effect that since the ability of a teacher to bring about given outcomes in the schools depends upon some set of knowledges and skills preparatory programs should focus upon the mastery of such knowledges and skills. While the logic is sound, and there is little disagreement with the desirability of developing training programs that focus on the mastery of knowledges and skills as predictors of success

---

[6] Some of the shifts in thinking about measurement that will be required to implement an output referenced teacher education program are put forth by the writer in the chapter on measurement in The National Research Training Institute Manual. Monmouth, Oregon: Teaching Research, 1969.

rather than as its uncertain enablers, the fact of the
matter is that at this point in time there is no firm
evidence as to the knowledge or skill base needed to effect
desired educational outcomes. The hard reality is that if
one wishes to have confidence that prospective teachers can
in fact effect learning outcomes in pupils prior to
certification there is little alternative to moving to an
output referenced program. This does not mean, however, that
as a discipline education should cease to work towards a
model of training that has greater efficiency. But the
training model based upon knowledge and skill mastery assumes
predictable relationships between that which has been
mastered and successful performance as a teacher, and at the
moment these relationships are unknown. Moreover, perhaps
the best way of establishing such relationships is to move to
the kind of product referenced training model that has been
proposed. By moving to such a model it will be possible
over time to establish the kind of empirically demonstrated
relationships between knowledges, skills, and task performance that ultimately may permit a more efficient model
to operate, but until that time--at least if certifying or
hiring agencies wish to have evidence that prospective
teachers can in fact perform the tasks for which they will
be responsible as professionals--there is little option to
moving to other than an output referenced training program.

More will be said in subsequent paragraphs about how
such empirical relationships might be established within the
context of ongoing training programs.

The economics of operating an output referenced program
are also bothersome to many. The cost of collecting output
related information (assuming that it can in fact be
collected), and the cost of moving students to the point
of being able to effectively produce expected outputs, would
seem to force such programs to be more costly than traditional teacher education. Once such a program has been
developed this is not necessarily the case. Feasibility
studies have shown that the cost to colleges of operating
such a program can be no greater than traditional, experience based programs, as schools are willing to assume
many of the costs associated with them.[7] Development costs

---

[7] See for example the final report on the feasibility
study of the ComField model. Schalock, Kersh and Horyna
(Eds.) A Plan for Managing the Development, Implementation
and Operation of a Model Elementary Teacher Education Program.
Final report of a Phase II study in the U.S.O.E. sponsored
Elementary Models Program. Superintendent of Documents,
U.S. Government Printing Office, Washington, D.C.

are high, however, so the economic issue is a real one,
In the end, the decision to support the development of such
programs will rest upon the value that is given the increased
clarity and order that they would introduce to the field of
education generally.

3. A SHIFT FROM AN ESSENTIALLY DATA FREE TO AN ESSENTIALLY DATA DEPENDENT MODE OF OPERATION

Most teacher education programs operate today on a minimum of information. Little is known about student interests
or abilities or background or projected plans; little is known
about the effectiveness of a given instruction-learning experience for students who vary on any of these qualities; and
little is known about the appropriateness or usefulness of the
learning objectives established for the preparatory program,
from either a short-term or long-term point of view. Even
students in preparatory programs rarely know whether what they
are doing has genuine utility for their performance as professionals. Upon close analysis it can honestly be said that
a great many educational personnel development programs operate without being at all clear as to what it is they are attempting to do, why they are attempting to do it and whether
or not they have been effective in doing whatever it is they
are trying to do. Students within such programs tend to suffer similar fates.

Such conditions cannot endure under a performance-based,
output referenced preparatory program. Under such a program
the outcomes that students are to be able to effect if they are
to succeed in the program must be specified, the indicators acceptable as evidence of their realization spelled out, the conditions that bring about such outcomes identified, the knowledge and skills and sensitivities assumed to be needed by personnel to create such conditions hypothesized--and then evidence
systematically gathered as to whether or not all of the above
hold. Most critically the collection of evidence starts with
an assessment of whether the students of teaching are able to
effect the outcomes for which they are being held responsible.
Data are also needed, however, on the effectiveness of each of
the various elements within the program in bringing about the
learning outcomes for which it has been designed. By systematically collecting data at all levels of program operation
empirically based decisions can be made about either the plans
of individuals within the program or the program as a whole as
it moves through time.

By and large the kind of data being called for here are
data that serve on-line decision making, and are thereby best
thought of as data that derive from either formative or sum-
mative-comparative evaluation activities rather than research
activities (see the definitions of evaluation and research in
the Glossary).

4. A SHIFT FROM AN ESSENTIALLY TRAINING FUNCTION TO A RESEARCH, DEVELOPMENT AND TRAINING FUNCTION

The need to identify increasingly more powerful conceptions of teaching and learning, the need to establish a more efficient preparatory system than one that depends upon indicators of output for certification purposes, the need to establish strong "principles of instruction" on which to build teacher education programs--that is, empirically demonstrated relationships between instructional strategies or tactics or moves and the emergence of desired learning outcomes for given kinds of learners in given kinds of settings--and the need to understand the emergence and interaction of different kinds of learning outcomes in different kinds of pupils over time are all matters of greatest urgency in education and teacher education. They are matters, however, that will find their solution primarily through research and development activities (see the Glossary for a definition of these terms) rather than evaluation activities. It follows that the effective, efficient operation of educational personnel development programs over the long-term is dependent upon such activities, and it is proposed here that a performance-based, output referenced and data dependent training program provides the best possible context within which to mount research and development programs that will be able to provide answers to such questions. The essential conceptual frameworks, the organizational structures, and a significant portion of the data base needed to carry out such R & D functions will be available as a necessary adjunct to training programs so designed. It would represent a terrible waste if such contexts were not utilized to their fullest.

5. A SHIFT FROM AN ESSENTIALLY IMPERSONAL, INSTRUCTOR ORIENTED LEARNING ENVIRONMENT TO ONE THAT IS PERSONALIZED AND STUDENT ORIENTED

The plea for the personalization of the instruction-learning process in teacher education comes from many sides. On the part of students there is the plea to "increase the relevance" of teacher education programs, where relevance is defined personally and from the point of view of the broader social context within which education functions. They plea for a greater opportunity to exchange on a personal basis with instructors and other students; for an opportunity to take from a program that which makes sense to them in terms of their individual interests, plans and preferred mode or style; and for the right to have the assessment procedures that are applied to them and their work be appropriate in terms of the goals, objectives and contexts within which that work is taking place.

The experience of the writer has been that teacher educators also wish to personalize the instruction-learning process-- both for the sake of making the learning experience as meaning ful as possible to each individual involved in it and for the sake of increasing the probability of personalizing the instruction-learning process at the elementary and secondary level. Educators are increasingly of the opinion that in order for instructional staff to personalize instruction at the elementary-secondary level they probably will have to have experienced a personalized program in the course of their own educational history.

There is also a concern on the part of students and educators that a "performance based, output referenced, and data dependent" mode of operation in teacher education will force programs and students within them into a stereotype or common mold. To persons first introduced to the language of such programs this appears to be a genuine danger, and as a consequence an insistence upon the personalization of learning within them assumes major importance.

Actually, the designers of such programs have little option but to personalize both the instruction-learning and the assessment process, for the demonstration of the ability to effect desired educational outcomes is always situation specific. To illustrate the concept, consider two demonstrable outcomes: getting a six year old child in a group of ten who is bright but visually handicapped to be able to distinguish between all letters of the alphabet and getting a thirteen year old boy of average ability in a class of thirty, with little exposure to cultures other than that of hiw own relatively isolated mountain community, to place value in cultures other than his own. Competence in bringing about such outcomes simply cannot be thought of in an abstract or generic sense; competence in a prospective teacher must always be thought of in terms of the ability of that teacher to bring about a specific outcome for a specific child or set of children who have specific characteristics and who are operating in a specific instruction-learning context. Operationally this means that competence in effecting educational outcomes is always defined in terms of an idiosyncratic mix of output oriented operations, the nature of the output to be effected and the context within which it is to occur.

What does the translation of such concerns into program management look like? What are the dimensions of personalization? Schalock and Garrison[8] have suggested that seven conditions must be met in order for a preparatory program to become genuinely personalized:
(1) person-to-person experience must be a part of the planned program;
(2) a variety of instruction-learning options must be available to meet individual needs within the planned program;

[8] Schalock, H.D. and Garrison, J. The Personalization of Teacher Education Programs. In New Directions In Teacher Education: Problems and Prospects Ahead. M. Vere Devault Ed. In Press.

(3) students must participate in the design of their own programs
(4) students must have the opportunity to participate in the design and development of the overall teacher education program;
(5) there must be a mechanism, for example, sponsorship, negotiation or performance contracting, that will carry the personalization process;
(6) students and staff must hold perceptions that permit the personalization mechanism to operate; and

(7) there must be an approach to assessment that is consistent with the philosophy of personalization.

6. A SHIFT FROM AN ESSENTIALLY COLLEGE OR UNIVERSITY CENTERED PROGRAM TO A FIELD CENTERED PROGRAM

If a performance based program adopts output criteria as its point of reference there is little option but to have a significant portion of the program take place within a field setting. For a prospective teacher to demonstrate that he can bring about a particular learning outcome in a particular child or set of children he must have access to children, preferably in a school setting. Moreover, the access must be of a continuing nature over a relatively long period of time in order to demonstrate that meaningful learning outcomes on the part of pupils can be effected. To establish such close and continuing contact with the schools requires essentially that colleges and universities enter into partnership with the schools in the operation of the teacher education program. While it is possible for performance based programs that are knowledge referenced to operate within the context of a university, and it may even be possible through the adept use of simulation strategies such as microteaching to operate skill referenced programs within a university, it is literally impossible to operate an output referenced program within a university context alone.

7. A SHIFT FROM A RELATIVELY NARROW AND ESSENTIALLY CLOSED DECISION MAKING BASE TO ONE THAT IS BROAD AND ESSENTIALLY OPEN

Historically decision making in teacher education has rested largely within the colleges and universities. State departments of education, as agents for teacher certification, have obviously had some influence upon the field, and so have professional education and teacher education associations, but by and large influence outside of the colleges has been relatively weak. Increasingly this picture is changing. Professional groups within education, teachers' unions, community groups, and students in preparatory programs are demanding an increased voice in decisions relative to the conduct of such programs.

The adoption of an output referenced, performance based strategy for teacher education would serve to further broaden this decision making base. As has been pointed out repeatedly,

such programs rest squarely upon the explication of the kinds
of learner outcomes expected from the schools, and this
requires some degree of consensus between the colleges, the
schools, the community, the state boards of education, and
the students and pupils involved. So too does agreement as
to the indicators acceptable as evidence of the realization of such outcomes, and the role of prospective teachers
in bringing them about. It is also likely that such programs would lead to increased involvement of professional
education associations in the business of teacher education,
in part because of the same issues that draw other groups
into the decision making structure of such programs, but
also because of the implications of such an approach for professional licensure and job maintenance over time. As a
consequence, one of the major tasks that output referenced,
performance based teacher education programs will have to
face is the design of a decision making mechanism that
provides for representation from these various groups, and
which orchestrates their input with the design and operation
of the program.

Do the Five Thrusts Constitute the Necessary and Sufficient Conditions for Teacher Education Programs to Meet the Requirements Outlined Above?

In the writer's judgment the answer is an unqualified
YES, provided that the potential of each of the five thrusts
is fully utilized! The performance based certification
thrust provides the wherewithall to move on to an output
referenced mode of operation, and thereby move teacher education to a level of accountability that will force not
only teacher education to be certain that it is preparing
personnel that can in fact bring about the goals set for
education but to force education as a whole to become
clearer about its goals. The thrust represented by the
elementary models provides the wherewithall to move to a
data dependent mode of operation, and to integrate research
and development with training. They also provide for the
design and operation of preparatory programs that are
committed to output as a point of reference for certification,
for the integrated use of protocol and training materials
throughout the instructional process, and for the personalization of the instructional process. The protocol and
training materials development thrusts can provide the conceptual and theoretical leadership needed in establishing
the content of teacher education programs, as well as
leadership in the design, fabrication and development of the
materials base needed in support of such programs. Finally,
the training complex thrust provides the structure within
which to establish the necessary working relationships with
the field and within which to establish the broadly based
decision making mechanisms needed to reach concensus as to
the products to be developed within the field.[9]

---

[9]
Several of the elementary models also provide a framework for linking to the community and a more broadly based
decision making structure. Syracuse University's "Proto-
cooperative" notion, Florida State University's "Portal
Schools" notion and the ComField Model's concept of
"coalitions" are cases in point.

In the writer's opinion the crux of the matter is the criterion level set for certification. If it is set at only the knowledge level the five thrusts in combination will produce little more than teacher education now produces. If it is set at the knowledge and skills level the potential contribution of the five thrusts will be more fully exercised, but as pointed out in the discussion of the desirability of an output referenced criterion the education profession would still be lacking the essential element that would give it leverage to "turn itself around," and a base for confirming that having turned itself around it is making a difference in the lives of children and youth. The criticalness of the criterion issue has been elaborated more fully by Turner in a paper prepared for Task Force '72 entitled "Programmatic Themes and Mechanisms in Teacher Education."

What is Needed to Effect the Kind of Change Envisioned for Teacher Education on a National Scale?

Assuming optimal utilization of the five thrusts within any given personnel development program, and by so doing implementing preparatory programs that will truly make a difference in the education of children and youth, there is the second order problem of diffusing that which has been developed throughout the nation as a whole. This is a concern that is obviously of high priority to the Office of Education but to the writer's knowledge it is a concern for which no formal solutions have been either sought or found. The Office of Education has systematically attacked one aspect of the problem, namely, the dissemination of information through its ERIC system, but dissemination is only one dimension of the diffusion process. (For a definition of diffusion see the Glossary.) For the majority of teacher education programs in the nation to adopt the kind of program that has been described the on-line demonstration of such programs will in all likelihood be required, banks of protocol and training materials that can be drawn upon fully and easily will be needed, resources to provide the necessary support systems for such programs will have to be found, and elaborate information and materials exchange networks will have to be established. It is probably fair to say that at present education has no good examples of nor models for such a massive diffusion effort. Accordingly, in the "preferred plan" that is outlined in the pages which follow, considerable attention is given to the nature of the diffusion mechanism that is likely to be needed if a major diffusion effort is to be a success.

And Where Does One Start In Relation to All of the Above?

With first questions first! In the writer's judgement it is inappropriate to take as a point of departure in the design of education personnel development programs the question "What kind of training programs do we want?" In the language of the everyday this is simply getting the cart ahead of the horse. Training programs must be responsive to the question "What kind of personnel do our schools need, and what competencies should such personnel possess?" But

this too is out of order as a place to begin. The first
question to be asked, and it is the question from which all
else must flow, is "What do we want our children to learn?
How do we want them to feel or believe? What should they be
able to do? What adults do we want them to become? What
should they know or be able to do or be able to accomplish?
And toward which of these ends should the schools contribute?"

Once answers are in, in relation to first level
questions, second level questions can then be asked. "What
kind of schools will it take to achieve the desired ends?
And how do we want such schools to function? Are schools
to make explicit and public their goals and objectives? What
indicators are to be used as evidence of the realization
of such? In what sense are the schools to be held accountable
for realizing their goals and objectives? Are they to present evidence as to cost/benefit relationships for alternative
goals, or for alternative programs in relation to a particular goal?" As answers to second level questions begin to
emerge it then becomes possible to ask third level questions,
namely, "What kind of personnel are needed to operate
schools of the kind required to achieve the ends desired?"
When answers are finally obtained to this level of question
it then becomes possible, but only then, to sensibly
design an education personnel development program that has
some hope of providing the personnel that are needed to
operate the schools that are needed to effect the outcomes
that are desired by a community (or a state or a nation) for
its children.

Rather obviously, ongoing personnel development programs
do not have the time or the human and financial resources
to carry out such fundamental analyses prior to or while
they proceed with their training function. Nor do school
systems. Nor can such an anlysis be done once for
example by a state, or a region or the federal government,
and have it translate functionally into the variety of
personnel development programs that crisscross the nation.
While the latter may be a place to start, simply as a means
of providing a real-life example of how such an analysis
works and the power it generates once it has been done, in
the end each training program in concert with representatives
from the community it is intended to serv e must make its own
analysis and design its own program on the basis of it. Anything less denies the reality of the differences that exist
within and between training programs, within and between
communities and the strength of the tradition in America
that insures local control of education.

So again, where does one start? Again the answer
"With first questions first!" And in the opinion of the writer,
the federal government, each state and each personnel development program in conjunction with representatives from
the community it serves should begin with such questions. If
the kind of analysis suggested were undertaken simultaneously
by all of the above it is likely that enough progress could
be made and enough wisdom gained to permit preparatory programs

to become relevant, functional units within the larger
education enterprise. Without such progress, however,
it is questionable whether this will ever be the case.

PART II: A PREFERRED PROPOSAL

The proposal which follows represents an attempt to integrate the five thrusts with which the paper is to deal within a statewide teacher education program that reflects the characteristics outlined in the previous section of the paper. Specifically, the proposal has five purposes:

1) develop broad specifications for a prototype education personnel development program that combines within it the essential features of the five foundational thrusts within BEPD in such a way as to optimize their impact in relation to the point of view expressed previously;

2) link to these specifications a plan by which to incorporate the research, development and evaluation functions that will be needed to insure effective operation of the proposed program;

3) develop specifications for a state-wide network of such programs;

4) suggest ways in which the costs involved in the development and operation of a state-wide network be shared between federal, state and local agencies; and

5) suggest ways in which state-wide networks could be linked nationally and to industry in order to insure maximum spread effects.

The proposal is set forth in a series of guidelines that speak to the five purposes.

Guideline #1: Define certification standards in terms of PERFORMANCE CRITERIA and set those standards at the OUTPUT rather than the KNOWLEDGE AND/OR SKILL level.

Of the five thrusts to be dealt with in the paper the concept of performance based certification has within it the greatest leverage for change. This is especially so when certification criteria are set at the output rather than the knowledge or skill levels. By insisting that preparatory programs spell out in advance what it is that prospective teachers or administrators or instructional support personnel be able to accomplish in an ongoing educational context prior to certification, and insisting that each candidate show evidence that he can in fact effect such accomplishments, there is little opportunity for anyone to "weasel" on their obligations.

Persons responsible for preparatory programs must make explicit that which graduates of their programs will be able to accomplish in the schools; they must make explicit the indicators they will accept as evidence of such accomplishments; and they must devise a program

that insures the majority of students in it are
able to develop to the point where they are able
to realize such accomplishments. They must also
make explicit the kind of systematic linkage
called for in the previous section of the paper
between the expected outputs of their program and
the personal needs of schools, and these in turn
to the outcomes expected of schools.

Students who wish to become certified must show
that they can "put it all together." They cannot
just talk about it; they cannot win brownie points
by regurgitating the contents of books or lectures
or discussions; they cannot make it with a few
highly developed "performance skills." Performance
based certification at the output level requires
that they know what it is that they wish to
accomplish with the children they wish to work with,
and that they can in fact accomplish those things
with at least the majority of children with whom
they do work. Anything less and certification
will simply not be forthcoming.

State department personnel must be responsible
for insuring that such is the case or else the
entire process will be a mockery. These are
harsh guides to action for everyone involved
but such is the leverage of performance based
certification with criteria set at the output
level.

   In the writer's judgment none of the other thrusts
being dealt with has anywhere near the power to effect
change of such magnitude and on so many fronts simultaneously
as does performance based certification. As a consequence
the position can be taken as it is in fact in the present
paper, that the remaining four thrusts are simply means
to effect the conditions established by Guideline #1.

   While powerful as a lever to effect change, and
therefore attractive to those who wish to bring change about,
it needs to be reiterated that performance based certification
at the output level carries with it some extremely complex
problems that are in need of solution before it is free to
fly. Many of these have already been alluded to, for
example, the necessity of explicating the goals of education,
and designing educational systems that have a high
probability of realizing those goals, as prerequisites to
the design of personnel development programs; the need to
involve the schools and community in such an effort; the
need to personalize the entire preparatory process so as to
furnish a negotiated choice for students as to school
contexts within which to work, and, the outcomes to work
towards within those criteria and criteria by which to be
judged successful or unsuccessful in bringing about such
outcomes.

   There are also other problems. One of the most critical

132

of these is the certification of persons who demonstrate markedly different sets of competencies. Given the need to personalize output referenced programs, and the fact that such programs will vary by the nature of the schools to which they link, it is probable that persons from preparatory program A, which is linked to school districts that are pressing toward open classrooms, individualized learning programs for pupils and decisions about pupils resting upon performance or other recorded data will present markedly different portfolios of demonstrated competencies than persons from a preparatory program that is linked to schools reflecting a different mode of organization. This is the case even when the students applying for certification have worked with reasonably similar groups of pupils toward reasonably similar kinds of outcomes with reasonably similar materials. When kinds of pupils vary, for example by grade level and ability, and kinds of outcomes and materials and school contexts vary, and when these all interact with the differences that exist in prospective teachers and the personnel responsible for operating preparatory programs, the variation in the portfolio of demonstrated competencies that will be presented to the state department for certification purposes staggers the imagination.

How is the state department to cope with such variance? Will the vehicle of the approved program handle it? Probably not in the way it presently operates for it is vehicle designed primarily to handle variance only between course oriented, experience based preparatory programs, not between individual candidates who vary in demonstrated competencies. Will the "committee" strategy developed in the state of Washington handle it? Perhaps, but only so long as the data base required about performance is minimal. If hard performance data are required as a basis for certification the committee strategy will have to be supplemented to accomodate the generation of such data and its use in decision making. Considerable attention must be directed to the solution of this problem if output referenced performance based certification procedures are to be implemented.[10]

---

10 Performance based certification programs with criteria set at the knowledge and/or skill levels do not face such sever difficulties for it is possible to insist (and even convince some people) that all students in preparatory programs should know whatever it is they need to know about children, methods, subject matter fields, etc. and that all students should be able to perform essentially the same set of skills---since such knowledges and skills are assumed to be essential prerequisites to effective teaching. Because some tough issues can be avoided by choosing intermediate performance criteria for certification purposes, at least for a little while, is not a good reason in the writer's judgment to do so.

Another serious problem that is encountered immediately
when attempting to implement an output referenced program
is the fact that such a program requires a significantly
different structure, content and mode of operation than does
an experience based program at the knowledge and/or skill
level. So long as experience based programs are defined
primarily in terms of courses, or performance based programs
focus only at the knowledge level, the business of teacher
education can go on relatively unchanged in the college and
university setting. It can even continue there when performance criteria are defined at the level of skills
provided creative uses of "simulation" or "microteaching"
techniques are used, and the criteria of skill demonstration
are kept rather simple, i.e., without regard to the performance of skills within the context of real-life
educational settings with real-life children who may or may
not be responsive to a particular skill. Teacher education
programs cannot remain cloistered if they adopt an experience based mode of operation that places students in
contexts outside of the college or university, or if they
adopt a performance based mode of operation with
certification criteria set at the output level. In the first
case, students must access to other contexts, whatever
they may be. In the second, they must access to schools,
and students within schools. Such a requirement forces
preparatory programs to link functionally to contexts
other than the college or university, and that fact forces
a set of structures and operating procedures on such a
program that represents essentially "a new ball game".

But this is not the only kind of change that adoption
of an output referenced certification strategy forces on
program operation. As indicated previously, it forces the
personalization of the program, attention to data, attention
to self correction, attention to schools and schooling,
attention to children, attention to community, attention to
what life is all about. All of these matters have major
implications for program operation, and they are simply
inescapable. For those who wish details of the Oregon
College of Education adaptation of the Teacher Education,[11]
see Schalock, Kersh and Horyna (Editors): A Plan for the
Development, Implementation and Operation of a Model
Elementary Teacher Education Program. Final Report of the
Phase II study in the U.S.O.E. sponsored Elementary Models
Program. Superintendent of Documents, U.S. Government
Printing Office, Washington D.C.

---

[11]
    The ComField Model is one of the nine elementary
teacher education models developed under the sponsorship of
NCERD. It is the only model of the nine to advocate
output referenced criteria as a basis for certification.

Guideline #2: As a context within which to implement an
output referenced, performance based certification plan,
establish on a cost sharing basis illustrative state-wide
networks of Training Cooperatives, with each Cooperative
having the organizational characteristics of a TRAINING
COMPLEX and the structural, functional and operational
characteristics of one or more of the ELEMENTARY MODELS.

As suggested in the previous section of the paper
adoption of an output referenced, performance based
approach to certification forces preparatory programs to
assume two dominant characteristics: (a) a functional
linkage to the field, and (b) a data dependent or "confirmatory" mode of operation. A functional linkage to the
field is demanded by the requirement that such programs rest
upon an explication of the kinds of learning outcomes a
community wants for its children, the kinds of schools
needed to effect those outcomes, and a context within which
prospective teachers can demonstrate that they can or cannot
bring such outcomes about. A reliance upon a data
dependent or confirmatory mode of operation is forced by the
commitment to performance as a basis for certification.
Within such a framework each candidate for certification
must provide evidence of acceptable performance in relation
to the established criteria for certification. Also, given
the responsibility of the programs to prepare personnel to
meet these criteria within a reasonable length of time with
a reasonable outlay of energy, it is essential that evidence
be obtained on the contribution of each component within a
program to the realization of the goal or goals that it is
designed to serve, the success of different types of
students with the component, etc. It is also essential that
evidence be provided on the appropriateness of the goals
pursued by the program, and on its long term consequences,
for example, its impact on the personal growth of teachers
three or five or ten years after graduating or on their
impact on children and the schools at those points in time.
Operationally, a functional linkage of a personnel development program to the field involves a full-fledged partnership between a community, its schools and a college or
university responsible for the preparation of education
personnel.[12] The implementation of a data dependent or
confirmatory mode of operation within such a program
involves reliance upon the principles of systems design and
operation.

Fortunately, through the work that has been done on
TRAINING COMPLEXES and the MODELS guidelines for such
partnerships and for the application of systems principles
to the design, development and operation of teacher education programs already have been established.

---

[12] It is this partnership that has been labeled in
Guideline #1 as a Training Cooperative.

On the basis of the conceptual work done thus far the
idea of a teacher educational model, as this has been
explicated in the elementary models, and the idea of a
training complex, as this has been explicated in <u>Teachers</u>
<u>for the Real World</u> and subsequent design efforts, seem to be
mutually supportive. In general terms, the training complex
provides a context within which a systematically designed
and operated teacher education program resides, and the
elementary models provide first approximations to the
structure, function and operation of such programs. As
indicated earlier, while some of the elementary models
proposed structures somewhat akin to a training complex none
took those ideas as far in their development as has Bunny
Smith and others in their thinking about training complexes.
Contrariwise, those who have been concerned with training
complexes have not pushed their thinking as far in regard
to the actual structure, function and operation of the
training programs to be housed within as have the elementary
models directors. By combining the work of both groups it
would seem that the efforts of each would be strengthened.
The combination of the two ideas can be illustrated
schematically as follows:

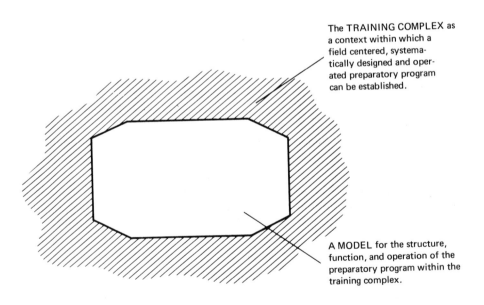

The TRAINING COMPLEX as
a context within which a
field centered, systema-
tically designed and operated preparatory program
can be established.

A MODEL for the structure,
function, and operation of the
preparatory program within the
training complex.

Figure 1.   The basic components that make up a
Training Cooperative for the preparation of educational personnel.

136

In the design of Training Cooperatives three
sensitivities should be kept in mind:

1. A Cooperative is seen as an integral part of all
    teacher education programs within a state, that is,
    it is not simply an illustrative or demonstration
    program for a state or region;

2. It is a school-community context within which
    only selected aspects of any given personnel
    development program will be housed; and

3. It will always be developed around exemplary or
    illustrative elementary-secondary programs.

Given these conditions it follows that (a) in order for
a state to adopt a competency based plan of certification it
must first establish a network of Cooperatives where desired
competencies can in fact be defined and demonstrated; (b)
that each Cooperative involve minimally a community, a
school within that community and a college or university
responsible for the preparation of education personnel; and
(c) only communities that possess one or more exemplary
schools, with exemplary being defined as a school that is
clear about its objectives and that has been designed with
the realization of those objectives in mind, will be
invited to become a part of a Training Cooperative. As
presently conceived the following activities will occur
within each cooperative:

> identify the outputs to be realized by prospective
> educational personnel within the Cooperative;
>
> identify the indicators acceptable as evidence of
> the realization of those outputs;
>
> carry out the instruction that leads to the actual
> development and demonstration of the competencies,
> required to bring such outputs about, including
> the skills associated with them; and
>
> carry out the formal assessment required in all of
> the above.

The mastery of the knowledge that is prerequisite to skill
and competence demonstration, and to some extent the mastery
of skills--to the extent that this is possible through
simulated training conditions--will be carried out within
the college setting. A state-wide network of such
Cooperatives is illustrated schematically as Figure 2.

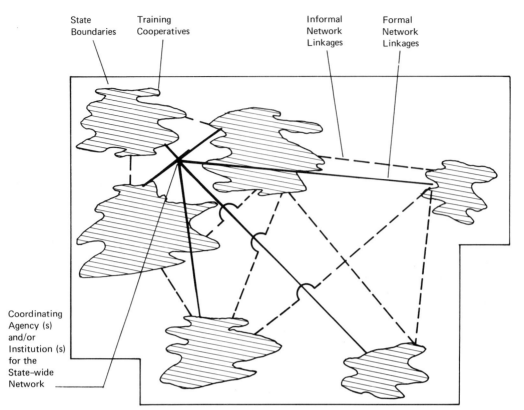

State Boundaries   Training Cooperatives   Informal Network Linkages   Formal Network Linkages

Coordinating Agency (s) and/or Institution (s) for the State-wide Network

Figure 2.   A schematic illustration of a state-wide
network of Training Cooperatives for the
preparation of educational personnel, and
the formal and informal linkage mechanisms
needed for the network to function
effectively.

Four further points need to be discussed: (1) the
rationale for utilizing a community and its schools as the
locus of a Training Cooperative rather than creating a new
institution on a "neutral ground"; (2) the rationale for
using a state as the primary organization for Cooperatives
rather than a region; (3) the rationale for cost sharing in
the development and operation of Cooperatives; and (4) the
rationale for establishing a nation-wide network of illustrative state-wide networks.

1.   The rationale for utilizing a community and its
schools as the locus of a Training Cooperative
rather than creating a new institution to house
it.

The rationale is relatively straightforward: communities are where the action is. Also they are the governmental
units that provide the bulk of funds for the support of
elementary and secondary education in the nation; they are
the units that have the schools; they are the units that have
the greater reason to care about the well being of schools;

and they are the units that ultimately control what happens within the schools. Finally, the schools represent established, understood, politically and economically supported institutions that have a good share of the economic and human resources needed to operate a Training Cooperative. They are also the ones to benefit most from such a Cooperative, both in the short and long term. To not utilize such resources to their fullest in the creation of Training Cooperatives (including intermediate education districts, or their equivalents) is unthinkable.

Not so by some writers. In reading the materials prepared on training complexes the plea for a new institution on "neutral territory" is repeatedly made. The assumption underlying the plea seems to be that schools, communities and colleges could never establish a relationship that would permit them to function as they would need to within a Cooperative. Such an assumption has not been borne out by the writer's experience. Prototype cooperatives have been in operation throughout Oregon for the past ten years, and within the last several years they have been established in Florida, Massachusetts, Minnesota, New York, North Dakota, Utah and Washington. In the writer's judgment the only real hope for Training Cooperatives is their integration within the ongoing educational enterprise. Obviously, such integration is a complex business, and can run aground in a thousand different places, but if done sensitively and with an awareness of what it is that is to be gained by all concerned it can take place.

The other factor that presses for the utilization of existing institutions and agencies in the design of Training Cooperatives is the fact that Cooperatives will be needed to facilitate training (both pre- and inservice) in all regions of a state. The image of a state having to create multiple new institutions in order to support its education personnel needs is disquieting at best. The likelihood of the success of such a venture, given the financial circumstances of the times and the history of the Regional Laboratories and R & D Centers, is probably next to zero.

2. <u>The rationale for establishing a state as the primary unit of organization, rather than</u> a <u>region</u>.

Granting the proposition that a Training Cooperative or something akin to it is needed to support each training program in teacher education, and recognizing that at this point in time the certification of teachers is a responsibility of states, and recognizing that legislation, funding sources, communication networks and other support systems to teacher education are defined primarily by state boundaries (although there are obvious moves afoot to increase the planning and operation of human service programs on a regional basis) it seems reasonable to think of the state as

the primary unit of organization for such Cooperatives. As
a means of facilitating nationwide resource sharing and
communication flow across state lines within a region makes
some sense, but beyond that the notion of organization
along regional lines would seem to have little to offer.

3.   The rationale for cost-sharing between
      participating institutions in the
      Cooperatives and the state and federal
      governments.

Colleges currently have budgets that support education
personnel development programs. School districts have
budgets for inservice education. Increasingly schools want
beginning teachers who have had a wide range of experience
with children. Colleges are following suit by seeking such
experience for their students, and for earlier and longer
periods of time. As schools move to open classrooms,
individualized instruction, team teaching, differentiated
staffing and the like they have more and more need for
persons in the schools with different backgrounds and
capabilities. College faculty are increasingly of the
opinion that persons in the schools have a great deal to
give in relation to the preparation of teachers.

In most instances the community and the state department
of education view these events with pleasure.

So should the designers of Training Cooperatives for
they provide not only the interpersonal and interinstitutional groundwork for Cooperatives but they also provide
the avenue for their financial base as well. A number of
schemes have been worked out whereby a school district and a
participating college have pooled their human and financial
resources so as to effectively create a prototype
Cooperative, and these seem to be working to the satisfaction of all concerned. [13] If such arrangements could become widespread, and there is no reason for believing that
they could not, a relatively firm financial base already
exists for the development and operation of Cooperatives.

Given the projected functions of these "new institutions"
however, it is unlikely that such a financial base would be
adequate for their full development and operation. As
always, one place to turn for additional financial help is
the state and federal governments. Assuming that the
installation of fully functioning Training Cooperatives of
the kind proposed would significantly influence education
throughout a state and the nation, and assuming that district

_____

[13]For information about such arrangement contact Dr.
Jim Ellingson, Oregon Board of Education, Salem, Oregon or
Dr. Bill Drummond, Washington State Department of Education,
Olympia, Washington.

and college contributions would cover operating instructional costs, a state might be willing to pick up the cost of program evaluation and instate diffusion and the federal government might be willing to pick up the cost of the research and development needs associated with launching a state-wide network of Cooperatives as well as the cost of nation-wide diffusion efforts. [14] whether federal monies for the support of such activities should be assigned to states on a "project" or "block grant" basis, or some other basis, is an open question, but the idea of shared costs at the federal and state level, in conjunction with shared costs at the college and local level, seems sound.

4.   The rationale for establishing a network of illustrative state-wide networks.

Much will need to be learned in the operation of Cooperatives both individually and on a state-wide basis before they become fully functional components within the education enterprise. It seems reasonable to assume, therefore, that some organizational structure which links the developing state-wide networks would be most useful. Through such a structure they could share on a regular basis the issues that they face and the solutions that they find.

Similarly, by pooling that which emerges from the various state networks and making it available to teacher education at large the utility of such networks would be greatly enhanced. Given the national scope of such an effort it seems reasonable to assume that the Office of Education would be the agency to effect such coordination. [15]

---

[14] The research, development, evaluation and diffusion needs associated with Cooperatives as well as more detailed suggestions for cost sharing relative to them are outlined under Guideline #4.

[15] It is also possible that each state-wide network initially funded could serve as a "pilot" or "lead" state in relation to a region, and thus insure a more intimate network for communicating the results of the overall development effort. As a pilot or lead state, a state would have to be willing to assume responsibility for establishing and maintaining regional linkages, invite other states within the region to review and perhsps advise relative to within state network development, arrange for on-site observation of on-going programs, and perhaps even establish demonstration programs within other states. Additional details are provided in this regard under Guideline #7.

<u>Guideline #3: Utilize within the proposed preparatory</u>
<u>program all PROTOCOL, TRAINING AND INTEGRATING materials</u>
<u>that are available to and consonant with that program.</u>

Strictly speaking, a teacher education model is
devoid of substance or content. It lays out specifications
for the structure, function and operation of a teacher education program but the specific content to be included within
it when fully developed is left to the designers of that
program (and thus the general utility of a model). Given
this condition a program of the kind proposed becomes a
ready consumer of the protocol, training and integrating
materials that are available to it. The incorporation of
these materials within the operation of a center is
illustrated schematically in Figure 4. [16]

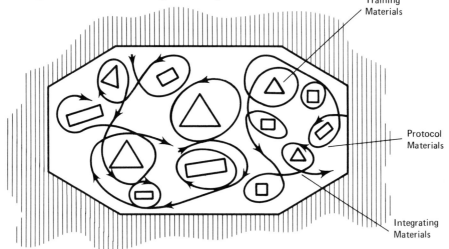

Figure 4.   An illustration of the manner in which existing
protocol, training and integrating materials
would be used within a preparatory program of
the kind proposed.

While the principle just stated and illustrated in
Figure 4 is appropriate as a principle a host of operational
questions revolve around it.

_____

[16] Strictly speaking, a large share of the available
training and protocol materials will probably he used in the
college setting, though many may also be used in or as
adjuncts to the field setting provided by the cooperative.
In this sense the schematic is a pictorial convenience.

1.   How likely is it that protocol and training
materials produced in other centers or in other preparatory
programs would be adopted by or would be able to be fit
within a second program? To the extent that a program
focuses upon knowledge and skill outcomes (which would run
counter to the proposal made in the present paper) it is
possible that "ready-made" materials would receive wide use.
This assumes, of course, that the conceptual base for both
protocol and training materials has been well established,
that such materials have been well produced, and that there
is evidence that they in fact bring about the outcomes that
they are intended to achieve. If the second program is
output based, however, it is likely that protocol and
training materials developed elsewhere--at least if they have
been developed independently of an analysis of the outputs
that educational personnel have to bring about--will have
more limited utility. In an output referenced program the
outputs which educational personnel are to achieve in a
given educational context become the primary organizing unit
for the professional education curriculum,and if protocol
and training materials have been developed independently of
those intended outcomes it is likely that they will have a
restricted utility within the curriculum. [17]

2.   Even if protocol and training materials developed
elsewhere could be readily adapted to a wide range of programs
how likely is it that the present production schedule for
such materials will meet the needs of such programs? At the
moment a limited number of protocol materials are under
development (probably no more than 50 or so sets of
protocols will be in a finished state by the end of this
academic year) and plans for the production of training
materials are only now getting under way. While some training
materials already exist in the field there is no where near
the mass of materials that will be needed ultimately to
support a fully operational performance based program. At the
present rate of development, or even at a ten-fold expanded
rate of development, how long will it take to accumulate the
needed mass of such materials?

3.   At the present time no integrative materials
(see Glossary)are being developed. In fact, so far as one is
able to determine, no one in the nation is sytematically
addressing the question of the kinds of learning outcomes
that educational personnel are expected to develop to

---

[17] The implications of a performance based, output
referenced program in teacher education for concept identification and organization is spelled out in detail in a paper
by the writer entitled "Tasks to be Performed by Teachers
as a Basis for Identifying and Ordering Concepts in Teacher
Education." The paper was prepared for use as a discussion
vehicle within the Protocol LTI, February. 1971.

facilitate the realization of learning outcomes.[18]   Given
the definition of integrating materials, it is quite obvious
that they cannot be developed until questions of this kind
have been answered. If certification criteria and
preparation programs are to become output referenced there is
simply no way to avoid dealing with such issues for they
constitute the beginning and end of both curriculum development and competency assessment.

Assuming the correctness of this assessment it seems
essential that a task force comparable to that which exists
for protocol and training materials be established to begin
the process of identifying the outcomes expected of schooling,
the kinds of school arrangements needed to effect such outcomes, the criteria to be used in judging whether prospective teachers are able to bring them about, the measures
to be used in assessing performance relative to those
criteria, and in the nature of the learning experiences that
must be engaged in by prospective teachers to develop the
competence to perform them. Within this context learning
experiences will need to include those designed to sensitize
the prospective teacher to all of the above.

4. Given such concerns should the proposed
illustrative statewide networks of Training Cooperatives become primary producers of protocol, training and integrating
materials? If so how should production responsibilities be
divided amongst them? And what critical mass of human and
non-human resources would be needed to support the development of such materials within a reasonable time frame? If
heavy production were commissioned for the cooperatives what
would their responsibilities by for producing multiple copies
of the materials for distribution? For actually distributing
or marketing the materials that they do produce? For
corrdinating their development? If the cooperatives were not
to become involved in production would they in fact be field-
test centers for producers? More is said under Guidelines 6
and 7 about the production and distribution of such materials.

18
     Since writing this an RFP has been discovered that has
been let by BEPD (RFP #71-27) for "The Design and Conduct of
a Program to Qualitatively Assess the Educational Needs of
Children Through a Broadly Based Literature Review and to
Determine Quantitatively the Implications for Educational
Manpower." This is surely a much needed step in the right
direction

Guideline 4:   Incorporate within one or more of the training
cooperatives within each state the functions of RESEARCH,
DEVELOPMENT, EVALUATION and DIFFUSION. [19]

The major research, development, evaluation and
diffusion activities that need to be carried out within a
Training Cooperative, or within a state-wide network of
cooperatives, have been alluded to at various places and in
various ways throughout the paper. The rationale for including such activities has also been advanced in pieces and parts.
The purpose of this section of the paper is to summarize these
proposed activities and the rationale for them in one place,
and to speak to their distribution within a state-wide network of cooperatives.

1.   Development. In the previous section of the paper,
questions were raised about the generalizability or the
transportability of materials, be they protocol, training or
integrating, across programs. It will be recalled that in the
writer's judgment the bulk of materials designed to support
educational personnel development programs will be sub-
mitted to some degree of modification by each program that
relies upon them. If this is true it will mean that each
program will have to assume responsibility for some adaptive
developmental activities in order to arrive at an integrated
use of materials that become available through multiple
producers. Since this is not a major developmental activity,
however, it will not be dealt with further at this time.

A more critical issue for the purpose of this discussion is whether major program development efforts, such
as the one that has been proposed in the present paper, should
be considered as a primary locus for materials development.
The history of experience in the protocol projects and in the
development of instructional modules in support of Teacher
Corps efforts suggests that the process of materials
development is much more complex than people initially
realized. This has also been the experience of the Regional
Laboratories. Accepting the complexity of the task, would
it make sense to add such a responsibility to all the other
responsibilities that will accompany a program development
effort of the magnitude that has been proposed? In one
respect, yes, for the development of such a program
represents a natural context within which to launch the
development of the materials needed to support it. Also, if
the program development effort is viewed as exemplary, then
materials developed within it should be optimally useful.

---

[19] This section of the paper, and the three sections which
follow, deal with topics that extend beyond the five thrusts
with which the paper is intended to deal. They have been
included in the paper, however, because of their criticalness
as adjuncts to the five thrusts in the overall design and
operation of personnel development programs that have some
hope of making a difference.

In another respect, however, the requirements of materials development could be so severe as to threaten other aspects of program development and operation. This is an issue that needs to be tested on a trial and error basis.

Assuming that a Training Cooperative or a network of such Cooperatives should become involved in the production of materials the next question is whether all three kinds of materials, that is, protocol, training and integrating materials, should be produced at a single site? One of the inevitable problems that would arise with multiple centers producing multiple products is that of overlap or duplication. If exemplary programs were to assume major responsibilities for materials development some coordinating mechanism would have to be established at the national level to oversee such efforts.

Another development problem exists in relation to an output referenced, performance based teacher education program which has not been spoken of heretofore. That is the problem of the design and development of the support systems needed to operate such a program. Generally speaking these pertain to the design, development and operation of the instructional program, the generation of information to support instruction and the assessment of its results, the management of information, the selection, preparation and maintenance of staff, the provision of facilities and supplies, costing, program management, and policy setting.

One of the results of the feasibility study conducted in Oregon on the implications of adopting the ComField model was the finding that the development and operation of the systems needed in support of instruction were roughly equivalent in cost to the development and operation of the instructional program per se. [20] Since each program must develop its own support systems in order to operate, it is likely that these will be developmental costs that cannot be significantly reduced through "system sharing" across programs. This is not to say that design and development costs could not be reduced by having exemplary systems available, but it is to say that support systems are not likely to be able to be transported and used by operating programs in the same way that instructional materials can be.

---

[20] See the report of the feasibility study that is cited elsewhere for a detailed description of the mechanisms needed in support of such a program and the costs projected by mechanism.

In summary it is likely that every performance based
teacher education program will encounter some adaptation
developmental costs in relation to instructional materials,
and that they will encounter considerable costs of this kind
in relation to support systems. If the decision is made to
have exemplary programs become the locus of materials
development efforts, or as the locus for the development of
exemplary support systems, developmental costs will climb
accordingly. Because of the highly specialized human resource
requirements involved in such activities, and because of the
relatively limited supply of such resources, it is not likely
that many programs will be able to be mounted that will be
able to assume major responsibilities for development.

2. Evaluation. For purposes of the present paper
evaluation has been defined as that set of activities that
generate information in service of on-line decision making
(see the Glossary). Ignoring the function of evaluation
within developmental activities, it would assume at least
the following functions within a program of the kind
proposed:

> determine for purposes of certification the
> success or lack of success of each student in
> realizing each outcome for which he is responsible;

> determine the contribution of each element
> within the program to its intended outcome;

> determine the effectiveness with which each
> element makes its intended contribution, that is,
> determine the range and proportion of students
> that achieve the learning outcomes that they are
> expected to achieve after engaging with a particular
> program element;

> determine the range and proportion of students that
> are able to reach the criteria required for
> certification as a function of engaging with the
> program as a whole;

> determine the amount of time and energy required to
> reach the criteria of certification;

> determine the long-term effects of students who
> have moved through the program upon the schools in
> which they work and the children with whom they
> interact;

> determine the long-term effects of the program
> upon the personal development and well-being of
> the students who have gone through it;

> continuously review the appropriateness of the goals
> of the program, especially those having to do with
> the learning outcomes desired for children.

One of the great strengths of a performance based program is that it has within it the data base that permits such evaluations to be made without undue effort. Without such information the program as a whole and individuals within it suffer from an inability to adapt wisely.

Evaluation efforts, like other instructional support efforts, will involve program specific development costs. While it is possible that exemplary systems can be developed, and to some extent adapted to the demands of individual programs, it is likely that they will not have the same degree of transportability that instructional materials will have. It is also likely that they will require a greater outlay of resources to operate for the information that derives from them must be processed, stored, and made available for retrieval upon call. While the costs associated with these activities can legitimately be considered as instructional support costs they do require considerable resources to develop, install and operate, and that fact should not be overlooked in planning for program development.

Since evaluation activities provide data that are designed to have utility only for on-line decision making, and are therefore not intended to be generalizable beyond the context within which they are collected, a question is often raised as to the defensibility of spending as much money as it takes to obtain such information. Questions are also raised as to whether or not such information might not be of use to other programs even though it is not gathered against the constraints of a design that is intended to force its generalizability. With respect to the first question the answer is simply that if one is to adopt a performance based mode of operation, and it is to be other than a mockery of the concept, there is no alternative to the systematic collection of evaluation data of the kind outlined. While it is true that such information does not have the properties that permit it to be generalizable that is not the intent of such information. Its purpose is to support decision making in relation to ongoing program operation and that should not be confused with the knowledge generation purpose of research.

The second question is obviously related to the first, and carries an answer that can alleviate some of the anxiety reflected by it. In the writer's judgment evaluation information, if carefully prepared and presented as documentary rather than the results of research, has considerable information value to persons beyond the program in which it is collected. The results of another's experience can be studied, whether that experience is similar or dissimilar to that incurred in one's own program; procedures that have been used in generating, presenting, or utilizing the information presented may be of value to someone else; and the fact that documentation has occurred insures that some record will be preserved that can be viewed by others who at a later time may be thinking of pursuing a similar course. Information of this kind does not have the same utility that generalizable knowledge possesses, but it has some utility. For this reason it would seem advisable, at least at a state level, for Training Cooperatives to maintain such documentation and share it with one another. Since case histories have been found to be highly useful documents in other disciplines, considerable utility may be found in sharing such information nationally.

3. Research. Given the output focus of the proposed program, the multi-state linkage of the program to those output, that is, through schools designed to bring about such outputs, the personnel needed to maintain such schools, etc., and the necessity of evaluation data relative to the adequacy of all the linkages that have been made, an extremely rich "natural" context for research on human learning and instruction becomes available. To not take advantage of such a circumstance would be a phenomenal waste.

From the writer's point of view the great advantage gained by such a context is that it provides a relatively natural setting within which to conduct the kind of multi-variate research that ultimately must be done if principles of instruction are ever to be identified. As used here, an instructional principle refers to an empirically demonstrated relationship between one or more classes of instructional strategies and one or more classes of learner outcomes when the characteristics of learners and the conditions under which learning is taking place are known (within such a scheme the substantive content that links to a strategy is considered as part of that strategy). By forcing explication of classes of learning outcomes, and by systematically gathering data as to their realization, an output referenced preparatory program provides the critical context needed for such research.

The nature of the research that could be undertaken within the program that is being proposed need not be limited, of course, to the kind just outlined. Research into the nature of learning environments, the nature of learner characteristics, the dimensions of instruction, small group processes, or any other dimensions of social behavior and settings would be appropriate as foci of investigation. To prevent researchers from jumping into such a context too quickly, however, with what could turn out to be a discordant array of research activities, it needs to be recognized that any ongoing educational program can tolerate only so much activity above and beyond the business of its operation. Thus, while a wide variety of research is possible within a context of the kind proposed, and the tolerance of the program for research activities is likely to be much greater than that found in traditional programs, there is obviously an upper limit to the range and amount of research that can go on there. For this reason researchers who enter such contexts should choose well their research priorities.

In the writer's judgment the kind of research that has been proposed should receive the highest of ratings in this regard. Somehow, more powerful paradigms for research on teaching and learning must be developed than we presently

have at our disposal, and they must be applied in a context
and with a level of support that offers some hope of results
that have immediate payoff. As things now stand the development and operation of education programs and teacher education programs have to take place essentially without benefit
of empirical data, and that is a circumstance that cannot be
permitted to exist. If the proposals made in the present
paper were acted upon it could begin its alteration.

4.   Diffusion. If a Training Cooperative is designed as an illustrative program within a state, or if a
state-wide network of such Cooperatives is designed as
illustrative for a region or nation, the realities of the
diffusion process must be faced. As used in the present
paper diffusion refers to that set of activities that lead
to the adoption by another of that which is attempting to be
spread (see the Glossary).

As such diffusion involves a great deal more than simply
the dissemination of information. While it is not clear what
in fact the diffusion process requires in order for it to be
effective [21] it is probable that in addition to the
dissemination of information it must also involve demonstration,
testing on a trial basis, support during implementation and
service following adoption. If this is true diffusion becomes a very complex and costly business, and the mechanisms
to carry it must be extremely carefully constructed. Because of the complexity of the matter Guidelines 6 and 7
are devoted to the topic specifically.

Given the nature of the RDD&E activities proposed for
inclusion in a Training Cooperative what is the optimal distribution of such activities within a state-wide network of
cooperatives? Undoubtedly this will vary by state, depending upon the extent to which information management
capabilities crosscut an entire state, the distribution of
research, development and evaluation capabilities within a
state, etc., but something on the order of that which
follows seems reasonable: one or perhaps two Cooperatives
in a state become identified as "lead" institutions, and
in that role assume major responsibility for receiving resources for research, development (including the development of an exemplary evaluation system) and diffusion. These
institutions would be expected to carry the brunt of the research and development efforts needed within a state, and
also the major responsibility for in-state diffusion of those
efforts. Other programs would receive some support for research and development, on the assumption that situation-
specific demands will always force some adaptation on materials
or systems developed elsewhere, and on the assumption that research needs to be an ongoing process in all contexts. Each

---

[21] See for example Havelock, R. A Comparative Study of the
Literature on the Dissemination and Utilization of Scientific
Knowledge. Ann Arbor: Michigan University, Institute for
Social Research, 1970 (ERIC Document No. ED 029171).

program would receive also some support for the diffusion
function and all programs would receive essentially equivalent funding for the execution of the evaluation function.
Such a formula reflects several related assumptions: (a)
that resources of the kind needed for initial developmental
work can best be utilized by "bunching" them within a single
or limited number of contexts; (b) that some contexts are
better equipped to accommodate such resources than others;
and (c) that different contexts within a state will be
ready to engage in RDD&E activities at differing points in
time. While some may feel that such a plan is elitist and
doomed to failure because of the politics of inter-insti-
tutional cooperation, it can only be pointed out that at
least one state has supported such a plan and is of the
opinion that it's functional. [22]

Guideline 5: Federal funds for the operation of each state-
wide network of Cooperatives, and for the coordination of the
various statewide networks at a national level, should come
jointly from various Bureaus within the Office of Education.

The concept of shared funding between local school
districts, cooperating colleges and the state and federal
governments has already been outlined. The purpose of the
present discussion is to suggest a way in which federal
funds could be shared across Bureaus within the Office of
Education so as to integrate several related thrusts within
OE and at the same time optimize resource availability for a
training program.

It will be recalled that the cost sharing strategy called
for school district and college resources to be directed
primarily to the costs of instruction within the program, the
extra resources of the state to be directed to the costs of
evaluation and to some extent the costs of development and
diffusion, and federal resources to the major costs associated
with research and development and to the costs of diffusion
at the national level. With this as a point of departure it
is proposed that BEPD and the Experimental Schools Program
share in both development and diffusion costs, and that NCERD
assume responsibility for research costs. Such a division
would seem to fall logically within the domains of responsibility for these three operating units, especially in the
light of the new organizational structure within the Office.
The opportunity to participate in an activity that would hold
so much joint interest should provide a convenient vehicle
for cross-bureau programming.

In terms of OE's history cross-bureau activities have
never been particularly common, and those that have been tried
have never been particularly successful, so the hopefulness

---

[22] See Chapter 3 in Part I, and Part VII in Volume I of
the Final Report on the ComField feasibility study.

about such cooperative efforts has to be viewed with re-
straint. Nevertheless. there are seeds for such activity
afoot and there is the expressed desire to let such seeds
flower, so there is some reason to be hopeful about its
possibility. An output oriented model of teacher education.
with its linkage to schools and the intended outcome of
schools, should be ideal as a place to begin. It would be
unfortunate if a vehicle so right for exploitation at the
bureaucratic level was bypassed

Guideline 6: As a means of bringing the knowledge and
capability of the private sector to bear in support of the
diffusion process each state-wide network of Cooperatives
should link to industry for assistance in the design and
development of its instruction and support systems.

     As discussed previously, the diffusion process is one
which is not well understood and, with the exception of its
ERIC program, one in which the Office of Education has not
had a great deal of experience or success. In part this is
undoubtedly due to a limited understanding of what is required to carry out diffusion successfully. In the writer's
judgment, however, even if the requirement of an effective
diffusion effort were known the likelihood of carrying out
such efforts with federal funds is minimal. It is simply too
costly a process. For this reason it seems in the best
interests of education to turn to the private sector for
help.

     Given the notion of packaged and therefore reasonably
transportable instructional materials being available for
use in preparatory programs in the future, a number of
questions as to the diffusion of such materials arise: (a)
After being developed, how are they to be mass produced and
distributed? (b) How is a demand for their use to be created?
(c) Once a demand has been created, who is going to see that
the demand is met? In the judgment of the writer, the only
feasible way to mass produce and distribute (market) such
materials and provide the services needed in support of their
adoption and use is to involve the private sector. These are
precisely the kind of services that private enterprise is
accustomed to providing and they have the financial
wherewithall to carry them out.

     While the nature of the working relationship that would
have to be struck between industry, the Office of Education
and the initial producers of materials is unclear it could
assume something like the following:

          Education materials production firms would
          consult with the initial producers of materials
          during their development (each producer should
          probably work with a different representative
          from industry);

          Once developed and appropriately field tests, the
          distributing firm will "package" the materials,
          reproduce them in the quantities needed, market

them, and provide the service functions needed in
support of their adoption and utilization;

As materials become available for distribution the
distributor will provide ERIC and the regional
laboratory network with detailed description of the
materials that are available, the requirements for
their utilization, cost, how they might be obtained,
etc. This information can be disseminated through
ERIC and the laboratories as well as through the
channels ordinarily used by industry;

Each of the training cooperatives within a state or
region that is a part of the nationwide develop-
ment-diffusion network will develop an efficient
and effective means of demonstrating the materials
being distributed for those who wish to make an
on-site inspection of them in operation.

Whether such a procedure would prove to be functional is
open to debate, but given the magnitude and significance of
the task it seems critical that OE begin to explore seriously
something approximating it.

Guideline 7: In addition to a national pool of transportable products to be used in performance based teacher
education programs, made available largely through industry,
regional dissemination-diffusion networks should also be
established.

As indicated previously one of the key elements in the
diffusion process seems to be an opportunity to see that
which is being considered for adoption in operation. Trans-
lating this to teacher education it requires that demonstration programs be reasonably abailable in terms of dis-
tance from satellite programs so that persons who wish to get
to them can. Granting this necessity, it would seem that
demonstration programs must be provided on at least a
regional basis. By linking such programs to ERIC, and perhaps to regional laboratories, the more personal aspects of
the dissemination function might work as follows:

Each demonstration institution would assume
responsibility for developing prototype materials
that describe the program being implemented;

Staff from the ERIC Clearinghouse on Teacher
Education would take these prototype materials,
refine them, and reproduce them in quantities
sufficient for distribution by ERIC, the laboratories, and the demonstrating programs;

Each of the regional laboratories would be
responsible for personallt informing each of the
teacher preparation institutions in their region
about each of the illustrative programs underway,
how additional information might be obtained about

those programs, how they might gain access to
specific materials and/or procedures developed
within them, etc.;

Each of the demonstration institutions, and their
sister institutions within a state, would establish
a procedure whereby persons coming for on-site
inspection of the program could be accommodated
efficiently and effectively.

Again, while it is not at all clear that that which has been
proposed will work, the issue to which the proposal is
addressed is critical, and the Office of Education must
develop a plan to deal with it seriously.

As a first approximation to such a plan a proposal
made by the writer as a followup to the feasibility study
on the ComField Model is attached as Supplement I. It needs
to be pointed out that the proposal is dated, and that it
contains the language of the models, but in its time it was
intended as a relatively complete proposal.

PART III: SOME IMPLICATIONS OF IMPLEMENTING
A PROGRAM OF THE KIND PROPOSED

The major implications of the proposals that have been
made for program operation have been spelled out in the preceding pages or in the supplements attached to the body of
the paper. Implications have not been spelled out specifically,
however, for those involved in or affected by the program.
The purpose of this section of the paper is to do so, and
attempt to do so in cost/benefit terms. In order to keep
the analysis short and as easy to read as possible, costs
and benefits are put forth in summary form for each group of
individuals affected. Only those implications which must
necessarily follow from the implementation of such a program
have been listed; possible or hoped for implications do not
appear.

Implications for Institutions
Responsible for Program Operation

It will be recalled that the operation of an output
referenced, performance based personnel development program
requires a partnership between a community, one or more
schools within that community, one or more colleges or
universities and the State Department of Education. It will
also be recalled that the partnership functions within the
context of a Training Cooperative. The implications for
members of this partnership are the first set to be
summarized.

The Schools

BENEFITS

1. An increase in clarity as to the goals of education and how those goals are to be translated
   into the goals or objectives of indicidual schools.

2. An increasingly better fit between a school and
   its programs and the goals or objectives it is to
   realize.

3. An increased awareness of the expectations which
   members of the community have for their schools.

4. The contribution of all of the above to a vital,
   continuing in-service education program.

5. A prototype system for the assessment of a school as a whole or any of the elements within it against desired pupil outcomes.

6. A prototype model for the operation of schools that are output referenced, performance-based, personalized, field-dependent, data dependent, etc.

7. A continuously available supply of new personnel with known capability so far as performing the functions required within a particular school is concerned.

8. A relatively inexpensive source of personnel to fill positions at the lower end of a differentiated staffing structure.

9. A built-in, rational change mechanism.

10. Direct and active involvment in the preservice as well as the inservice development of education personnel, at the levels of policy, management and operations. [24]

COSTS

1. The added responsibility of and additional re- sources required for participation in such a pro- gram, though resource requirements will be offset by the availability of students to fill supporting staff roles and the contribution of the program to in-service training.

2. Having to share with the community and a college or university decisions relative to the goals of education and the nature of schools and schooling as it pertains to the realization of those goals.

3. An increased number of adults in the schools.

4. The hard work of having to continuously engage in decision making relative to the goals of education and the nature of the schools and schooling that will lead to the realization of those goals.

5. The intellectual and emotional wear and tear that is attndent to work in a context that is committed to continuous, data dependent change.

6. The demand placed upon continuously updated in- service education that accompanies work in an institution committed to continuous change.

---

[24] The implications cited are in no particular order and they are not intended to be exhaustive.

7. The threat of a data dependent, output referenced mode of operation--both philosophically and in terms of personal performance.

8. The potential threat of incoming staff having demonstrated levels of competence.

The Residents of a Community

BENEFITS

1. All of the benefits that accrue through the schools (see above).

2. A prototype system for generating information as to the success or lack of success that the schools are having in bringing about the outcomes expected of them.

3. A prototype system for obtaining cost/benefits indices relative to the operation of programs within a school as well as a school system as a whole.

4. An opportunity to influence the utilization of a broad range of resources within a community and state in service of the education of children.

COSTS

1. All of the costs, to the extent that they are real rather than perceived, that accrue to the schools (see above).

2. The expenditure of the time and energy required as full participants in the preparatory program.

3. The shared responsibility for seeing that the schools, the personnel that operate the schools, and the programs that prepare those personnel are of a quality to insure the realization of the outcomes desired of schooling.

4. The shared responsibility for insuring the resource base needed by (3).

The College and/or University

BENEFITS

1. All of the benefits that accrue to a community and the schools within it as a strengthened base on which to design, develop and implement a preparatory program.

2. The resources of the schools and the community in assisting with the design, development and implementation of a program.

157

3. The provision of the real life context within which an output referenced, performance based program must function.

4. The functional integration of the preparatory program within the profession that it serves.

COSTS

1. Having to share the responsibility for decision making about teacher education with other institutions and agencies within the Cooperative.

2. No longer having the luxury of conducting a preparatory program within the walls of a college or university.

3. Having to engage in the continuing and difficult intellectual task of identifying the pupil outcomes desired from schooling, the nature of schools with the greatest probability of bringing about such outcomes, etc. as a basis for the design, development and implementation of the preparatory program.

4. Having to establish new structures and modes of operation, both within and without the college and university, and having to adopt significantly different role behaviors within them.

5. Having to perceive students in the preparatory program as individuals able to make decisions relative to their own ends, and the means to get to them, and then act in terms of it.

6. The threat of data relative to the effectiveness of a program, and the effectiveness of one's own performance in relation to it.

7. The emotional wear and tear that is an accompaniment to a program that is designed to be continuously adaptive.

The State Department of Education

BENEFITS

1. All of the benefits that accrue to the schools, participating colleges and universities, and the residents of participating communities.

2. An information base which permits an analysis of the outcomes desired from education on a statewide basis.

3. An information base which permits an analysis of the kinds of schools deemed appropriate for the realization of those outcomes.

158

4. An information base which permits the projection
    of personnel needs on a statewide basis for the
    manning of such schools.

5. An information base which permits the assessment
    of the competencies of existing education personnel
    on a statewide basis.

6. An information base which permits an analysis of
    the contribution of existing personnel development
    programs in a state to projected personnel needs.

7. An information base which permits an analysis of
    the adequacy with which ongoing preparatory pro-
    grams are preparing needed personnel.

8. An information base which permits the linkage of all
    of the above to the effectiveness with which the
    schools in the state are able to bring about the
    learning outcomes expected of them.

9. An information base which, given all of the above,
    would permit a State Department to rationally and
    systematically coordinate educational activities
    so as to effect optimally the learning of children
    within a state.

COSTS

1. Assuming that the benefits outlined above wish to
    be exploited, a complex information generation and
    management system must be developed and maintained,
    with its attending resource requirements.

2. Still assuming that all possible benefits wish to be
    exploited, a state department would have to assume
    an even more active and pervasive coordination/
    leadership function than it now assumes, with its
    attending resource requirements.

3. The working out of a solution to the problems
    associated with certification when certification is
    based upon situation specific demonstrations of
    competence in effecting desired educational out-
    puts rather than the completion of program specific
    course sequences.

Implications for Students in the Program

Thus far a great deal has not been said about the
specific implications of such a program for students in it,
although it is likely that the reader of Parts I and II of
the paper sensed that the nature of learning experiences within such a program would be considerably different than they
are within existing programs. Three major differences would
appear: (a) students would be spending a great deal of time
with real outcomes; (b) knowledge and skills would be seen

only as enabling conditions in relation to certification, rather than criterion conditions; and (c) the whole process of instruction within such a program would be highly personalized. Beyond these points, however, little has been said as to the actual operation of the program from the point of view of students and personnel within it.

In order to provide additional information along these lines, two pages of narrative from a synopsis of the Oregon College of Education's adaptation of the ComField model have been reproduced. These pages are intended to introduce the reader to both the structure and function of output referenced programs, though obviously the model presented is only one of a variety of arrangements that could be followed. With this minimal background, and with the background gained through reading Parts I & II of the paper, it is anticipated that the reader will be able to make reasonable sense of the implications statements that follow the insert.

The program involves three relatively distinct phases of work: the General Studies phase, the Clinical Studies phase, and the Intern phase. Operationally, the General Studies phase, is defined as that aspect of the program that does not involve responsibility for the learning of children; the Clinical Studies phase as that aspect of the program that involves responsibility for the learning of children under simplified (laboratory or simulated) conditions; and the Intern phase as that aspect of the program that involves supervised responsibility for the learning of children in fully operational, real-life educational settings. As such, the General Studies phase of the program corresponds most closely to that which has been traditionally labeled the "professional development" or "laboratory" dimension.

The Intern phase has no parallel in traditionally designed teacher education programs, and it in no way resembles the "intern" programs currently in vogue. As used in the program proposed by the OCE Coalition a prospective teacher enters the Intern phase only after he has demonstrated a specified set of competencies under laboratory conditions, and his task within the Intern phase is to demonstrate the same or a higher order set of competencies under real-life conditions. As an Intern a prospective teacher is to assume supervised responsibility for the full range of functions for which he will be responsible as a teacher, and he will be held accountable for the systematic demonstration of those functions.

Two levels of certification are included in the preservice program: INITIAL and CONTINUING. [25] These
correspond, respectively, to the completion of the
Clinical Studies and the Intern phases of the program.
As used in the proposed program INITIAL certification
designates a level of competency which permits the
assumption of supervised responsibility for the learning of children (a teaching Intern), and CONTINUING
certification designates a level of competency which
permits the assumption of full responsibility for the
learning of children. Certification criteria and
processes are described in greater detail in Part III
of the report.

As currently planned, no firm time lines are attached
to program phases but in general, for students declaring an interest in teacher education upon entry
as a Freshman, the General Studies phase will last for
a year or two, the Clinical Studies phase a year or
two and the Intern phase a year or two. Some students
may extend or shorten these estimates, and students
transferring from other colleges or students declaring
an interest in teacher education after a year or more
at OCE will undoubtedly move through the program on
some other time schedule. On the average, however,
most students will likely spend three or four years
completing requirements for INITIAL certification and
one or two years completing requirements for CONTINUING
certification.

A schematic representation of program structure, the
probable number of years required to move through the
program, and the certification levels within it is
presented in Figure 2. The broken lines in the figure
represent relatively flexible entry-exit requirements;
solid lines represent relatively inflexible entry-exit
requirements.

BENEFITS

1. As a consequence of the programs linking to desired
   learning outcomes in real-life learning contexts

        students would be able to gain first hand ex-
        perience with children;

        there would be an opportunity to determine
        whether they can or cannot effect the kinds of
        learning outcomes desired for children, and to

25
    A third level of certification, that of CONSULTANT, is
also used in the program but it is reserved for persons in
the field who have demonstrated the competencies needed to
perform as Clinical Supervisors. As such, this is a level of
certification that occurs outside of the preservice program
and is not dealt with in the present context. It is planned,
however, that certification at the CONSULTANT level will be
as stringent and systematic a process as it is at the preservice level.

The General Studies Phase	The Clinical Studies Phase	The Intern Phase	Teaching
Program entry as a Freshman	2 years ($\pm$1)	3 years ($\pm$2) INITIAL CERTIFICATION	4 years ($\pm$2) CONTINUING CERTIFICATION

Figure 2. A schematic representation of the structure of
the preservice elementary teacher education
program proposed at OCE

> continue their learning until they are able to
> do so;
>
> there would be an opportunity to determine pre-
> ferred contexts, that is, level and type of
> children with whom to work, the educational
> settings in which to work, the subject or
> discipline areas in which to work, etc.;
>
> there would be an opportunity to struggle
> seriously with the unending question of the
> outcomes desired from schooling:
>
> there would be increased meaningfulness of
> "relevancy" of the preparatory experience as
> a result of all of the above.

2.   As a function of the personalization of the instruction-
learning process there is

> an assured one to one or small group contact with
> staff and other students;
>
> an opportunity to contribute meaningfully to the
> design and development of the program as a whole;
>
> an opportunity to negotiate that which is to be
> taken from the program as a whole;
>
> an opportunity to negotiate the settings within
> which competence is to be demonstrated, and to
> negotiate the criteria by which judgment about
> competence is to be made;
>
> an opportunity to assess continuously the
> relevance of the objectives that have been
> negotiated and the relevance of the learning ex-
> periences being pursued in relation to those
> objectives;

162

an opportunity to progress through the program at a rate and in a sequence that optimizes the relationship between objectives, past experience, and present circumstances;

an opportunity to develop a minimal level of self-understanding as a basis against which to make judgments of the kind required in all of the above;

an opportunity to develop an overall "style" of teaching that is in concert with one's self-understanding.

3. As a function of treating knowledges and skills as enablers of competence

the mastery of knowledges and skills needed to bring about a particular outcome in children, or to develop instructional support outputs such as curriculum units, evaluation designs or assessment tools, is each student's responsibility[26] and as such is not a matter of direct relevance for certification;

a student already in possession of a particular knowledge or skill, as determined by criterion referenced measures, need not engage in learning experiences designed to bring about mastery of that knowledge or skill;

a student has the opportunity to demonstrate a particular competency prior to or independently of the demonstration of mastery of the knowledges and skills that are assumed to relate to the demonstration of a particular competency;

a student has an opportunity to cycle repeatedly through attempted competency demonstration or the mastery of knowledges and skills assumed to facilitate that demonstration.

4. As a function of all of the above, with their emphasis upon personally appropriate and self directed learning experience, it is assumed

that prospective teachers will develop into independent, self-directed, continuing learners; and, that systematic, personalized and self-

---

26
It is, of course, the responsibility of those in the program to provide the learning experiences that will insure that the knowledges and skills needed to bring about a given output are in fact available within the program.

directed instruction of the kind encountered in the preparatory program will transfer to the education of children in the school.

COSTS

1.   The increased responsibility placed on students in such a program for their own learning.

2.   The harshness of certification criteria.

3.   The indeterminate time required to complete criteria for certification (sometimes this may extend considerably beyond the four years now typically associated with certification, but it may also require fewer years than this).

4.   The emotional wear and tear that may accrue as a result of being free from the constraints (and security) of the highly structured cource approach that now dominates preparatory programs.

Implications for Others in Society That Would Be Directly Affected by the Program

While the implications that emerge from a program of the kind that has been proposed are most far reaching for those responsible for its implementation, or for students enrolled within it, it also carries with it implications that spread throughout a relatively large sector of the social system. In the paragraphs which follow some of the more obvious of these are spelled out for a selected set of persons who would feel its impact.

Pupils in the Schools

BENEFITS

All of that which would accrue from the benefits accrued by other who make a difference in the lives of children, and results of implementing in the schools the kind of systematically designed, data dependent and personalized approach to instruction that characterizes the preparatory program. It will be recalled that such an approach to instruction is likely to result in relatively independent, self directed learners, two benefits of the highest priority.

COSTS

Assuming the adoption by schools of the approach to instruction that has just been outlined it is likely that pupils would respond to it in much the same way that college students are expected

to respond (see above) Also, as in the case of
students in the preparatory program, pupils at
the elementary-secondary level will in all
likelihood encounter some emotional wear and
tear during the time that a shift in program
operation is underway.

Parents and Citizens of a Community, a State or the Nation

BENEFITS

All of the benefits which accrue to the
children in the schools of a community or state
that moves to such a program, or which accrue
to the personnel who operate such programs (see
earlier statements). Another kind of benefit
stems from being able to hold schools and preparatory programs accountable, in a costs/
benefits sense, for effecting the kinds of
learning outcomes which are held collectively
to be of importance.

COSTS

All of the costs encountered by pupils
affected by such a program (see earlier statements)
and the possible increase in dollar costs to
support such programs.

Schools and School Personnel Generally

BENEFITS

In time all the benefits that accrue to
the schools that are members of a training
cooperative should extend to schools throughout the educational system of a community or a
state or the nation.

COSTS

Using the same logic all of the costs that
schools are likely to assume as partners within
a training cooperative should also be encountered
by other schools in a community, or a state or
the nation as they enter into similar working
relationships. It may be, of course, that over
time the costs assumed will diminish as new means
are found to help the transition, but it is
unlikely that costs will ever be able to be
attenuated completely.

Colleges and College Personnel Generally

The rationale in relation to both benefits
and costs outlined for schools would seem to
hold in relation to colleges. For a summary of

the benefits and costs likely to be encountered
by colleges and college personnel, see pages
49 to 50.

Professional Education Associations and/or Unions

BENEFITS

All that would accrue from the increased
status of the education profession if it were able
to perform in the way anticipated as a consequence
of initiating the kind of program that has been
proposed. Whether this would forge an increasingly
important or less important role for professional
education associations and/or unions within the
overall conduct of education, however, is an open
question.

COSTS

The loss of traditional bargaining points,
such as number of working hours, reduced class
size, and vacation rights to such matters as the
learning outcomes most appropriately the responsibility of the schools, the resources required
to effect those outcomes, and personnel benefits
such as salary and staffing positions as a
consequence of the realization of given outcomes.
In a sense the loss is one of moving from the
relatively comfortable, non-threatening environment
of a non-accountable model of education to the
harshness of an accountability model.

Implications for the U.S. Office of Education

As indicated at the outset of the paper two Bureaus
within the Office of Education, and the Experimental
Schools Program, are particularly appropriate sources for
support in implementing a program of the kind proposed.
In the paragraphs which follow the implications of such
a program are summarized specifically for these units,
as well as for the Office as a whole.

The Experimental Schools Program

BENEFITS

The requirements that an output referenced
preparatory program take as a point of departure
the nature of learning outcomes desired from
schooling, and the nature of schools required to
effect those outcomes, would parallel in effort
the kind of thrust that is represented by the
Experimental Schools Program. That program is
centrally concerned about the consequences of
schooling and the nature of schools that can
effect those consequences, and they must have
evidence that schools so designed are in fact

bringing about the consequences desired. Functionally this means that all which derives from the Experimental Schools Program should be of immediate and critical use to the kind of preparatory program that has been proposed, _and vice versa_. It is also clear that neither program would be able to wait upon the results of the other. Operationally, then, it would seem essential that both efforts maintain intimate contact, if not sharing the funds.

COSTS

It is unclear where any costs would be encountered by the Experimental Schools Program unless some of the resources that would ordinarily be used to support such a school within the context of an output referenced personnel development program.

The Bureau of Educational Personnel Development

BENEFITS

1. An integrated application of the five basic thrusts currently emerging within the Bureau.

2. Through the application of those thrusts the development of a generic preparatory program which would serve as a primary source of input to the target programs within the Bureau.

3. The linkage of all preparatory programs supported by BEPD to schools and the process of schooling.

4. The legitimizing of a research, development, evaluation and diffusion within BEPD operations (through cooperation with NCERD and the Experimental Schools Program).

5. All of the benefits that accrue a state department, multiplied by fifty (see pages 72 and 73).

COSTS

1. Assuming that the benefits outlined above wish to be exploited, a complex information generation and management system must be developed and operated, with its attending resource requirements.

2. Continuing to assume that the benefits outlined above wish to be exploited, the Bureau would have to provide a more active and persuasive

coordination/leadership function than it now
provides, with its attending resource requirements.

The National Center for Educational Research and Development

BENEFITS

The essential benefits that would derive for
NCERD from such a venture is the context that would
provide for the pursuit of the R&D activities that
are functionally dependent upon such a context.
Some of the specific benefits that would emerge
from the conduct of R&D within an output referenced personnel development program have been
spelled out on pages 37 to 42.

COSTS

No undue costs to NCERD are apparent. There
would have to be resource allocations, of course,
in the support of R&D activities within the
context of preparatory programs, but these are
funds that would be channeled in support of
activities elsewhere so no "direct costs" are
seen accruing in that sense.

The U. S. Office of Education Generally

BENEFITS

1. An instance of cross-Bureau coordination that
   is more than perfunctory.

2. An instance that illustrates the functional
   integration of on-line schooling, the preparation of personnel to man those schools and the
   pursuit of RDD&E activities that relate thereto.

3. An instance of all of the above activities
   being linked directly to specified learning
   outcomes in children, and in a real sense being
   accountable for the realization of those
   outcomes.

4. An instance of partnership in funding at the
   state, local and federal levels that seems to
   be economically feasible, and sensible from
   the point of view of the differentiated use of
   resources.

5. An instance of an economically feasible and
   sensible linkage of industry to federal, state
   and local education efforts.

6. A basis for a natural experiment on the
   effectiveness of a nation-wide diffusion
   strategy.

COSTS

No apparent costs other than those normally
encountered in support of similar activities
(for an estimate of cost by supporting agency see
Part V of the paper) and for some possible
emotional wear and tear that could accompany the
"reordering of priorities" or "rethinking of
strategy" of "the establishment of cross bureau
linkages" within the Office of Education as a
result moving to a cooperative effort.

A Teacher Education Model: an integrated set of specifications that establish boundaries or parameters for
the structure, function, content and operation of a
teacher education program. A model is not an
operational program; it simply provides a framework
within which operational programs can be created. Fact,
theory and accumulated wisdom dictate the substance or
content of model based programs, and as a consequence--
because different people have access to or accept
different sets of facts, theories and accumulated
stores of wisdom--each model based program will vary
in its substance. All model based programs, however,
will share the parameters established by the model on
which they rest.

A Training Complex: a social institution designed to serve
teacher education by providing "neutral ground" on
which all institutions and agencies that have an
investment in teacher education--especially the colleges,
the schools and State certification agencies--can
direct their resources toward the improvement of that
enterprise. An essential feature of the institution
is the concept of "parity" or "equality of representation" for those participating within it.

Protocol Materials: "packaged" and thereby sharable or
distributable learning experiences that lead to the
mastery of a particular concept or set of related
concepts by given class of learners with a known
degree of reliability, and with assurance that the
concept that is mastered has meaning in terms of
"real life" referents. A basic assumption underlying
protocol, materials development is that the "real life"
referents necessary for concept mastery can be provided
through simulation technology, i.e., through films,
tapes, video tapes and the like.

Training Materials: "packaged" and thereby sharable or
distributable learning eaperiences that have a known
degree of reliability in getting a particular class or
learner to execute a particular skill or set of related
skills at a particular performance level in a particular instruction-learning context. The demonstration
context may be simulated, for example, a micro-teaching
situation, or it may be a real-life situation. In
either case practice and corrective feedback--two
essential elements in skill training--must be able to be
provided. [1]

---

[1] It should be noted that those aspects of "packaged"
training materials that deal with practice and corrective feedback will assume the form of instructions and
suggestions rather than substantive materials with
which to interact.

<u>Integrating Materials</u>: "packaged" and thereby sharable or
distributable sets of instructions and suggestions that
have a known degree of reliability in getting prospective teachers with particular characteristics to be
able to demonstrate that they can produce <u>a particular</u>
<u>output or set of outputs that they will be responsible</u>
<u>for producing as professional educators</u>. Examples of
educational outputs include bringing about desired
learning outcomes in pupils, developing a particular
curriculum segment, designing a particular evaluation
scheme. [2]

<u>Performance Based Teacher Education</u>: a teacher education
program where the learning outcomes that are to emerge
and the indicators acceptable as evidence of the realization of those outcomes are specified and made public.
Learning outcomes may be at

> the knowledge level (the result of interacting
> with "protocol" materials)

> the skill level (the result of interacting with
> "training" materials)

> the output level (the result of interacting with
> "integrating" materials).

<u>Research</u>: the generation of knowledge (facts, principles,
generalizations, theories, laws) that can stand the
test of empirical verification.

Development: the generation of technology (procedures,
hardware, materials, organizational frameworks) that
have a known degree of success in bringing about a
particular outcome or in performing a particular
operation.

---

[2]   Educational outputs are always situation-specific, that
is, the realization of pupil outcomes always pertains to a
specific outcome or set of outcomes for a specific child or
set of children under a specific set of learning conditions;
the development of curriculum always pertains to the statement of goals, objectives and learning experiences for a
specific body of knowledge for specific sets of children
under specific sets of learning conditions, etc. As a
consequence the demonstration of the ability to effectively
carry out professional responsibilities must be done in real-
life settings where there are real pupils learning, real
curricula to be developed and real evaluations to be designed.
   As in the case of skill mastery, practice and corrective
feedback are critical to the development of the ability to
produce particular sets of educational outcomes and a large
proportion of the "packaged" materials designed to bring
about such abilities assume the form of instructions and
suggestions.

Evaluation: the generation of information that facilitates decision making in a specific context within
a given time frame.

Diffusion: the generation of linkages (dissemination and
installation networks) that lead to the adoption and
utilization of knowledge, technology, and/or information.

NOTES ON MAXIMIZING THE INFLUENCE OF
DEMONSTRATION PROGRAMS ON TEACHER EDUCATION
REGIONALLY AND NATIONALLY

H. Del Schalock
Teaching Research

From the outset the strategy of the OE Models Program
has been straightforward and sound: through competitive
proposals generate a set of alternative models for elementary teacher education programs; through a second set of
competitive proposals undertake careful feasibility
studies of the implementation of the initial set of models,
or any combination of them; and finally, if the feasibility
studies are at all encouraging, implement 2 to 4 model based
programs as exemplary programs for elementary teacher
education in the nation. The rationale underlying the
strategy for the first two phases was basically one that
relied upon the productivity of competition, governed by
the strengths of carefully planned projects. The rationale
underlying the third phase is that which underlies all
demonstration or experimental programs, namely, the power of
ideas in operation. John Dewey built the case for such
programs before the turn of the century:

"...I heard once that the adoption of a certain
method in use in our school was objected to by a
teacher on this ground: 'you know that it is an
experimental school. They do not work under the
same conditions that we are subject to.' Now, the
purpose of performing an experiment is that other
people need not experiment; at least need not experiment as much, and that they may have something
definite and positive to go by. An experiment demands particularly favorable conditions in order that
results may be reached both freely and securely. It
has to work unhampered, with all the needed resources
at command. Laboratories lie back of all the great
business enterprises of today, back of every great
factory, every railway and steamship system. Yet the
laboratory is not a business enterprise; it does not
aim to secure for itself the conditions of business
life, nor does the commercial understaking repeat the
laboratory. There is a difference between working out
and testing a new truth, or a new method and applying
it on a wide scale, making it available for the mass of
men, making it commercial. But the first thing is to
discover the truth, to afford all necessary facilities,
for this is the most practical thing in the world in
the long run. We do not expect to have other schools
literally imitate what we do. A working model is not
something to be copied; it is to afford a demonstration
of the feasibility of the principle, and of the methods
which make it feasible. So (to come back to our own
point) we want here to work out the problem of the unity,

the organization of the school system in itself, and to
do this by relating it so intimately to life as to
demonstrate the possibility and necessity of such organization for all education."

Assuming that the Phase I and II strategy has been
successful, that is, that strong models have been developed
and that it is feasible to implement them, the long range
success of the models program depends upon the impact which
the demonstration program will have upon the educational
community. In the judgment of those who have been respon--
sible for working with the ComField Model thus far, maximum impact will not come from simply establishing an
exemplary program at an institution and then making it known
to the educational community that such an institution exists.
Rather, the widespread diffusion of an educational change as
far reaching as that proposed in most of the models will
require more than a purely demonstration and dissemination
effort. The purpose of this section of the report is to set
forth a proposal as to how the impact of the third phase of
the models program can be maximized.

The Proposal in Brief

Fund at least two and preferably three or four exemplary programs; establish a functional information and
materials exchange network between exemplary programs; nest
each of the exemplary programs within a statewide plan for
implementation; and nest all of the exemplary and statewide
programs within an integrated network of the regional
laboratories and private enterprises. Operationally the plan
calls for: (a) two to four exemplary programs to be established across the nation (the criteria for selection of such
programs are yet to be established;) (b) implementation of
each exemplary program on a state-wide basis; (c) link each
exemplary and state-wide demonstration program to all regional
laboratories for the dissemination of information about them
to all institutions within a region which have elementary
teacher education programs; and (d) link each exemplary and
state-wide demonstration program to the educational publishing industry for the mass production and marketing of
the materials and/or procedures developed by those programs
and for the services required by institutions in attempting
to implement them in their own programs. In addition, each
exemplary program would need to link effectively to the research and development efforts occurring within the nation
that contribute to either elementary education or elementary
teacher education. The interdependencies between the exemplary program, the state-wide implementation of those programs, the regional laboratories, the educational publishing
industry, research and development activities in education
across the nation, and teacher education programs throughout
the nation are illustrated schematically in Figure I.

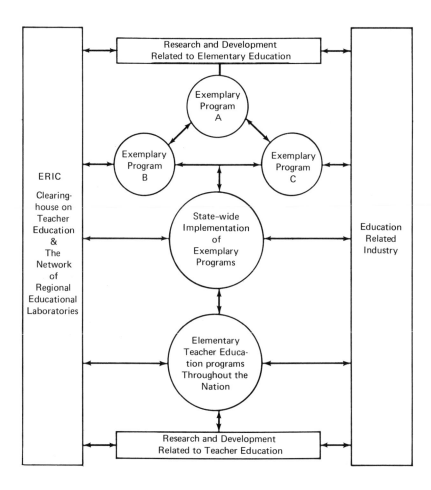

Figure I   A schematic illustration of the interaction of
            institutions and agencies in a plan designed to
            maximize the impact of Phase III of the OE
            Models program in elementary teacher education
            in the nation.

Rationale Underlying the Proposal

The central assumption underlying the proposal just sketched is that to effect change in elementary teacher education on a national scale, such change will have to be carefully planned for, and all the resources available in the nation in support of such change will have to be brought to bear in a finely coordinated fashion. This includes not' only the coordination of exemplary programs, but the coordination of teacher education programs within the states in which the exemplary programs rest, the coordination of the regional laboratory network in a massive dissemination effort, and the coordination of education related industry with all of the above. Attending assumptions are:

1) that the basic development work in support of the exemplary programs needs to be carried out within the context of the institution responsible for the implementation of the program;

2) that the materials and procedures developed within the exemplary program need to be validated against a wide variety of institutions before they are made available generally to teacher education institutions throughout the nation;

3) that private enterprise is best able to take the prototype materials that have been developed within the exemplary and state-wide programs, refine them, mass produce them, market them across the nation, and provide the supporting services (including in-service education) required for their utilization in other teacher education programs;

4) that the ERIC Clearinghouse on Teacher Education is best equipped to take the prototype materials describing the exemplary programs and the materials that have derived from them, refine them, and prepare them for use in nation-wide dissemination;

5) that the regional educational laboratories are best equipped to utilize the materials developed by ERIC in a nation wide effort to disseminate information about the exemplary programs and the products that have derived therefrom (the efforts of the laboratories will be supplemented by advertising efforts on the part of the materials publishers); and

6) that the products of research and development efforts throughout the nation have to be monitored consistently for their utility in the exemplary programs, and in those institutions utilizing materials that derive from the exemplary programs.

It is recognized in making such a proposal that none of the institutions mentioned carry on in pure form the functions assigned them: regional laboratories carry out developmental

as well as dissemination functions; education related
industries disseminate huge amounts of information; and the
exemplary programs will, in all likelihood, be involved in
research as well as developmental activities. Nor does the
proposal assume that such an interplay of functions will
cease. It does assume, however, that the institutions
assigned a primary function in the plan are those that are
best able to carry out major responsibility for those
functions, and if carefully coordinated could bring those
functions to bear in a manner which would maximize the
impact of the overall effort.

Rationale Underlying the Creation of Several Exemplary Programs

As a general rule planners find it dangerous to "put
all of their eggs in one basket." This is particularly
true when the various "baskets" available have not as yet
been tested operationally for their effectiveness. At the
present stage of knowledge, and in light of the complexity
of the various models being proposed, it would seem
imperative to test as many of the model programs as is
economically possible. Since it is likely that all eight
of the models available will not be implemented with equal
federal support, choices will have to be made. While the
criteria for making such choices have not as yet been
defined, a general rule to follow would seem to be one that
would maximize differences, given equal quality on other
criteria. Another factor to consider, again assuming
equality on other criteria, is the geographic location of
the exemplary programs selected. Geography is a significant
variable politically, logistically, and as a source of
identification. What weight it should have in the matter of
institutional selection for implementation purposes is
unclear, but it is a variable that must be considered.

Rationale Underlying the Creation of an Information and Materials Exchange Netwoek Between Exemplary Programs

The magnitude of the materials development task facing
those implementing exemplary teacher education programs, the
commonality of the logistical and operational procedural
problems to be overcome, and the commonality of the subject matter around which instructional materials are to be
developed suggests that considerable economy could be
effected if those responsible for implementing a given
program had free access to that which was being developed in
other programs. This is not to imply that all materials developed in one program will be directly or indirectly
applicable to another. It does imply, however, that much of
what is done in one program will have some degree of utility
in another, and whatever savings in time and resource expenditure can be effected thereby, should be effected.

Given this rationale it could be argued that institution A should be responsible for developing one aspect of
an overall program, institution B another aspect of the

177

overall program etc. On the surface there is a logic to
such an arrangement and the likelihood of considerable
economy. Operationally, however, it is doubtful that it
would be an effective way to proceed. While there will be
obvious commonalities between programs each will be
relatively idiosyncratic with respect to how such commonalities are put together. Also each program will have
characteristics unique unto itself. The major strength in
the entire models development effort has been the
opportunity to synthesize and integrate the knowledge and
ideas and procedures that are common to the field into a
unique and interdependent whole that represents a given
model. To not honor that integrity at the time of
implementation would be to deny the fundamental strength that
has derived from the program up to this time. Farming out
pieces and parts of a program to various institutions to
develop, or attempt to develop only those pieces and parts
that are common to all models, would lead in effect to a
kind of dismemberment of each of the models that would
destroy the strengths inherent in them.

Rationale Underlying the Implementation of Exemplary Programs on a State Wide Basis

To have maximum impact upon elementary teacher education
nationally, demonstration programs must have high visibility.
They must also have high credibility. The proposal being
made suggests that one of the best ways possible to gain both
is to implement the program on a state-wide basis. Such a
strategy would provide evidence as to the feasibility of
implementing the program under a variety of contexts, it
would provide a range of alternative institutions with which
an adopting institution could identify and/or work with, it
would provide a natural setting for the field testing of
materials before they were marketed, it would be of sufficient
political significance that it would not be ignored nationally,
etc., etc. The full range of arguments in support of state-
wide implementation have been provided in Chapter 3 and
Part VII.

Rationale Underlying Linkage to the Network of Regional
Laboratories

While implementation on a state-wide basis would provide
for program visibility and credibility, there remains the
problem of getting detailed information about the program to
institutions interested in its adoption. Are the demonstration institutions to carry out the dissemination function?
Will the ERIC Clearinghouse on Teacher Education? While
both will undoubtedly play major roles in the dissemination
effort, it is doubtful that they would be able to reach all
institutions in the nation that prepare elementary teachers
in a way which lets those institutions come to fully understand the nature and scope of the exemplary efforts.

Another logical resource available to the dissemination
effort is the regional laboratory network. The involvement
of the laboratories in such an effort would be in keeping
with the original intent of the system, and would make use
of the extensive information networks that most laboratories
have established with teacher education institutions. It would
also permit the dissemination process to be more personalized
in that personnel within a laboratory are generally knowledgeable of the idiosyncracies of the institution within
their regions having elementary teacher education programs,
and they could help interpret the demonstration programs
accordingly.

Operationally, by linking the demonstration institutions and ERIC to the laboratory network, the dissemination
function could work as follows:

1. Each demonstration institution would assume
   responsibility for developing prototype
   materials that describe the program being
   implemented;

2. Staff from the ERIC Clearinghouse on Teacher
   Education would take these prototype materials,
   refine them, and reproduce them in quantities
   sufficient for distribution by ERIC. the
   laboratories, the demonstration programs, etc.;

3. Each of the regional laboratories would be responsible for informing each of the institutions
   within their region that prepare elementary
   teachers about each of the exemplary programs
   underway, how those institutions might get
   additional information about such programs, how
   they might gain access to specific materials
   and/or procedure developed within those
   programs, etc.; and

4. Each of the demonstration institutions, and their
   sister institutions within a state, would establish a procedure whereby persons coming for on-
   site inspection of the program could be accommodated efficiently and effectively.

Rationale Underlying Linkage to the Educational Publishing
Industry

While the dissemination of information about the demonstration programs is a necessary condition to widespread
impact, it is not a sufficient condition. In addition to
information, adopting institutions must have access to the
materials and procedures needed to make such programs
operate. A critical question to be faced is how such access
is to come about.

As in the case of dissemination, the demonstration institutions will simply not be equipped to produce and distribute materials on a scale that would support wide scale

adoption. While resources are expected to be made available in support of materials and procedural development within demonstration institutions, that which derives from them will be in "home made" form and in a limited number of copies. Even if materials were available for wide scale distribution, demonstration institutions would be in no position to pro- vide the consultants, training, and follow-up services that will be needed by adopting institutions to effectively integrate the new materials and procedures into their ongoing programs. If the fruits of the implementation efforts are to have maximum payoff nationally there must be provision for the production and distribution of the materials that emerge from the demonstration programs on a scale which will make it possible for every institution in the nation desiring their use to be able to do so. In the collective judgment of those who have worked with the ComField Model the only feasible way to produce and dis- tribute the materials and services needed in support of widespread program adoption is to involve the private sector.

Operationally the relationship between industry and the other institutions involved in the implementation effort might be as follows:

1. Educational materials production firms would consult with demonstration institutions during the development of the materials and procedures needed in support of program operation (each exemplary institution would probably work with a different representative from industry);

2. Once developed and appropriately field tested, the producing firm that has been monitoring their development will "package"them, reproduce them in the quantities needed, market them, and provide the service functions needed in support of their utilization;

3. As materials become available for distribution the producer will provide ERIC and the regional lab- oratory network with detailed descriptions of the materials that are available, the requirements for their utilization, cost, how they might be obtained, etc. This information can be disseminated through ERIC and the laboratories as well as through the channels ordinarily used by industry; and

4. Each of the exemplary institutions and the institutions within a state committed to the implementation of a model based program will develop an efficient and effective means of demonstrating the materials being marketed for those who wish to make on-site inspections.

Rationale Underlying the Linkage to Research and Development Activities Across the Nation

By and large the elementary teacher education models
that have derived from the phase I and II efforts have a
minimal empirical base. Also the materials to be used
within the program are by and large in a "projected state"
rather than an existing, empirically tested state. This is
not the fault of the model builders, for in all cases they
have used that which has been available to them. It does
suggest, however, that all of the proposed programs are
only approximations of what they could be, and in order to
continuously grow in effectiveness they will need to
continuously expand the knowledge base, the materials and
the methodology on which they rest. This can be done by
closely monitoring that which emerges from educational
R & D efforts around the nation and by carrying out a
vigorous research and evaluation program within context
of the demonstration effort. [1]

Management Procedures Needed to Implement
the Proposal

Specifying that linkages of the kind described should
occur between institutions and agencies of the variety
proposed is one consideration; developing the wherewithall
that permits such linkages to function through time is
another. Obviously, an extremely complex management system
would be required to make such relationships work. Some
preliminary ideas as to what such a management system might
look like are outlined in the paragraphs which follow.

---

[1] Actually, the implementation of the demonstration program will provide a unique opportunity to extend our
understanding of the educative process because in all cases
the models are data dependent. Without exception the models
are committed to systems design principles, and this requires
that empirical data be continuously gathered on the
effectiveness of program operations. As such, vast amounts
of data will be available to those who operate the program
and it would be an indefensible waste of resource if that
information is not used to its limits in extending our base
of understanding in the teacher-learning process. While it
is true that much of the information that will be collected
within the context of the program will be done so outside
of the constraints of traditional research paradigms, and
therefore may be lacking in its generalizability, the absence of such rigor in design does not render such data useless. Assuming that the measures used are valid, and that
the questions being asked are of a kind that do not require
the rigor of experimental design, great amounts of information can be obtained that has high usability to both persons
attempting to operate the program and to extend the
empirical base of the discipline.

A Structure that Could be Used to Link Demonstration Programs

An informal structure characterized by frequent "coordinating contacts" between project directors and the director of the models program in the U.S. Office of Education; periodic cross-site visitations by key personnel within each of the implementing institutions.

A Structure that Could be Used to Link Demonstration Programs to State-Wide Implementation Efforts

The structure proposed to support the state-wide implementation effort in Oregon (see Chapter 3 and Section VII), provides an example.

A Structure that Could be Used to Link Demonstration Programs and State-Wide Implementation Efforts to the ERIC Clearinghouse for Teacher Education and the Network of Regional Educational Laboratories

A formal structure wherein the individuals responsible for dissemination functions within the demonstration programs would meet periodically with representatives from each of the regional laboratories, the ERIC Clearinghouse for Teacher Education, and the director of the models program from the Office of Education, to plan and coordinate the national dissemination effort. This body could be labeled the "Dissemination Council."

A Structure that Could be Used to Link Demonstration Programs and State Wide Implementation Efforts to the Educational Publishing Industry

A formal structure wherein the persons responsible for overall program development and dissemination within each of the demonstration institutions, representatives from the private sector working with demonstration institutions, director of the OE models program, meet regularly to plan and coordinate materials distribution and program support efforts. This structure might be called "the Products Development and Utilization Council."

A Structure that Could be Used to Link Demonstration Programs to National Research and Development Efforts

A formal structure wherein the person responsible for overall program development within each of the demonstration institutions, a representative from each of the federally supported research and development centers across the nation, and the director of the OE models program, meet periodically to review emerging knowledge and/or products that might have utility to the models program, and to make known the needs of the models program to those charged with responsibility for R & D efforts. This group might be called "the Research and Development Council."

A Structure that Could be Used to Coordinate All Facets of the Dissemination and Diffusion Effort

A formally constituted structure wherein the project directors at each of the demonstration institutions, a representative from the network of regional laboratories, a representative from the network of federally supported research and development centers, a representative from the industrial firms supporting the dissemination-diffusion effort, a representative from the ERIC Clearinghouse for Teacher Education, a representative from each of the states committed to implementing the demonstration program, and the director of the OE models program, meet at regular intervals to establish policy governing the overall implementation-diffusion effort. The group might be called "the Coordinating Council."

Evaluating the Effectiveness of the Overall Dissemination-Diffusion Effort of the OE Models Program

Because of the magnitude of the dissemination-diffusion effort, its criticalness, and its potential contribution as a model for other nationwide educational change efforts, the entire procedure needs to undergo careful and continuous evaluation. In this regard it would seem appropriate to let independent bids for the evaluation effort, thereby assuring the best evaluation design possible within the present limits of our knowledge and a relatively independent or unbiased assessment of that which actually emerges from the program. Minimally, however, the request for evaluation proposals should require an evaluation design that is "formative" in nature, that is, continuous in its provision of corrective feedback from the initiation to the completion of the project, and "summative" in nature, that is, a final assessment of the impact of the overall program upon teacher education in the nation. In addition the request for proposals should require that the evaluation design attend specifically to the operation of each of the institutions and/or agencies contributing to the overall effort, as well as the effort as a whole.

Allocating Resources for the Management and Evaluation of the Dissemination-Diffusion Effort

It is assumed that resources must be set aside within the OE models program to accomodate the energy required to carry out such management functions.

CHAPTER 7

FACILITATING LOCAL OPTIONS
AND COORDINATION OF PROGRAMS

Charles E. Stewart

It is clearly evident that the training of an educator is never completed. The process begins long before the
career decision is made and continues--systematically or
not--as long as the educator remains in the profession.
Such a concept of teacher education as a continuing process
has an obvious advantage in that it permits a local school
system to assist in designing training programs to fit
local needs, limitations, and resources. It also permits a cooperating higher institution to make use of inservice training activities as a basis for the assessment
and redesign of preservice programs.

Indeed the notion of gearing training programs to local
needs is so crucial today that many educational leaders have
come to the rather extreme view that local school systems--
especially large cities--should assume a teacher education
function. For example, Chandler and others have said,
"In effect, cities must produce their own teachers and
school administrators. Metropolitan colleges and universities
must join with urban school systems to design programs of
preparation for educational personnel that are geared to the
educational problems and opportunities present in cities. " [1]

This is not to suggest that a "good" teacher in a large
city school classroom will look or behave sharply different
from her counterpart in a rural school, although many would
argue that this must be the case.What is crucial here is the
requirement of differing arrangements for training, involving
new cooperative roles and relationships which will vary
among school-university partnerships across the country.

The reassessment of role and function for the various
members of the partnership is, in itself, a formidable task
among institutions whose record of successful cooperation
has been a sometime thing, highly individualized and

---

[1]   Chandler, B.J., Stiles, L.J., and Kitsusue, J. I. (Eds.)
Education in Urban Societies. New York, N. Y.: Dodd, Mead
and Co., 1962, p. 259-260

personalized according to the tastes of those choosing to
participate at any given time. Moving towards the sounder
basis of institutionalized collaboration in continuing
teacher education certainly will require great skill in,
and commitment to, the task of building the partnership at
the local, regional, or state level. But it will need also
all of the nurture and assistance to be gained from a
maximum flexibility in any design for allocating national
resources to this purpose.

It is perhaps axiomatic to state that a variety of
regional influences, including urban-suburban-rural factors,
must be allowed to have an important bearing upon program design and implementation at the local level. Moreover, as
pointed out elsewhere in this report, one must take into
account existing patterns of school-community-university
relationships as illustrated by a large city university
deeply involved with its immediately surrounding urban
complex of school systems, as opposed to the more widespread service area of, for example, a large Midwestern
university area--or a sparsely settled state which looks to
its State Department of Education for strong organizing and
planning leadership.

Beyond these factors, however, is the hard reality
that there are as many important differences among large
cities as there are between the large city and the small. To
begin with, school systems in the main are not organized in
a manner which facilitates institutional collaboration in the
teacher education enterprise. Consequently, an examination
of large-city school system organizational structures will re-
veal notable differences which, in many cases, will inhibit
such collaboration. In such instances it will be necessary to install costly coordinating mechanisms to cut across
bureaucratic lines of authority and ensure easier access to
an appropriate locus of decision-making where cooperative
teacher education is concerned.

Furthermore, no two large cities are alike in the nature
of the school system's relationships with its teacher organization or organizations. Despite the militant adversary
posture assumed by most big-city bargaining units, the
underlying nature of the relationships varies from a city in
which the teacher organization insists on being involved in
planning and implementation as an organizational entity to
one in which the teacher organization views itself as a part
of the school system and expects to be involved as such by
means of appropriate intra school system coordinating
mechanisms.

Similarly, few if any large cities are at the same point
in the transfer of power from the tightly controlled central
administrative bureaucracies to some type of wider community
base. Even in cities that have attained some measure of
"decentralization" there remain important differences regarding both the nature and extent of real power dispersion.
This reality has implications for the teacher education
coordination function within a large school system. It also,
together with some of the factors mentioned above, emphasizes

they need to rethink the concept of "parity" and the means by which to make that concept an actual force in cooperative teacher education ventures.

The term "parity" is not perceived to mean the same thing from city to city, depending largely upon where the same city is in its progress towards the decentralization of power. In most communities, parity is looked upon as an opportunity for community representatives to review a plan of action before implementation. But there are some communities in which parity means participation in the writing of the plan, with total disregard for built-in constraints such as negotiated personnel policies and categorical funding directives, as well as payment for participation in the process.

Obviously Federal guidelines are essential if there is to be Federal leadership in a clear-cut, well-coordinated thrust for improvement in teacher education. It seems equally obvious that organizationally negotiated school system policies cannot be dealt with in a capricious fashion by a group planning for a specific program or plan of action, particularly when the consequences may affect other school, community, or university personnel not involved in the program. The latter point is partly illustrated by the fate of a school-university collaborative effort in one city where the demand by the community to "screen and select" university faculty participants resulted in no faculty participants.

Most of the foregoing discussion argues for a flexibility which would: (1) permit a more productive consideration of local needs and realities in program planning and implementation; and (2) allocate Federal resources in a manner which would provide greater assistance in gearing up for programs which properly take into account those local needs and realities. But much of what has been said here suggests also that, while there is need to work on strategies and arrangements for more effective institutional partnerships, there is an accompanying need to improve the coordination and integration of the various federally funded "programs" which now serve as "delivery systems" for new ideas in education. It would appear from experience that the notion of a consortium of programs is as valid as that of a consortium of institutions for program implementation.

Programs such as COP, Teacher Corps, TTT and the like have demonstrated a certain effectiveness as agents for desirable change in teacher education despite the fact they have often operated as autonomous, self-contained, and controlled units. Each has its own administrative apparatus with the one hand little knowing, or understanding--or caring--what the other is up to. Each has its own university affiliation in which the university project leadership usually enjoys no better internal communication than is the case in the school system.

Each delivery system has its own liaison officer in the Federal regime with whom relationships are zealously and jealously guarded by the local administrators. This is not, of itself, bad and is mentioned here only as a further illustration of the separatism which inhibits efforts to effect a coordinated thrust at the local level.

Finally, each funded project has its own community participation machinery ranging in one city from a rather elaborate COP Advisory Council which serves without pay-- and at some cost to community participants least able to afford it--to a paid "community representative" plus un- paid local school advisory councils serving the Teacher Corps project. Again these variations are not cited as necessarily demaging effects of program autonomy; however, they do not appear to be planned variations to test several approaches. Rather, the variations seem to exist without a reason in most instances.

In summary, it is the intent of these comments to focus on some problems confronted by local education agencies as they attempt to engage in cooperative teacher education improvements efforts. Some, such as the hidden cost of after- school building use for "on site" classes and seminars, appear minor, but they add up over time to a considerable local expense. Others, such as the factors of program coordination and integration, are more obvious but no less troublesome. Together with the varying interpretations of the concept of parity, these problems give rise to a serious need for more flexibility for local planning and, at the same time, more leadership from the Federal education agency.

Greater flexibility might well result from Federal guidelines which would recognize local differences and encourage and support the reflection of those differences in sharply varying program approaches within a given framework. Increased Federal leadership might well take the form of support for an integrated "national" program thrust based upon accepted "essential elements" such as those recommended by experts inside and outside the Federal agency, and a coordination of Federal liaison functions so as to facilitate program integration at the implementation level.

CHAPTER 8

RELATIONSHIPS BETWEEN TEACHERS FOR THE REAL WORLD AND THE ELEMENTARY MODELS PROGRAMMATIC THEMES AND MECHANISMS PAYOFFS, MECHANISMS AND COSTS

Richard L. Turner

The three papers which follow were selected from among the six somewhat specialized papers written by the author for the Committee. The three deleted papers were addressed to very specific problems faced by the Committee at particular points in its progress and are considered too specialized to be included here although certain concepts from them appear in the final recommendations of the Committee. The three papers selected for inclusion, although specialized, are more closely tied to the original charge of the Committee: (a) to articulate and integrate the five thrusts (protocol materials, training materials, training complexes, performance-based teacher certification and the Elementary Models) examined by Task Force '72, and (b) to examine the feasibility (cost/payoff) of these thrusts.

In general accord with this charge, the first paper provides one articulation of the relationship among the five thrusts as evidenced in Teachers for the Real World and the Elementary Models. The second paper provides one way to integrate these five thrusts into broader themes and programs, while the third establishes a set of criterial payoffs, then suggests programs and mechanisms which might be considered feasible from the standpoint of costs while at the same time remaining targeted on the payoff. Considerable disjunction occurs between the second paper and the third. A careful examination of the payoffs suggested that several of the mechanisms proposed in the second paper and, indeed, proposed by other authors were expensive and poorly targeted on payoffs, thus requiring a substantial modification of the mechanisms to bring them within the range of cost feasibility.

RELATIONSHIPS BETWEEN TEACHERS OF THE REAL WORLD AND THE ELEMENTARY MODELS

The problem addressed in this paper is to explore the relationships among the five thrusts in teacher education currently under consideration by BEPD. Of the five thrusts, three are drawn from Teachers for the Real World (5): (1) the development of protocol materials, (2) the development

of training materials and (3) the creation of training
complexes. The remaining two thrusts, (1) the actual models
for the in-service and pre-service education of elementary
teachers and (2) the use of performance criteria, are drawn
centrally from the final reports attendant to NCERD's
Comprehensive Elementary Teacher Education Models (3).

The over-all position taken in this paper is that the
five thrusts broadly overlap and intersect; indeed, that
they are, when properly arranged, responses to different
aspects of a single question.

What is the Question?

What should a teacher education curriculum, pre-service and in-service, be like? Although this question can
be phrased in a great many different ways, the point in
phrasing it as it is phrased above is to make the basic
issues clear. They are <u>curricular</u> issues; issues about the
sets of experience that preparatory and in-service teachers
might have under tutelage, and especially about the range,
content and sequence of these experiences. The precise
nature of the curricular issues and the way in which the
thrusts drawn from <u>Teachers</u> and from the Models bear on them
may be most easily identified if one draws out of the
preliminary question those subordinate questions intrinsic
to it, These questions are:
> What should the goals of the curriculum (or
> curricula)be?
> How will you know (verify or confirm) that the
> goals of the curriculum have been met?
> What will the students experience in the curriculum?--
> What will be the bases of these experiences?
> Do the experiences have to come in a particular order?
> How will you know that a particular order of
> experiences is a good order?
> How will you know (verify or confirm) that the
> experiences lead to the goals of the curriculum?

The way in which an individual or a group will respond
to these questions, indeed, the questions to which they will
respond, depends on the stance or orientation of the group.
With respect to the groups involved in the five thrusts,
two different stances may be identified. First, the Models
group, on the whole, takes a "knowledge,""confirmation" or
"research" stance. This group is willing to address all of
the above questions, but in addressing them it is always
concerned with a nagging underlying question: "How will we
know?" "How will we conform?" Because of the latter question,
this group tends to be criterion or performance-criterion
oriented. One cannot verify or confirm his hypotheses or
speculations about curriculum components unless he specifies
the criteria against which he will make the terminal or
confirmatory ¹udgments.

Second, the <u>Teachers</u> group takes an "action." "mechanism"
or "development" stance. The underlying question is, "What
do we need to invent to improve the teacher education
curriculum? On the whole, this group emphasizes questions
involving curricular goals, student experience and the

189

curricular treatments or mechanisms through which these
experiences are delivered. It does not emphasize the procedures or criteria for confirming that the student experiences, their order or the curricular treatments or
mechanisms do precisely what they are supposed to do. Hence,
this group responds obliquely, if at all, to questions of
confirmation.

Some Resolutions of Subordinate Questions

Q.1. What should the goals of the curriculum (a) be?
One of the two noticeable differences in curricular
goals between Teachers for the Real World and most of the
Models is that the curricular aims in Teachers are predominantly bound to the preparation of teachers who will be
successful in teaching disadvantaged groups, especially those
in the inner city, while the curricular aims of many, but not
all, of the Models are successful performances of teaching
roles. This difference undoubtedly arose in a quite logical
way. The initiators of the Models are college and university
groups. These institutions prepare teachers for a broad
spectrum of teaching contexts, hence cannot logically address
themselves to preparation for success in a particular context.
What they can prepare for is success in performing teaching
roles, since roles presumably transcend particular teaching
contexts. One broad thesis in the Models seems to be that,
if one learns to perform his various roles as a teacher very
well, he can easily adapt his performance to a particular
teaching situation or context. Teachers for the Real
World does not deny the relevance of teacher role performance; indeed, various roles are discussed in it, and
skillful performance of them is emphasized. What it appears
to challenge, however, is the concept that role performance
can be easily adapted from one context to another, for example, from a middle class school to a ghetto school. Indeed,
much of the thrust of the early chapters in Teachers is that
the teacher must understand the context in which he is to
teach if he is to be successful in that context.

The product of the differences between the curricular
aim of contextually adaptive or successful behavior, as
suggested by Teachers for the Real World, the aim of
successful role performance, as suggested by the Models, seems
to the author to be an expansion of the Models toward the
inclusion of role performance in a spectrum of particular
contexts, including disadvantaged urban and disadvantaged
rural, as well as suburban middle class and small-town,
mixed socio-economic contexts. Expansion toward this
contextual aim vastly complicates one of the five major BEPD
thrusts, as will later be noted.

A second noticeable difference in the curricular aims
between Teachers for the Real World and the Models lies in
the sharp distinction between theory and practice in
Teachers and the relative absence of this distinction in
most of the Models. Perhaps because the Models are highly

performance oriented, a whollistic or integrated view of
the relationship of theory to practice is implied, if not
openly espoused. There is, for example, virtually no
distinction between concepts and skills, although there are
distinctions between liberal or general education and professional education. The latter distinction is not, however,
germane to the point at issue. In Teachers, on the other
hand, the aims of the professional curriculum are split, one
part dealing with the interpretive use of concepts (theoretical)
and the other with skills (practical). This split is a
fundamental one, since the theoretical aims ultimately give
rise to protocol materials as an instructional mechanism,
while the practical aims give rise to training materials.
The welding of these two to the contextual aims of the
curriculum is partly accomplished through the use of reality-
based materials (protocol and training both), but the chief
mechanism for welding theory, practice and context is the
training complex.

A reconciliation of the differences in expressed
curricular aims between Teachers and the Models is perhaps
easier than one might anticipate. The question is largely
one of how to group the behavioral outcomes or competencies.
Theory-practice is one kind of grouping, separation of
competencies by roles is another, delineation of integrated
concept-skill sequence is a third. A precise reconciliation
does, however, present a substantial practical problem. To
show the interrelations among the groupings, one would have
to start with a pool of competencies or behavioral objectives,
then sort them into the cells of a two, or possibly three,
dimensional matrix, with each dimension of the matrix representing the different ways of expressing curricular aims,
e.g., understanding teaching contexts, theory-practice, roles,
or integrated concept-skill sequences.
Q.2. How will you know (verify or confirm) that the
goals of the curriculum have been met?
This question is an extremely difficult one because the
answer to it has two parts, one apparent and one hidden. The
apparent part of the answer lies in establishing performance
criteria which, in sum or in toto, are taken to be equivalent
to the goals of the curriculum. In the Georgia and Michigan
State Models, these criteria are specified in great detail,
coded and stored on computer tapes. Verification that these
criteria have been met, hence, verification that the goals
of the curriculum have been accomplished, requires a set of
procedures, measurement and observation of teacher behavior,
through which one certifies that the teacher does in
actuality perform to the criteria. These processes seem
sound, yet the hidden problem is partially revealed by the
ComField Model, which requires not that the teacher demonstrate
that he has particular behaviors, but that he demonstrate
that he can bring about a specific type and level of learning
in students. The ComField Model thus suggests that the
validity criterion for the teacher education curriculum lies
in the performance of the students of teachers trained in the
curriculum. Under the ComField Model, then, student learning
is revealed as the hidden performance criterion for teachers.

Unfortunately, there is also a hidden issue in the
ComField Model. If one is to rest his case on student
learning, he must be able to implement this criterion first
by acquiring the relevant measures of student learning,
second by showing that the teacher is the factor responsible
for whatever learning takes place and third by showing that
the teacher can replicate his performance in a variety of
situations, i.e., that ability to bring about student
learning is not merely a one-shot affair on the part of the
teacher. Although it is not logically impossible to
implement these procedures, within current resource constraints and know-how, it is probably impossible to implement
them on a practical basis. The objective is sound, but
reaching it seems unlikely in the foreseeable future

Teachers for the Real World does not deal in any
systematic way with the question of confirming that the goals
of the teacher education curriculum have been met. Insofar
as performance criteria appear at all in Teachers, they
appear by implication from the nature of the teaching complex,
since performance with students in intrinsic to the complex.

The issues which surround verification that the goals
of a teacher education curriculum have been met are of course
the very same issues which surround "performance-based
certification." From the viewpoint of the author, Task
Force'72 should recognize from the outset that the basic
question involved is the degree of confidence that one is
willing to place in the procedures by which attainment of
the goals of the curriculum is defined or by which the
meaning of "performance-based certification" is specified or
operationalized. Different procedures will yield different
levels of confidence. Moreover, it is quite possible to
scale the degree of confidence one has in a given set of
procedures. For example, student teaching supervisors now
judge the performance of student teachers, either against
criteria specified by the training institution or by
criteria generated by supervisor himself. The question is
how much confidence is produced by this procedure. Would
judgments by multiple supervising teachers as might occur
in a training complex increase confidence? Would judgments
of performance by panels of experts still further increase
confidence? Would demonstration that the teacher brings
about student learning increase confidence still further?

As one may observe in the above progression, as
confidence in the procedures for appraising performance
increases, the complexity of the procedures for making the
appraisal also increases. Indeed, at the more advanced levels
of appraisal, very substantial sophistication in research and
evaluation methodology is required. For the latter reason,
the author believes that resolution of questions surrounding
the verification of curricular goals or the utilization of
performance-based certification will require substantial
long-range support from NCERD as well as from BEPD if the
answers to them are to be scientifically justifiable and
defensible in the public eye. Almost any teachers' organization, any educational research organization and many lay
groups have the capability to destroy the concept of
"performance-based certification" if the procedures by which
it is operationally defined are in any way unsound and by

implication, unfair.
      Q. 3. What will the students experience in the
              curriculum?--
              What will be the bases of these experiences?
     The responses to these questions in the Models and in
Teachers might be interpreted as being in agreement on the
first question and as different, but complementary, on the
second. Both are in broad agreement on the first question
in that both view the teacher as experiencing both general
or liberal education or education in the academic disciplines and professional education. With respect to the
education of elementary teachers, both also recognize the
possibility of specialization in a particular discipline,
or in an area, or at a grade level, hence skills in teaching
several subject areas and typically a range of grade levels.
Both are in agreement that the curriculum provides for
direct experience with pupils in school.
     The responses of the Models and Teachers to the question,
"What will be the bases of these (curricular) experiences?"
are of three different types. These types arise because
there are different ways of construing what the "significant
bases" of curricular experiences are.
     In Teachers, the significant bases of curricular
experiences are interpreted to be the materials encountered
by the student. There are probably several reasons for this
choice of interpretation. First, an emphasis on materials,
and especially on protocol and training materials, in-
trinsically permits one to represent different kinds of
teaching contexts while at the same time teaching particular
concepts or skills by means of the materials. Second, the
use of carefully constructed materials yields an extremely
 high level of control over the nature and efficiency of
student learning. In one sense, "curriculum" means a set
of controlled experiences for the student, and the method
of control in most curricula lies in the material which one
chooses to have the student study or learn. For example,
protocol materials permit one to take a controlled slice of
a particular kind of experience, say in a classroom, and
utilize it to help a student acquire specific concepts,
enrich concepts which he already has by showing instances of
them in contexts not before experienced, and help him gain
functional interpretive uses of the concepts. The use of a
controlled slice of experience in this way may generally be
interpreted to be more efficient than exposing a student to
a very broad and complex experience, since the number of
elements to be interpreted in a complex experience, say
working in a classroom full time, are too confusing to enable
him to sort out and deal with what is going on in an analytic
manner. Similarly, skill learning can be made more
efficient by controlling the training material encountered.

     A third reason for emphasizing the development of
materials as the basis for curricular experience is that
they are exportable or diffusable. They therefore potentially
provide a basis for the curricular experiences of a wide range
of students in a variety of institutions. Moreover, to the
extent that the materials enhance the learning concepts and
skills relevant to teaching and facilitate the understanding

of teaching contexts, the total impact of carefully developed materials is probably greater than could be realized
from any other single instructional mechanism.

In the Models, the significant basis of the curriculum
is not explicitly interpreted to mean materials, although
materials development may be implicit to several of the
Models. Rather, the significant bases are, first, how the
experiences are organized and, second, how the student is
to make his way through the organization. One type of
curricular organization in the Models deals with the way
in which the curricular content is grouped. On the professional training side of the curriculum, this grouping is
typically by the anticipated roles and functions of the
teacher, as noted earlier. More importantly for this section
of the paper, however, is the fact that many, if not most,
of the Models attempt to reorganize standard college
curricular structure by doing away with the "course" and
substituting some other type of curricular unit, for example, modules, phases, sub-components, and activities.
The intent of this type of reorganization is undoubtedly
to increase the flexibility of the curriculum so that a
wider and more diverse set of experiences can be incorporated into it over a particular period of time. There
is little question that such flexibility is desirable.
Certainly there is little reason other than the traditions
of colleges and professors for perpetuating the "course"
as the principal curricular unit.

How a student negotiates or makes his way through a curriculum is not a material or content basis for a curriculum,
but it is an extremely important basis for curriculum organization. Most of the Models take the stance that the preservice teacher should be able to negotiate his way through
the curriculum on a personalized or individualized basis.
Moreover, in many of the Models, the curricular structure
is laid out in such a way that the major points for students
are readily apparent. The student can know beforehand what
his potential experiences might be and can to some degree
choose which experiences he will have contingent on his
capabilities, interests and objectives. Again, there seems
to be little question that a curriculum which offers distinct
choices within a well-defined structure and can be individually negotiated by a student is desirable when judged against
the apparent values current in American society.

By almost any measure, the interpretations of the
significant bases of the curriculum in Teachers and in the
Models are complementary. Teachers addresses and specific
kinds of experience which teachers should encounter in their
curricula in the form of the materials with which they are to
interact. The Models, on the other hand, are addressed to
the way in which the curricular units might desirably be
organized and how students might negotiate their way through
these curricular organizations and thus determine in part the
content of their own educations. In an innovative curriculum,
protocol and training materials might indeed be used as the
most important materials in a modular curriculum individually
negotiated by students.

Q.4. Do the (curricula) experiences have to come in
any particular order?

With respect to this question, <u>Teachers for the Real
World</u> seems to the writer to be an implicitly theoretical
document. The order of experiences implied by <u>Teachers</u> is
that theoretical knowledge is antecedent to the acquisition
of teaching skills and that, in the final round, theoretical
knowledge and teaching skills must be webbed together in an
actual teaching context. Thus, the use of protocol materials
and the attendant concept learning is generally antecedent
to the use of training materials and the attendant learning
of skills. The final integration of concepts, skills and the
understanding of teaching contexts occurs last, in the
training complex, which is, for pre-service teachers, a kind
of specialized finishing school. It is important to recognize, however, that for in-service teachers the training
complex is more nearly a "refinishing" school, a place where
the in-service teacher may expand his skills, a re-tool,
up-grade.

Inherent to the general sequence of professional development which appears to characterize <u>Teachers</u> is also an
implicit notion about successive levels of concept and skill
development and the understanding of teaching contexts.
Protocol materials may not be anticipated to perfectly develop all needed concepts; training materials will not produce
the ultimate or finished form of a skill; neither will it
produce final understanding of a teaching context. It is in
part because the total task to be accomplished by the curriculum cannot be completely accomplished by the use of protocol and training materials that the training complex is
needed. In the main, there are sound psychological reasons
for this view. Conceptual interpretations of behavior and
skill sequences must be "cued off" by the appropriate en-
vironmental stimuli if they are to be effective. The problem
is one of both appropriateness and timing. Quite typically these cues cannot be made fully available through either
protocol or training material; thus, neophyte teachers must
spend considerable time "learning their cues," so to speak,
by being engaged in actual teaching situations. The purpose
of direct classroom experience is <u>not</u> to learn the skills,
but rather to finish them. If the neophyte teacher simply
lacks certain concepts or skills, one purpose of having a
training complex is to enable her to return to the protocol
and training materials through which the basic components of
the concepts or skills, or both, amy be acquired.

Like <u>Teachers</u>, most of the Models have an order or sequence to the curricular experiences. It is for this reason
that students reach successive choice points in negotiating
the curriculum. Elaboration of the precise type of sequence
for each Model goes beyond the bounds of this paper, but
they may be observed in the original documents and certain
summaries (3) of the Models.

Perhaps an important point to keep in mind in differences in sequences between particular Models and <u>Teachers</u>
is that the Models are virtually all university-based, and
the feasible sequences are in some degree bound by this fact.
<u>Teachers</u>, on the other hand, makes some distinction between

the work most appropriate to the university, that which is theoretical, and orders to the training complex many, if not most, of the training tasks.

Q. 5. How will you know that a particular order of experiences is a good order?

Teachers for the Real World does not deal with this question in any systematic way, probably because the order of experiences implicit to its theoretical position is very general. Most of the Models also do not deal with this question in a very direct way, i.e., they do not state specifically how the goodness of a proposed order will be ascertained. Nearly all of them do deal with this problem indirectly, however, by creating some kind of evaluation mechanism, which, presumably, has within its capabilities securing the information necessary to make decisions about the effectiveness of the proposed order of experiences.

Q. 6. How will you know that the (curricular) experiences lead to the goals of the curriculum?

In one sense, the answers to this question are precisely the same as the answers to Question 2 above, i.e., one will know whether experiences lead to the goal when he examines the products of the curriculum, the teachers prepared, against the performance criteria which are equated to the goals of the curriculum. Certain of the Models, including Georgia, MSU and Syracuse, have, however, a slightly different way to answer the question. These Models include explicit sequences of performance objectives. These objectives in turn make possible an appraisal of the extent to which any particular set of experiences do in fact bring about a particular level of performance. Thus some formative appraisal is possible. They do not, however, completely answer the question since it is always possible that meeting the intermediate performance objectives does not predict how one will perform in the end when the actual classroom performance of the teacher is used as the criterion against which the ultimate utility of the curriculum must be appraised.

PROGRAMMATIC THEMES AND MECHANISMS

The contention in this paper is that to lead a successful reform movement in teacher education BEPD-NCERD should (1) focus on two programmatic themes and the policy positions attendant to them and (2) fund selected mechanisms drawn from the classes of implementing mechanisms coordinate to these themes. The two programmatic themes may be expressed as follows:

1. The development of a nation-wide system for the confirmation of the outcomes of teacher education.
2. The development of curriculum intervention strategies to increase the power of teacher education programs.

These themes are implicit to Teachers for the Real World and the Models for Preparing Elementary Teachers, although they are not explicit in these documents. The explicit components of Teachers and the Models are more nearly implementing mechanisms than themes. These components suggest particular

devices and organizational structures which might be used
in the reform of teacher education. Viewed together, Teachers
and the Models may be seen as presenting several instances
of mechanisms which may be divided into classes with each
class of mechanisms coordinate to a theme.

Theme 1
The Development of a Nation-Wide System for the
Confirmation of the Outcomes of Teacher Education

The possibility that the nation-wide system for the
confirmation of the outcomes of teacher education could be
established as a theme arises from two sources. First, of
the five thrusts initially proposed by BEPD, "performance-
based certification" may be recognized as a potential policy
position rather than as a mechanism. This position involves
a clear intervention in the criterion which might be
employed for teacher licensure or certification. The criterion
implied is that certification is to be based on the observed and measured capabilities of the teacher, not on infer-
ences about capabilities based on courses taken and credits
received.

A second source from which the possibility of a nation-
wide confirmatory system arises is the Models. A key feature
of all of the Models is the espousal of a "systems" approach.
Although a major selling point for the "systems" approach is
that all the components of the system are integrated or
coordinated, the critical feature of this approach is the
confirmatory-feedback mechanism. As the Wisconsin Model
suggests, it is this feature of the system which makes it
correctable, self-renewing and capable of reform. Moreover, as suggested in the first paper by the writer, it is
the confirmatory mechanism which permits one to know
(verify or confirm) the extent to which the experiences
within a teacher education curriculum are valid when
appraised against the criteria, goals or ends for which these
experiences were designed.

Development of a Policy Position

The development of a policy position bearing on a
nation-wide confirmatory system involves at least three
steps.

Step 1. The first step entails creation of a value-
laden proposition. This proposition might be cast in the
following way:

> The reform of teacher education requires the de-
> velopment of a confirmatory-feedback system by
> means of which (1) changes in teacher education
> programs may be appraised for their efficacy, (2)
> teachers may be certified and (3) both public and
> professional confidence in the professional
> qualifications of teachers for their work may be
> assured.

The intellectual burdens of this proposition are very great.
The immediate intent of the proposition, however, is to
demonstrate recognition at the national level that an over-
arching, confidence inspiring system for quality control in

the preparation of teachers and for entry into the teaching profession is an unconditional requirement for intelligent reform.

Step 2. The second step entails coping with the intellectual burdens generated in the first step. Although these burdens may be dealt with from several different perspectives, the writer believes that the key point to be examined is the development of several levels of criteria. These levels should make clear the points at which feedback to teacher education programs could be generated and the points at which performance-based certification could occur. In addition, they should, as a group, increase confidence in the quality controls exercised in teacher education. The several levels of criteria are suggested below.

Criterion Level 1. At the highest level, the criterion against which teachers (or teaching) might be appraised consists of two parts. The first part is observation of the acts or behaviors in which the teacher engages in the classroom. The observations must be conducted with a set of instruments which permit classification of teacher behaviors in both the cognitive and affective domains. The second part is systematic analysis of the level of outcomes achieved by the teacher with the pupils he teaches. Outcomes in both the cognitive and affective domains must be included. Because of variation in the entry behaviors of students and variations in teaching contexts, the residual outcomes in pupil behavior (the terminal behaviors corrected for entry behaviors and moderating variables) should be used as the criterion measures. To be placed at criterion level 1, the above two-part appraisal of teacher performance must be conducted over a relatively long period of time, probably at least two years (on a time sampling basis), with both the observational and residual pupil behavior components assessed during each of the years. The reason for the two year period is that both teacher and pupil behavior are open to some random fluctuation and care must be taken to obtain a sufficient sample of behavior from both sources to assure fair conclusions.

There are two principal uses to be made of the data obtained at criterion level 1. First, if the data are obtained during the teacher's first three years of teaching experience, they might be used to certify that the performance of the teacher is at a level to warrant relatively permanent certification. How permanent the certification might be depends on whether a cyclical pattern of certification (e.g., re-certification once every ten years) becomes a socially acceptable policy, or whether life certification remains as the socially acceptable policy. Second, if observational data on teacher as well as pupil performance data are included in the criterion, the relationships between the observed behavior of teachers and pupil performance can be utilized as general feedback to teacher education programs. These relationships will indicate which types of teacher behavior are most likely to be influential in bringing about particular changes in pupil behavior. Teacher education programs would thus be able to increase the amount of confidence they have in intermediate performance criteria which involve only the actions of the teacher.

Criterion Level 2. This criterion level is identical to criterion level 1 except that a shorter performance period is involved. Current thinking about performance-based certification, such as that in the ComField Model, appears to assume a teacher performance period of one year or less, after which certification might be awarded. Although a performance criterion involving the latter period of time is at a high criterial level, it is sufficiently open to error attributable to fluctuations in teacher behavior, pupil behavior and the teaching context that it inspires considerably less confidence than does criterion performance based on wider sampling over a longer period of time. One may also note in this context that the ComField Model focuses almost wholly on pupil outcomes and largely eliminates observation of teacher classroom behavior. It therefore is of very limited utility in providing relevant feedback to teacher preparation programs.

Criterion Level 3. This criterion level differs from criterion levels 1 and 2 in that pupil performance data are eliminated from the criterion. Judgments about competence or proficiency are thus based on the observable behaviors of the teacher rather than on the pupil outcomes associated with these behaviors. Nonetheless, this criterion level is still performance-based in the sense that the teacher actually does engage in teaching and is gauged on the quality of his professional actions. How "good" or valid this criterion level is depends almost wholly on whether empirical relationships between teacher actions and pupil performance have been established through research or through data obtained by use of criterion levels 1 and 2.

The degree of confidence in criterion level 3 lies in the upper intermediate range. In the judgment of the writer, this criterion yields sufficient confidence to be useful in the provisional certification of teachers. It is also highly useful in teacher education programs since one may observe teachers to explicitly determine whether they evidence the behaviors which a particular teacher preparatory program claims to be producing, and by means of this observation may provide the basis of feedback about efficacy to the program.

Criterion Level 4. This criterion level differs from criterion level 3 in that both the teaching context and the range of teacher behavior observed are restricted. The context might be a typical micro-teaching context involving a few pupils or even peers acting as students. The teacher behavior observed would be restricted to a few categories in the cognitive or in the affective domain.

This criterion lies in the intermediate range, but it inspires very modest confidence and cannot be construed as an adequate basis for performance-based certification. Rather, its utility lies in providing feedback about the efficacy of particular segments of the teacher education program and in providing diagnostic feedback to students about their own progress. It tells whether a student has acquired certain behaviors or skills and whether he can integrate these skills under specially arranged teaching conditions.

Criterion Level 5. This criterion level differs from criterion level 4 in that the teacher need not perform before live students (simulated students would be satisfactory).

He must, however, be able to produce or show in his behavior at least one teaching skill, e.g., probing.

This criterion inspires virtually no confidence as a
criterion for performance-based certification, but it is very
useful for providing feedback about the efficacy of targeted
training materials or sub-components of instructional
modules or of courses. Its "goodness" as a criterion depends in substantial part on the extent to which the skill
being assessed can be shown to be a skill associated with
pupil performance outcomes as established either by research
or by use of data obtained in using the higher order
criteria noted above.

Criterion Level 6. This level differs from criterion
level 5 in that the teacher need not engage in producing a
performance, but rather, only show that he understands some
behavior, concept or principle germane to teaching. Within
this criterion several levels of "understanding" can undoubtedly be identified. These levels of understanding can
be operationalized by varying the kinds of problems the
teacher is asked to respond to in accord with some type of
taxonomy, such as Bloom's. Like criterion level 5, the
utility of this criterion is primarily to provide feedback
about the efficacy of particular program components within
teacher education. Similarly, its "goodness" as a criterion
level depends largely on the extent to which knowledge of
particular behaviors, concepts or principles may ultimately
be shown to be useful in predicting attainment of one or
more of the higher criterion levels.

Step 3. The third step in the development of a policy
position requires a careful distinction between types of
mechanisms relevant to a confirmatory system. At the present
time, at least two types of mechanisms can be identified.
First, because the development of sequential criterion
levels for assessing the outcomes of teacher education, as
elaborated in the preceding step, one set of mechanisms must
deal with the operationalization of these criteria. If one
is to talk about performance criteria at any level, he must
ultimately specify the permissible range of devices and
instruments by which the actual assessment might occur. He
must, moreover, produce the actual devices and instruments;
otherwise, the actions suggested by the policy will remain
theoretical and practice will remain unaffected. In addition,
if the use of such instruments and devices is to result in
renewal and change, some system for reporting the results of
their use must be established. For example, protocol materials
may be used, if properly designed, for testing concept
mastery. The results of using them in this way must,
however, be fed back into the system if one is to learn about
the efficacy of their use for this purpose, the efficacy of
the components of teacher education programs in which they
are used as tests and, ultimately, their efficacy in
eliciting behavior which may be used to predict other, subsequently employed, criteria.

Second, the various criterion levels previously noted
cannot be brought into being without creating some kind of
institutional or organizational vehicles to provide a context
in which they can exist. For example, it is virtually

impossible to imagine performance-based certification of the ComField type (level 2 criterion) without simultaneously imagining the institutional structure or mechanism which can manage the procedures required to actually implement the criterion. The teacher seeking certification must be placed in a classroom, his pupils must be tested for entry behaviors, some observation of the classroom surely must occur, terminal tests must be given and an analysis must be made. A certification decision must be delivered. Who will do all of this work? Who will support him? What will his career line be like? The answers to such questions lie in some kind of institutional mechanism which is designed to carry on the needed work functions.

Implementing Mechanisms

Of the two types of implementing mechanisms described in the immediately preceding section, creation of the institutional structure through which the confirmatory system can operate should be given the higher priority. There are a number of reasons for assigning top priority to these structures. First, a nation-wide confirmatory system must be composed of a decentralized, regionally distributed network of centers, complexes, institutes or cooperatives. Although such centers or cooperatives must be coordinated by some central agency, the actual operations which comprise confirming the outcomes of teacher education programs, giving feedback to these programs and, potentially, offering performance-based certification must occur at a local level. Second, the creation of institutional structures should facilitate the more rapid development and adoption of devices, instruments and procedures necessary to implement the various criterion levels described earlier, hence, the implementation of the processes by which performance-based certification and feedback systems actually come into being.

The Class of Institutional Structures. Members of the class of institutional structures which might be used to implement a nation-wide confirmatory system must have certain characteristics in common, but the members of the class need not, and probably should not, be identical. Those characteristics which these structures should have in common are as follows:

1. Each should be connected to one or more institutions of higher education. All of these institutions must prepare teachers, but some must, in addition, have distinct R and D capabilities. Connection to teacher preparation institutions will help ensure a functioning feedback system and ease certification problems. Connection to R and D sources will greatly facilitate the development of functional devices, instruments and analytic procedures necessary for accurate feedback and for the confirmation of outcomes.

2. Each should be connected to a diverse group of schools and their attendant communities. These schools should not only be diverse in setting, but highly diverse in their practices and in the types of teaching roles functioning within them.

3. Each must agree to return to the nation-wide
    system the results of its confirmatory and
    feedback findings and practices and must de-
    velop a mechanism for assuring that this re-
    turn occurs on a regular basis.
Aside from these few characteristics, each institutional
structure should be permitted wide latitude to experiment
with its own organization and functions.

Theme 2
The Development of Curriculum Intervention Strategies to Increase the Power of Teacher Education Programs

Unlike theme 1, theme 2 is quite explicit in Teachers
for the Real World and in the Models. These documents are
clearly aimed at developing interventions which increase the
power of teacher education programs and thus serve as the
principal sources undergirding this section of the paper

Development of a Policy Position
The development of a policy position for the development of curriculum intervention strategies involves at
least three steps.
Step 1. As under theme 1, the first step is to assert
a value-laden proposition; it might be cast as follows;
> The reform of teacher education requires vastly
> increasing the power of teacher education pro-
> grams by means of (1) the development of in-
> structional materials which increase the scope
> of concepts and skills acquired, the depth in
> which they are acquired, and the speed with
> which they are acquired, (2) the development of
> indepth professional experiences for the
> functional consolidation of these concepts and
> skills, (3) the development of accomodating
> curricular organizations and (4) the development
> of intervention strategies which facilitate the
> installation of the materials, the experience and
> accomodating curricular organizations.
BEPD has quite obviously already accepted and begun to
implement the first two components of this policy position.
In the opinion of the writer, these implementing moves are
in precisely the right direction, and only increased refinement and targeting of the protocol and training materials
thrust and the accomodation of the training complex thrust
to the confirmation-feedback system suggested in theme 1 are
needed.
The immediate difficulty with the policy position
already developed in BEPD is that it does not reach far enough
to provide reasonable assurance that the power of the teacher
education programs will actually be increased. To give greater
assurance, component three and especially component four of
the above proposition need substantial development as policy
positions. These components are therefore those focally
addressed in step 2 below.
Step 2. One of the major difficulties with teacher education programs in the nation is that their curricular

202

organization is designed as if education is a discipline in the social sciences and has as its aim the production of social scientists rather than as if its aim is to produce practicing educators. This point is recognized not only in Teachers, but also in many of the Models. The response to the point in Teachers was to shift a major portion of the basis of instruction to protocol and training materials and to the training complex. The response in the Models is more diverse. Most of the Models appear to have responded to the general point by moving toward a modular curricular organization and the possibility of a substantial amount of individualized instruction. Some, such as Columbia and Michigan State, seem also to have incorporated in their designs the concept that a teacher education curriculum is a distinctly laboratory-based curriculum.

If the responses of Teachers and the Models are combined to produce a more general policy position, something like the following emerges.

> The teacher education curriculum should be developed around instructional modules and should incorporate two types of laboratory instruction. The instructional modules should be constructed around those families of concepts and skills which are on the one hand germane to the interpretation of human behavior and on the other germane to engaging in actions which maintain behavior or bring about changes in it, whichever is dictated by the goals of instruction and the interpretations of the teacher. The conceptual content and objectives of some of the modules suggest that they can most successfully be utilized under conditions of group or classroom instruction under laboratory conditions. Typically, these modules would be those which require the student to examine a performance, produce a performance or acquire or exhibit a skill, and those which require the student to invent or develop some form of instructional material or aid.

> To maximize the impact of instructional modules and to increase the flexibility of the earlier portions of the curriculum toward greater individualization of instruction, each teacher education program should be characterized by a large, in-house component of laboratory-based instruction in which problems in the interpretation of behavior are solved and in which teaching skills are practiced. In the later portions of the curriculum, the student should move from the in-house laboratory to an external laboratory which, for all practical purposes, is identical to the training complex.

From a policy viewpoint, the aim of the foregoing prescription is that BEPD-NCERD should incorporate among its reform efforts a thrust toward reorganization of the teacher education curriculum. The central components of this thrust would be (1) curriculum organization by modules, with the modules tied to the protocol and training materials thrusts, and (2) the development of college and university based laboratories in which the modules formed the foundation of instruction.

Step 3. The third step in the development of a policy
position to facilitate the installation of curricular reforms in teacher education programs requires the development
of one or more installation strategies. Neither Teachers nor
the Models cope in any adequate way with installation
strategies. Nonetheless, two general strategies may be
recognized as having developed within BEPD -NCERD. One of
these strategies may be identified as the dissemination
strategy, the other, the concentration strategy.

A dissemination strategy is typically based on the
assumption that the provision of information about new
developments, together with some advisory help concerning
how to take advantage of the developments, will gradually
bring about acceptance and use by groups and organizations
functioning in the areas in which the developments occur.
The ERIC system functions on this premise, the Elementary
Models were diffused on this premise and the R and D Centers
and Regional Labs operate predominantly on this premise.
Although a dissemination strategy may be useful for the
diffusion of R and D findings, that it leads to the
installation of new developments or the institutionalization of major reforms seems to the author to be doubtful.
It is indeed difficult to think of instances of major change
in education which seem to have come about as a consequent
of a dissemination strategy. Why a dissemination strategy
does not rapidly lead to change, reform or installation is an
open question. One may only hypothesize that the possession
of new information does not add sufficient incentive for
change to overcome the barriers which militate against
change.

A concentration strategy rests on the premise that a
major barrier to change lies in trying to divert a finite
set of resources from an established use to a new use. To
remove this barrier, sufficient new resources must be made
available to establish the new use (typically a program,
device, or curriculum), which then competes effectively with
the old use of resources and drains the resources from the old
to the new use. One example of this type of strategy may be
found in the support of computers and their utilization on
college campuses during the late 1950's and all of the 1960's
by NSF. By 1970, computer utilization was sufficiently
established to eliminate external support, and the NSF program has consequently recently been phased out. The
Elementary Models would themselves have been an example of
a concentration strategy had the development phase been
followed, as presumably planned, by an installation phase.

In the opinion of the writer, the development of a
policy position to facilitate the installation of curricular
reforms in teacher education should be based on a concentration strategy. Under this strategy, sufficient funds would
be made available to selected institutions to permit them to
reorganize their curriculum to incorporate all of the developments (modular construction, protocol and training
materials, laboratory--based instruction, and participation
in a training complex) proposed by BEPD-NCERD as an alternative to the former curriculum. Once the reorganized
curriculum is fully functioning, external funds can be
withdrawn and placed elsewhere. Subsequent changes in the

new curriculum could then be introduced on a more modest basis as a consequent of the feedback returning to the institution through the nation-wide confirmation-feedback system.

Implementing Mechanisms

The question of the implementing mechanism for the policy position described above is largely an after-the-fact question. Protocol and training materials and training complexes are already under development. Various models of curriculum reorganization are available from the Elementary Models. The issue is basically not one of the development of mechanisms but, rather, one of timing the concentration of resources for the reform of particular teacher education curricula. A key part of this issue is whether selected ones of the institutions which orginally developed the Models have arrived at a point at which a concentration of resources would permit a powerful teacher education program, limited though it may be to elementary teachers, to emerge.

PAYOFFS, MECHANISMS AND COSTS

Unlike preceding papers by the author, this paper begins not with potential themes and mechanisms for BEPD programs, but with an examination of types of payoffs which must be achieved by these programs if they are to be considered successful, especially when gauged against the needs of the poverty community. These payoffs are separated into three levels: those related to pupils or students, those related to professional personnel in schools and those related to colleges and universities. The nature of the payoff at each level is examined and the priorities within and between levels are rationalized. Subsequently, the mechanisms believed most likely to bring about these payoffs are differentiated and examined in some detail. In this examination, the feasibility of previously suggested themes and mechanisms is tested. Finally, the costs attendant to the various mechanisms or interventions are examined relative to projected payoffs, and suggestions for funding are made. Broadly, the objective of the paper is to suggest ways in which the payoffs might be optimized, relative to costs, when the central control over inputs lies in the mechanisms to be created.

Levels of Payoff

First Level Payoffs

The first level of payoffs may be viewed as those criteria which must be achieved if federal programs are to have relevant impact and are to be described as successful. All such criteria lie in the behavior of pre-school, primary and middle school pupils and secondary school students from the poverty community.

Beginning with secondary school students, at least four types of payoff may be viewed as criterial:

  1. Retention of students for a steadily increasing number of years of schooling, with

the ultimate criterion being high school grad-
uation for virtually all students. This criterion
is drawn centrally from the report by Levin and
all (4) who suggest that number of years of
schooling completed is the best single predictor
of subsequent economic success.

2. Increased growth in general information (in the
   development of concepts and vocabulary) as
   evidenced especially in increased reading comprehension across a range of applied content
   areas. This criterion is also drawn from Levin
   and all, but is re-defined from general
   achievement into general information and reading
   comprehension so that the emphasis is on coping
   behaviors and on potential for continued growth
   by means of reading. This criterion overlaps the
   first criterion in that retention both reflects
   and is reflected in increases in conceptual
   development.

3. Growth in citizenship. On the negative side, this
   criterion is evidenced in decreased rates of crime,
   delinquency, vandalism and drug abuse by high
   school students and increased feelings of political
   and economic potency and involvement (or decreased
   feelings of alienation and political and economic
   apathy).

4. Increased opportunity to learn. This criterion is
   indexed by the range of alternative education programs of high quality available, including not
   only vocation education programs but also general
   education programs which increase the coping behaviors of students in poor social environments.

For pre-school, primary and middle school pupils, the
payoffs are coordinate to those for secondary school students.
In addition, part of the status of these payoffs may be viewed
as lying in the predictive relationships they hold to payoffs
at the secondary level. These payoffs are as follows:

1. At the pre-school, primary and middle school levels,
   increases in general information, i.e., in the development of concepts and the attendant vocabulary
   by which concepts are communicated.

2. Expression of satisfaction with the schools by
   the community, in conjunction with (a) decreased
   pupil absenteeism from school (a predictor of
   secondary school retention) and (b) expression of
   satisfaction or happiness with school by pupils.

3. At the pre-school level, increased oral language
   facility and increased facility with the
   fractional components of language and perception
   linked to reading readiness; at the primary level,
   increased attainment of reading and arithmetic
   skills; at the middle school level, increased
   attainment in reading comprehension and vocabulary,
   especially as related to the content areas or
   areas useful to increasing real life coping
   behaviors.

Second Level Payoffs

When instructional personnel are considered the central variable in influencing pupil outcomes (first level payoffs), the second level payoffs are those which bear on the careers and behaviors of these personnel. The payoffs relative to instructional personnel are as follows:

1. Placement in school practice according to training and specialization. As in any man- power training program, investment in specialized training, but a failure to place the trainee in a position relevant to his skills, severely damages the payoff possibilities attendant to training. Collaterally, placement of inappropriately trained personnel in positions demanding skills these personnel do not possess also decreases payoff, not only by damaging the probability of better first level payoff, but also by displacing appropriately trained personnel, thereby damaging second level payoff.

2. Retention of personnel. High attrition of trained personnel immediately following training or during the first year or two of practice increases training costs relative to payoff, since the cost of training many persons must be distributed over the productivity of the few who remain in practice. In addition, supervisors costs attendant to beginning teacher personnel, as well as turnover costs, must be defrayed against fewer and fewer productive personnel if the attrition rate for beginning personnel is high during the first two years of practice.

3. Performance. The direct connection between first level and second level payoffs lies in teacher performance. Placement and retention are the conditions or precursors of per- formance. As noted in the preceding paper, the ultimate criteria for the measurement of teacher performance are pupil outcomes. Pupil outcome criteria are difficult to employ fairly and accurately, however, An intermediate set of criteria, those based on the observa- tion and appraisal of teacher skills and personality variables, are consequently important intermediate criteria in the payoff matrix, as suggested in the preceding paper.

Third Level Payoffs

Third level payoffs are those that meet two criteria. First, they must be a direct consequence of personnel train- ing and/or selection. Second, because of the sequential nature of the levels of payoff, third level payoffs must be predictors of second and third level payoffs. The direct consequences of personnel training must be expressed in what teachers know and can do, i.e., in performance. The precise predictive relationships between particular performances, as level three payoffs, and the various payoffs at the second

and the first levels are, however, not known in any detail.
What is known are the general areas or domains within which
the predictive variables fall. These domains thus constitute
the areas within which the third level payoffs fall; discussion of the domains may be found in the Chapters by
Turner and by Rosenshine and Furst in a book edited by
Smith (6) and in the Elementary Models.

1. Increased knowledge of the substantive areas
   in which the teacher is to offer instruction;
   increased comprehension of the structural
   relationships within these substantive areas;
   increased ability to identify where a pupil
   stands in his knowledge of a substantive area;
   and increased ability to designate where he
   should next move in his knowledge of a substantive area.
2. Increased skill to perform teaching tasks in
   at least four domains as follows:
   (a) The diagnosis of pupil status and
       pupil learning difficulties.
   (b) The development of learning treatments
       to move pupils forward in their
       attainments.
   (c) The appraisal or evaluation of the
       efficacy of learning treatments,
       especially on the criterion of pupil
       performance.
   (d) Instructional support tasks, includ-
       ing classroom management.
3. Increased ability to perform over a range of
   instructional styles, i.e., didactic and
   heuristic, and within a variety of settings,
   i.e., individualized, small group and large
   group.
4. Increased skill in controlling and monitoring
   the affective consequences of one's own
   classroom behavior, hence increased control
   over one's own affective behavior and interpersonal sensitivity.

Optimizing Short-Range and Long-Range Payoffs
     Although several sequential levels of payoffs have been
described above, no attempt has been made to organize them
so that a coherent funding pattern could be generated. To
generate such a pattern, some particular first-level payoff
must be established as the criterion payoff or the thing one
is trying to optimize. The assumption made here is that
increased retention of secondary school students up to the
limit that all students entering secondary school also
graduate from it is the payoff to be optimized. It is to be
understood that this retention would not be gratuitous, but
that it would reflect increased intellectual and skill
attainments among the students retained. Retention is taken
to be the criterial payoff because, together with achievement,
it is the best predictor of economic success, which is in
turn taken to be the central and necessary factor in getting
members of the poverty community out of their condition of
poverty.

The most obvious funding strategy for optimizing retention in secondary school would be to place the most resources on the development of the quality in secondary school
personnel. This move, while good in the short run, would be
a poor long-range strategy because of certain well-known
empirical relationships.

As Bloom (2) has amply shown, and as is otherwise well
understood, the behavior of pupils, and especially the
intellectual or "achievement" behavior of students, is re-
markably stable. The achievements of a child in any one
year can be reliably predicted from his achievement in the
preceding year. It follows that a child who enters primary
school with poor achievement, relative to his peers, will in
all probability continue in this condition until high school,
at which time he has a high probability of dropping out. For
such children, an extremely powerful intervention must occur
relatively early if the probability of retention in secondary school is to be increased.

Although there is no point in arguing that a massive
up-grading of the quality of pre-school, primary and middle
school personnel will alone produce an intervention of
sufficient power to massively affect the probability of retention of students in secondary school, it is also true
that any intervention which does not up-date the quality of
these personnel is unlikely to be at all powerful. In short,
the argument is that the up-grading of pre-school, primary
and middle school personnel is a necessary but not sufficient
condition of increasing secondary school retention and,
moreover, that such up-grading is the key or crucial factor
in any strategy to optimize long-range payoff.

If the argument presented above is followed to its
logical conclusion, the optimum long-range funding pattern
would be one following an inverse relationship between
magnitude of resource allocation and the grade level at which
teachers teach (or for which preparatory teachers are
planning to teach.) Under this pattern, the greater resources
would be placed on the training of pre-school and primary
teachers, somewhat fewer resources on the training of teachers
of middle schools or of the intermediate grades and junior
high school, and still fewer resources on the training of
secondary school personnel. One must be careful under this
pattern not to construe "still fewer resources" to mean
virtually no resources or very minimal resources. If too
few resources are devoted to up-grading secondary school
personnel, short-range payoffs, as well as the optimization
of long range payoffs, will clearly be threatened. One
may note that this pattern is essentially the reverse of the
allocation of state and local tax dollars by grade levels,
since per pupil costs in high school typically substantially
exceed per pupil costs in elementary school.

If short and long range payoffs are to be optimized, a
second major factor to be considered is the distribution of
resources to up-grading personnel already in practice as
opposed to those preparing to practice. Again, certain
empirical evidence is germane to the way in which these resources should be distributed to obtain maximum payoff.
First, a very large proportion (approximately 50 per cent)
of practicing elementary teachers have five or fewer years

of experience. This fact is probably attributable to the extremely high attrition rate for teachers entering the elementary school. Second, there is some evidence that teacher skills remain relatively stable between the fifth year of experience and approximately the fifteenth year, with a gradual deterioration setting in (on the average) as experience increases. This pattern of deterioration is a relatively common one in the professions and should not be viewed as peculiar to teaching. Third, there is some evidence that teachers who remain in a school district for five years are very likely to remain as the stable core of teachers in the district (Turner, 1968).

Together, these factors suggest that the target population for in-service training are those teachers who have from five to fifteen or twenty years of experience. This group is most likely to remain in the school district and is perhaps most likely to benefit from up-grading. Moreover, new leadership in school districts is most likely to emerge from teachers in this population. To obtain the best short-range payoff, the greater resources should probably be allocated to the up-grading of this population. To obtain long-range payoff, however, several other factors must be considered.

As noted earlier, a central difficulty in obtaining payoff from training preparatory teachers, and in up-grading teaching as a profession, lies in the high attrition rate during the first five years of experience. Because of this attrition rate, further up-grading of this group is profitable only if it is conducted on an accurate, self-selection basis, i.e., those who intend to remain in the profession begin to up-grade themselves because of some foreseeable payoff (salary increases, prestige, advancement) from doing so. In point of fact, such self-selection already occurs and is almost universally tied to re-entering the university to seek a Master's degree. This fact is important because it means that this population can be up-graded in a university setting where preparatory teachers are already present, thus creating the possibility of a concentrated pool of resources which can be effectively used to up-grade not only preparatory teachers, but also a self-selected portion of the teacher group having from one to five years of experience.

To obtain maximum long-range payoff, not only must resources be concentrated where they will affect both preparatory teachers and teachers with 1-5 years of experience, but they must also be concentrated in locations in which the greatest numbers of preparatory teachers and early career teachers appear. Hence, they must be concentrated in the major teacher preparation institutions. Concentration in these institutions will not only increase the probability that any beginning teacher entering the poverty community will be appropriately trained, but also make possible better cost/benefit ratios by effecting economies of scale.

So that the pattern of funding suggested up to this point may be viewed quite clearly, the intersection of the funding pattern by grade levels of school, by in-service and pre-service teacher personnel and according to short and long payoff is shown in Table 1. Written in the cells of the table are the suggested priority ranks for funding, considering only the factors taken into account up to this point.

Table 1

	Pre-school and Primary	Middle School	Secondary School
IN-SERVICE Short range	third	second	first
Long range	first	third	fifth
PRE-SERVICE Short range	fourth	sixth	fifth
Long range	second	fourth	sixth

A major point to be considered in the priority rankings for funding shown in Table 1 is that they were generated by trying to optimize payoff without regard to the particular mechanisms through which the payoff is to be achieved. The consideration of mechanisms is of course a critical factor in arriving at final rankings. For example, although maximum short range payoff might be achieved by investing the most funds in in-service work for secondary school teachers, unless a mechanism is found by means of which payoff can actually be achieved, there is no point in expending the funds. "In-service work" is not a mechanism, but a theme within which mechanisms might be constructed.

Mechanisms

The criterion against which all mechanisms must be judged is workability. While the workability of a mechanism is always contingent upon specific (and frequently unforeseen) factors, a central consideration in workability is always the cost of creating and maintaining the mechanism. Thus, any mechanism which is not cost-feasible may be regarded as unworkable. In creating educational mechanisms, at least three assumptions about costs should be made.

1. Initial creation and maintenance costs must be within the reach of federal spending combined with some (usually minimal) state and local contribution.
2. Federal support will gradually be phased out, thus, throwing total costs on state and local support and possibly on individuals.
3. State and local tax elasticity in combination with multi-agency competition for resources will permit relatively little increase in cost for educational services in the foreseeable future.

A second criterion against which workability must be judged is, of course, whether the mechanism is targeted to

and achieves one or more payoffs. Considered in relation
to the levels of payoff outlined in the preceding section,
two types of mechanisms may be recognized as potentially
profitable. The first type should have immediate impact on
the retention of students from the poverty community in
secondary schools; the second type should up-grade the
quality of teachers in the poverty community, and indeed of
all teachers, over the long run.

Mechanism 1. Alternative Secondary Schools

Alternative schools for secondary school students for
whom withdrawl is imminent or who have already dropped out
of school already exist in several school districts and are
supported by state and local tax funds. One may recognize
that OEO supported Job Corps Training Centers are also a
functioning form of alternative schools. The clientel of such
schools is relatively predictable. As a recent paper by
Bachman (1) suggests, the intellectual abilities related to
success in traditional schools are primarily sex-linked
(girls do much better than boys) and to a lesser degree race
linked (whites do slightly better than blacks.) Thus
alternative schools are much more likely to have a large
male population than a large female population, and somewhat
more likely to have black males than white males. To put
the matter a bit differently, an alternative school would in
all likelihood have the greatest impact if it were targeted
on the education of males, and especially on the education of
black males. The least likely clientel is the population of
white girls, followed by the population of black girls.

The creation of alternative schools under (or in
conjunction with) existing BEPD programs is less difficult
than one might expect. Five existing programs seem clearly
relevant; other programs may be relevant in ways not
immediately apparent to the writer. The five programs are
Teacher Corps, Urban-rural, Career Opportunities, School
Personnel Utilization and Pupil Personnel Services.

Grants to create one or more alternative schools should
be made directly to school districts, preferably acting with
liaison arrangements to universities. The easiest vehicle
would probably be the urban-rural program. The initial staff
of the school would undoubtedly have to be drawn in substantial part from existing school system personnel. Working
with this staff should be three types of persons: (1) Teacher
Corps trainees; (2) paraprofessionals, especially black males,
and COP trainees; and (3) trainees from the Pupil Personnel
Services program.

In addition to the creation of alternative schools, an
Alternative Schools LTI and a consortium of directors of
alternative schools should be established. The leadership
and consortium groups are critical in this instance since
neither the types of curricula, the personnel roles, nor
the personnel training relevant to such schools is well
understood.

The alternative schools mechanism should be recognized
to be in reverse of the mechanisms subsequently to be suggested in this paper. It targets on first level payoff and moves
downward toward the second and third level payoffs, rather than
focusing on second and third level payoffs, as is characteristic of the remaining mechanisms.

Mechanism 2. Teacher Education as Laboratory-based Education

The intent in developing this mechanism is to find a way to achieve second and third level payoffs in the long run while at the same time keeping all sub-mechanisms within the feasible range and remaining congruent with the themes and mechanisms proposed in the preceding paper.

The first step in developing this mechanism is to recognize that <u>the training complex as an intermediate institution between the schools and the universities is not a feasible mechanism on the criterion of cost.</u> As presently conceptualized, the training complex would require the input of substantial new resources from school districts and universities, and probably also from general state funds, at the very time when each of these institutions is desperately short of resources. Elimination of the training complex as a mechanism requires that the functions which might have been discharged by it be covered by some other set of mechanisms.

A second step in developing the mechanism is to observe that performance-based certification for all entering teachers is not now feasible if the criterion for certification is set at either criterion level 1 or 2, i.e., demonstration of ability to bring about pre-specified changes in pupil behavior by either specified or unspecified means. At the present time there are no acceptable procedures by means of which one could fairly and equitably show the behavior of the teacher. This does not mean that the development of such procedures should be eliminated, but only that certification should not be predicated on currently available procedures.

The procedures which probably are sufficiently developed to consider as a potential basis for certification are those that focus on the skills of the teacher as evidenced in classroom settings. In essence, such procedures would be used to certify that the teacher engages in "good practice," i.e., professionally acceptable practice. Operationally, certification that a teacher engages in good practice would mean that the teacher had achieved the "performance" criterion previously designated as the target criterion among the second level payoffs. It is specifically to this criterion that laboratory-based teacher education is directed.

Laboratory-based teacher education should rest on two different laboratories, one based in the training institution, a college or university, and the second based in the field. This division in laboratory sites follows a separation in the level of skills to be attained by the trainee. The separation is marked by the attainment of criterion level 4 (demonstration of a single skill under micro-teaching or simulated conditions) in the university-based laboratory, while criterion level 3 (demonstration of integrated skills over a period of time in a classroom setting) is to be attained in the field laboratory.

The University-based Laboratory. To convert teacher education at the undergraduate level to a laboratory base, each course would be accompanied by a regular lab. For example, a three semester hour course in reading would be accompanied by a two hour laboratory. The materials used in this laboratory would in all likelihood be both protocol and training

materials since virtually all preparatory courses seek both
concept development and skill development among their objectives. In many instances, combined sequences of protocol
and training materials would be necessary since some concepts
lead directly into skill training.

The precise organization of both courses laboratories
should be left to the preparatory institution. The only
restriction is that students emerging from the sequence
would have to be capable of functioning at criterion level 3.
Operationally, this means that at the minimum a student would
have to be capable of demonstrating a set of skills. He
would be permitted to demonstrate these skills one at a time
or in related sets. He would not be required to demonstrate
his skills in an integrated fashion before a regular classroom group. The areas in which these skills would presumably fall are those noted in the description of third
level payoffs in the first section of this paper.

The Field-based Laboratory. The notion of field-based
laboratories differs from the notion of a training complex
in several ways. First, the laboratory would represent a
joint arrangement among universities and colleges, state
departments of education and individual teachers, with
school systems involved at a policy (or giving permission)
level, but not at a financial level. Second, the laboratories
would be extensions of the university-based laboratories,
not a separate institution. Third, certification would remain the joint venture of universities and state departments
without the direct participation of school districts as units.
To create such laboratories, a reasonably radical series of
steps needs to be taken.

1. Performance-based Certification for Master-Supervisory
Teachers. A major problem with both the training complex and
the field laboratory is that both depend on highly skilled
personnel to be drawn from a population sub-set of unknown
magnitude. The general population of teachers from which the
highly skilled group might be drawn is the stable core of
teachers with roughly 5-20 years of experience. To determine which members of this pool are highly skilled, a
separate, performance-based, state certificate must be
awarded. The group attempting to achieve this certificate
is to be a self-selected group.

2. Salary Incentive for Master-Supervisory Teachers.
Few teachers will opt for a certificate which does not bear
a salary differential. Thus, the certificate in question
must bear a differential, and the differential must be an
adjusted one. In operation, two adjustments would be
necessary. First the state, not the local school district,
would adjust the salary of each Master proportionate to his
base salary (salary schedule salary) directly from state
funds. To be feasible, this proportion should probably be
about five per cent. Second, Master Teachers in low income
schools in poverty communities should receive a second
adjustment of approximately five percent awarded through
Federal subsidies to states. These two adjustments should
create a differential of about ten per cent for Master
Teachers in the poverty community and should be sufficient
to encourage some migration of high quality teachers to these
areas as well as retention of teachers already located in

these communities.

3. <u>Certification by Observation.</u> If performance-based certification at criterion level 3 is to have meaning, award of this certificate could be made only after a systematic time-sampling of the classroom behavior of the teacher. This sampling could be done by video-tape or it could be taken on a "live" basis. In either instance, judgments about the performance of the teacher must be based on standard instruments used by trained judges, probably university personnel.

<u>Pre-service Field Laboratory.</u> Two uses should be made of the Master Teacher in the field laboratory at the under-graduate or Preliminary Certificate level.

1. <u>Pre-training and Diagnostic Semester.</u> The first contact between the Master Teacher and an undergraduate trainee should occur during either the first or second semester of the junior year in college. At this time the trainee should leave the college and enter the classroom of the Master Teacher to which he or she has been assigned. The role of the trainee would be essentially that of a paraprofessional. The role of the Master Teacher during this period would be (1) to acquaint the trainee with the range of tasks performed by the teacher and (2) to identify those areas in which the trainee would clearly benefit from additional substantive knowledge, better development of concepts and skill training; in short, to diagnose the areas to which the trainee should give attention. If the Master believed the trainee to be inadequate to the tasks of teaching, a recommendation for termination in the teacher education curriculum should be made. Following this semester, the trainee, if continued, should return to the college or university and continue study, with continued skill and concept development in the university-based laboratory.

2. <u>Preliminary Certification Semester.</u> At the end of the fourth year of training or during the fifth year of training the trainee should again enter the classroom of a Master Teacher for one semester. The role of the trainee at this time would be to assume the duties of a regular teacher, with the meaning of "regular" to be determined according to the type of instructional organization used by the Master Teacher. The role of the Master during this period would be to aid the trainee in finishing or integrating the skills at criterion level 3 and to certify whether or not the trainee had been successful in operating at this criterion level. Although certification would remain in the hands of the state and the colleges and universities, the recommendation of the Master Teacher would be required to issue the Preliminary Certificate.

<u>In-service Field Laboratory.</u> The development of the field laboratory at this level requires certain organizations and policies

1. <u>Advanced Skills Summer Training Schools.</u> Most teachers cannot both devote adequate time to their teaching and effectively up-grade their skills. For practicing teach-ers, the summer should be used for advanced skill training.

For the development of advanced teaching skills, in-struction in graduate education courses is not an adequate device. Such skills are highly complex and probably must be acquired through practice in actual school settings. Included among the skills might be those involved in flexible grouping, managing individualized instruction, utilizing an heuristic approach to teacher, conducting an "open" classroom effectively, diagnosing learning difficulties and the like.

So that these skills can be acquired in school summer training schools, centered primarily in schools serving low income groups, should be organized. These schools should be staffed by Master Teachers, with an advisory board of college and university personnel specializing in the development of particular skills, and financed directly by state funds with Federal subsidization. The children in the schools should be drawn from low income families.

2. <u>Restriction of Population.</u> Because many teachers leave teaching during the first three years, only teachers with three or more years of experience would be permitted to enter the summer training school. This restriction is probably essential to obtain a favorable cost-benefit relationship.

3. <u>Focus on the Master-Supervisory Certificate</u>. Although all qualified teachers who wish to enter the summer training school should be able to do so for purposes of improving their skills, the focus of this school should be on training teachers who aspire toward the Master-Supervisory Certificate. The school should not award this certificate, but it should train for it.

4. <u>Relationship of Advanced Skill Training to Graduate Degree</u>. There should be no formal relationship between the Master-Supervisory Certificate and a Master's degree or other advanced degree. Nonetheless, teachers who wish to obtain the Master's degree should be encouraged to take an advanced skills practicum and might be required to do so in certain university programs. The university would continue to be the source of work in the subject fields and in conceptual or foundational areas of professional training. It would not participate directly in the advanced skill training, however. This function would be left to the summer training school as the field laboratory at the graduate level.

Support Mechanisms

One set of major support mechanisms necessary to the field-based laboratory and performance-based certification are the instruments by means of which performance is judged at the Preliminary Certificate and at the Master-Supervisory Certificate levels. The development of quality instruments requires the participation of personnel on a nation-wide basis and should be nationally supported. Development of such instruments should be on a project basis.

The development of a national confirmatory-feedback system, as proposed in the preceding paper, is probably not a necessary system and probably would have a poorer cost-benefit ratio than locally controlled systems based on nationally developed instruments. Research relating teacher performance to pupil performance, and the development of procedures useful at some future time for certifying teachers

on the basis of pupil performance, should be placed on a
project basis.

A second set of support mechanisms for the field-based
laboratory are protocol and training materials. For the
immediate future, the development of prototypic materials
and the development of guidelines for developing and field-
testing such materials should continue on a nation-wide
basis. In three to five years, however, serious consideration should be given to (1) shifting materials
development to local laboratories, or (2) the preparation
of completely packaged laboratory units for use in colleges
and universities or (3) both.

Funding Patterns and
Speculation on Costs

Beginning with the funding pattern suggested earlier
in Table 1, the resolution of a final (suggested) funding
pattern requires taking the mechanisms suggested in the
preceding section, and the time required for their
development, into account. These mechanisms are
summarized below. Subsequently they are placed in a
second table (Table 2) and speculations about costs made.
The cost speculations are based on the assumption that from
10 million to 20 million dollars per year would be
available.

Alternative Secondary Schools

The assumption is that such schools would be funded from
State and local tax dollars, but that Federal support would
be offered for the training of personnel to staff the schools.

University-based Laboratory

The assumption is that the pre-service curriculum in
teacher education institutions would be converted to a
laboratory base.

Field-based Laboratory

From the viewpoint of Federal funding, the field-based
laboratory has three potential costs.

- (a) Certification costs attendant to the Master
Supervisory Certificate. Instrument development, observer training and the actual
procedures for certifying in specific states
must be included in these costs.
- (b) Salary subsidy. The salaries of Master Teachers in low income schools would be subsidized.
Probably not more than 20% of the population
of teachers would hold the Master Certificate.
About half of these would be expected to be
in low income areas.
- (c) Summer Training School. This mechanism should
become operational only if the Master certificate becomes operational. It is a very
long-range mechanism.

217

Protocol and Training Materials

These materials are viewed as the supporting materials for the university-based labs. In the long run they would be converted into a more nearly integrated set of materials labeled the laboratory package.

Year	Pre-school, Primary	Middle School	Secondary School	Support Systems	Certification and Salary Subsidy
1972-73	Lab. based curriculum 2.0 mil	Lab. based curriculum 1.0 mil	Training, alt. schools 2.0 mil	Protocol and training mat. 4.0 mil Instrument development 1.0 mil	0.5 mil
1973-74	Lab. based curriculum 3.0 mil	Lab. based curriculum 1.5 mil	Training, alt. schools 3.0 mil	Protocol and training mat. 4.0 mil Instrument development 2.0 mil	0.5 mil
1974-75	Lab. based curriculum 3.0 mil	Lab. based curriculum 2.0 mil	Training alt. schools 4.0 mil Lab. based curriculum 1.0 mil	Protocol and training mat. 1.0 mil Lab. packages 2.0 mil Instructional development 1.0 mil	2.0 mil

TABLE 2

Year	Pre-school,	Middle School	Secondary School	Support Systems	Certification and Salary Subsidy
1975-76	Lab. based curriculum 3.5 mil	Lab. based curriculum 3.0 mil	Training, alt. schools 3.0 mil Lab. based curriculum 2.0 mil	Lab.package 3.0 mil Training school feasibility 0.5 mil	Lab.package 4.0 mil
1976-77	Lab. based curriculum 2.5 mil	Lab. based curriculum 2.0 mil	Training, alt. schools 2.0 mil Lab. based curriculum 3.0 mil	Lab.packages 3.0 mil Training school feasibility 0.5 mil	Lab.packages 6.0 mil

TABLE 2 (cont.)

References

1. Bachman, Margaret E. "Relationships of Ethnicity, Socioeconomic Status, and Sex to Patterns of Mental Abilities." _American Educational Research Journal_ (in press for 1972).

2. Bloom, Benjamin. _Stability and Change in Human Characteristics_. Wiley, New York, 1964.

3. Burdin, Joel L. and Lanzilloti, Kaliopee (eds). _A Readers's Guide to the Comprehensive Models for Preparing Elementary Teachers._ ERIC Clearinghouse on Teacher Education and AACTE, Washington, 1969

4. Levin, Henry M. and all. "School Achievement and Post-school Success: A review." _Review of Educational Research,_ 41: 1-16, February 1971.

5. Smith, B.O. in collaboration with Saul B. Cohen and Arthur Pearl. _Teachers for the Real World._ AACTE, Washington, 1969.

6. Smith, B.O. _Research in Teacher Education, A Symposium._ Prentice Hall, Englewood Cliffs, N. J., 1971.

7. Turner, R. L. _Differential Association of Elementary School Teacher Characteristics with School System Types._ Final Report, USOE, CRP No. 2579, 1968.

Appendix A

DESCRIPTION OF THE FIVE PROGRAMS*

Training Complex

The training complex is an institution to facilitate
cooperation between schools, other human service agencies,
universities and colleges, and communities in improving
the preservice and in-service training of education and
other human services personnel. The training complex has
a clearly defined training mission. This training is
aimed at the development of complex integrated skills
appropriate for teaching and other human services in
education and other social service settings. The function
of the training complex is to provide an opportunity for
preservice and inservice teacher training to be conducted
in a variety of settings. Another function is the training
of individuals for a new or second career, in education
or other human services, building upon or extending
competencies and skills individuals already have. Features
which distinguish the training complex from other
institutions include:

1. establishment of training as the primary mission of
   the training complex;

2. provision for the active participation by all those
   concerned in decision making regarding the training
   of educational personnel, at a policy level;

3. access to the resources of the school, university,
   and community agencies to facilitate the efforts
   of the training complex; and

4. greater flexibility in employing and utilizing
   personnel from a variety of backgrounds, with or
   without the credentials applicable to specific
   institutions.

The training complex will be flexible in developing
needed training services, varying in specific character
according to the region and educational environment in
which it exists. It could be established on "neutral"
ground, or at one of the cooperating institutions. The
training complex could be funded federally, by drawing on
the funds of the cooperating institutions, or both.

---

* These descriptions were prepared as working definitions by the Committee in April, 1971.

Models for Elementary Teacher Education Programs

The Models for Elementary Teacher Education Programs are descriptions of teacher education programs which have been developed in considerable detail. They are an attempt to approach the description of teacher education from a logical, systematic analysis of the total program.

Ten "Models" or descriptions of elementary teacher education programs have been developed. While the Models differ in various approaches to the problems of setting instructional goals, overall program organization, curriculum design, institutional relationships and specific innovations, they share some common features. The features which distinguish the Models from other descriptions or definitions of teacher education programs include:

1. greater individualization and personalization of the teacher education curriculum;

2. orientation toward confirmation--teacher education programs are designed against a clear statement of goals or performance;

3. decision making on the basis of data--once a program is established, data is collected and used for decisions on revision and improvement;

4. monitoring of human and other instructional resources so that they are available to students as required--management and scheduling of resources; and

5. provision for breaking down the current course structure of teacher education programs, and placing teacher education on a non-course, e.g., module, basis.

An essential aspect of the systems approach is considering the teacher education program as in a continual state of development--as a process--with provisions being made for the cycle of: decision--feedback from data collected on the program--revision of the program. The cycle for decision making also means that the Models are "data-based" --data must be collected in sufficient detail for decisions to be made. This includes data on the students as they progress through the instructional units of the program, characteristics of students on entering and leaving the program, and data to manage the scheduling of students as they go through the program. The emphasis on data collection also points to the potential of the Model programs for answering questions about the education of teachers. The Models are researchable programs.

Performance-Based Certification

Performance-based certification is intended to make explicit what teachers know and can do (their skills) or

223

achieve when they leave a program of teacher training. It has been argued that the adoption of a performance base for teacher certification would enhance the credibility of the certification process, strengthen teaching as a profession, and improve the quality of education in the schools. The performance-based approach also would make explicit to the public the skills and knowledge which teachers are expected to possess. Two features of the performance-based certification approach seem to stand out. Performance-based certification would require the certification agency:

1. to ensure the explication of the nature of the performance standards which must be met for each type of certificate; and

2. to ensure the setting forth of the mechanisms or procedures by which specific performance standards will be established and judged (assessed).

The explication of the nature of the performance standards means that what might be called the _level_ of performance standards has to be decided. The level of performance standard required might vary with different certification agencies, from _knowledge_ of concepts or specific practices, to demonstration of _skills_ in laboratory or practice settings, to _demonstrated effectiveness_ in a classroom, i.e., producing stated changes in pupil behavior. Different levels of inference to the ultimate setting of teaching in a particular school context with specific children are apparent in these of performance standards. The inference to on-the-job effectiveness is greatest from the _knowledge_ level; somewhat less from the _skill_ level; and perhaps least from the _demonstrated effectiveness_ level.

The decision about the level of performance standards is a critical one, and has implications for the second feature, setting the procedures to establish specific performance standards and the methods of assessment. Setting the specific performance standards would force the criteria for certification to be made public, and would also have considerable impact on teacher education programs. The requirement of setting specific standards would encourage the teacher education institutions to train teachers to pass these performance standards, and would be a mechanism to effect change in teacher education. The training institution would have to be explicit, also, about the knowledge and skills that it has in its curriculum for preparing teachers.

Protocol Materials

Protocol materials are instructional materials that lead to efficient mastery of concepts. The basis of the instructional materials are "protocols," which are reproductions (audio-visual) of behavior that provide the means of learning concepts important in teaching and learning. The protocol materials enable the preservice of inservice teacher to study concepts that are educationally significant. Mastery of the concepts in the protocol materials means development of the ability to identify the concept in simulated or real life settings. The protocols and accompanying instructional materials are developed to be widely distributed and used in any program of teacher education. The features which appear to distinguish protocol instructional materials from other instructional materials are that they enable the student:

1. to identify the concept in simulated or real life settings;

2. to relate the concept to other concepts; and

3. to use the concept in interpreting behavior in teaching/learning contexts.

An important aspect of the protocol instructional materials is that they emphasize that those concepts acquired have real life reference. In this sense they are analogous to "protocols" as used in clinical settings: transcripts or reproductions of actual behaviors are studied to understand behavior.

The ultimate purpose of protocol materials is to facilitate interpretive competencies in teachers. The concepts which may facilitate interpretation of classroom behavior will be drawn from disciplines related to problems of understanding behavior, such as psychology, anthropology, sociology, and philosophy. Terms such as "self-concept," "aggression,""reinforcement," "culture," "role," and so on, designate concepts that teachers can use to interpret behavior. To interpret, however, is not to treat. The development of skills to deal with behavior in given contexts is the function of training materials.

Training Materials

Training materials are instructional materials which lead to the efficient mastery of skills. They provide for the identification of skills, description of situations in which they are to be practiced, description of the performance the skills entail, and ways of giving feedback to the student on his performance. The materials help the student identify his mistakes and see how to correct them. The fundamental purpose is the development of skills through practice and feedback. The features which appear to distinguish training instructional materials from other instructional materials are that they enable the student:

1. to identify the skill in use;

2. to perform the component parts of the skill; and

3. to exercise the skill under laboratory or simulated conditions.

Skill in the performance of such abilities as questioning, probing, performing reinforcement operations, performing in and with small and large groups, evaluating student achievement, and so on, would be developed through training materials. In training, it is the student's behavior that will be observed, analyzed and modified. Elements essential to the training materials include specification of the behavior, performance, feedback, and modification of performance, in a continual process until successful performance is attained.

Appendix B

EDUCATIONAL SPECIALTY BOARDS

Myron Lieberman

This memorandum proposes the establishment of a
system of extra-legal teacher certification tentatively
entitled "Educational Specialty Boards." These boards,
broadly based in governance, would certify teachers as
possessing a superior level of professional skill and
competence. Although such boards would be valuable for
many reasons, they will be discussed here largely in
terms of their potential for advancing the concept of performance based certification and for improving the quality
of teacher education generally.

First, it should be noted that extra-legal
certification is a common practice outside the field of
education. For example, in the field of medicine there
are about 20 medical specialty boards. These medical
specialty boards certify physicians in such fields as
surgery, internal medicine, radiology, and dermatology,
to cite just a few. The diplomate of the American
Psychological Association reflects the concept of extra-
legal certification in the field of psychology. The distinction between CPA's and accountants is also suggestive,
although CPA examinations are administered through state
agencies.

In education, certification by an educational specialty
board would not be required for a regular teaching
certificate. Specialty board certification should be accepted automatically as meeting the requirements for a regular
certificate in any state, but this will require understanding
and cooperation of the state certification agencies.
Presumably, they would not want to be in the potentially
embarrassing position of denying a regular teaching certificate to someone designated as a superior teacher by an
agency under the auspices of leading national educational
organizations.

In any case, one advantage of educational specialty
boards is that they would not require any change in state
certification procedures. This is extremely important.
The movement toward performance-based certification involves
many difficult problems. Before such a drastic change is
applied to the regular certificates, it would be extremely
helpful to have some broad, firsthand experience with the
process of performance-based certification. Extra-legal

certification can provide that experience in a meaningful way while avoiding controversy over existing certification requirements.

Another advantage of utilizing extra-legal certification as an alternative route toward performance-based certification is that the number of teachers involved would be manageable. For this reason, the performance-based criteria could be more intensively applied and evaluated. This memorandum does not take a position with respect to the proportion of teachers in any given field who should be board certified after the boards are fully operational. This is a policy issue to be resolved initially with representatives of appropriate organizations in the development process.

Moreover, the subject matter specialists will have to develop the standards for superior skill and knowledge in the subject matter fields. A third advantage, therefore, is that extra-legal certification would clearly constitute a unique opportunity for experts in arts and sciences and in pedagogy to work together to improve teacher education. Furthermore, experience in other fields suggests that representation from employer groups is helpful to prevent the lowering of standards of board certification, as it is extended to new fields of specialization. For this reason, it would be desirable to have representation from such organizations as the National Boards Association on the advisory group responsible for the development of the various specialty boards. It would also be desirable to have representation from agencies or organizations involved in civil rights and equal opportunity to keep the focus of the specialty boards on public rather than professional interests, and to encourage the acceptance of board certificates by the community at large. At the present time, certification and licensing procedures are under widespread legal attack for their tendency to reflect the interests of the occupational group rather than the public. The introduction of new certification procedures should take careful account of the valid criticisms of existing certification procedures.

Ideally, professors of methods and materials and supervisors in the public schools would be"board certified." It may be feasible to think of two levels, as in the field of medicine. Physicians are first required to pass an examination procedure which renders them "board eligible"; then, upon completion of all the requirements, they become "board certified." Regardless of whether there are one or two levels, however, the fact that the procedures are under the auspices of national organizations is extremely significant. For one thing, it means that the successful applicant (that is, the board-certified teacher) will be able to get additional compensation wherever he goes. This is a very important inducement for teachers to apply for and prepare themselves for the board examinations. In this connection, it is expected that teachers will pay for their board examinations inasmuch as the rewards for becoming board

certified will make such payment worthwhile. The same
practical logic underlies the willingness of accountants to
become CPA's or of physicians to become board certified in
the various medical fields. The basic issue is public
and professional confidence that the designation "board
certified" actually reflects a superior level of professional skill and competence.

The value of such board certification to institutions
of higher education and to school districts should also be
noted. Instead of relying upon letters of recommendation,
often from unknown sources with varying standards, institutions and school systems would now have a reliable way
of identifying superior individuals who can work with new
and inexperienced teachers, or with student teachers. For
example, a high school science department which finds
itself without a strong, experienced teacher or supervisor
would be in a much better position to employ one if board
certification were in operation. By the same token, a
college of education looking for outstanding individuals to
teach the methods and materials courses could also look
for board-certified professionals to meet their needs.

Note also that educational specialty boards would avoid
the historic objections to merit pay by teacher organizations.
Under educational specialty boards, the designation of who
is board certified would not be made locally; the local
employer would not be involved in board certification procedures. For this reason, there would be no employer
favoritism or subjectivity involved. Another important
point is that the national organization of teachers
(NEA and AFT) would be deeply involved in the research and
development effort to establish various specialty boards.
These organizations should have representation on the national
advisory bodies and would be in a good position to monitor
the development of the boards. At the local level, the teacher
organizations could bargain for the differentials for board-
certified teachers in the same way that they now bargain for
differentials for advanced degrees.

The crucial point for teacher education is that the
highest levels of skill and knowledge about teaching could
be built into the board examination. Significant research
carrying implications for teacher training could be incorporated immediately into the specialty board examinations.
This flexibility provides enormous leverage in upgrading the
quality of teacher education. If, for example, a superior
elementary teacher should know how to diagnose and prescribe
for certain reading difficulties, the board examinations can
test the teacher's ability to make the diagnosis and prescribe
for it--not on paper with pencil, but with actual students.
If a research study justifies a change in what a superior
teacher should know or be able to do, there is no need to
wait upon the legan machinery of state certification to give
force and effect to the change.

It is crucially important to recognize the potential
value of educational specialty boards to state certification

agencies. The boards would provide valuable feedback on all aspects of teacher education and certification. For example, they would provide data on the costs and technical feasibility of various performance-based criteria for certification. They would develop a pool of examiners capable of implementing performance-based certification for the regular certificate. They would or could provide valuable data on levels of subject matter competence, and of competence in dealing with guidance agencies, parents, and so on.

The Development Process

How could educational specialty boards be initiated? Funds from OE and/ or private foundations would have to be made available to an appropriate agency tentatively labeled the Educational Specialty Board Commission. The Commission would develop board procedures and examinations for a few fields. Position papers would be drafted on eligibility requirements, the content of examinations, cut-off points, costs, opportunities to retake the examinations, the duration of certificates, the location of the examinations, and so on. These position papers should be reviewed and discussed by the Commission with the persons who prepared the papers. Unquestionably, some attention should be given to the problems of extra-legal certification, especially of evaluating professional performance, in other fields. As various issues are discussed, analyzed, and tentatively resolved, an outline of board procedures in a few prototype fields should emerge. It would probably then be necessary to field test the tentative board procedures, perhaps several times under various conditions. After such field testing, the first few boards should be ready to operate, with meetings and conferences scheduled to generate interest and support. Initially, financial incentives might be needed to encourage applicants and establish the board certificates.

Perhaps the single most important point is that these boards offer a way to move ahead quickly on a national front to implement performance-based certification. The research and demonstration value and leverage of this approach should be enormous and should permeate all of teacher education within a relatively short time.

Appendix C

THE ROLE OF THE DISCIPLINES IN THE
TRAINING OF TEACHERS IN THE 1970's

Alan C. Purnes

This paper comments on the role of the subject-matter disciplines in the training of teachers in the 1970's, with particular emphasis on the development of five activities: protocol materials, training materials, teacher training complexes, the models for the training of elementary school teachers, and performance-based criteria for the certification of teachers.

It might be said that in the 1960's two strong impulses governed the training of teachers. The first, in part resulting from the writings of Conant, who decried a lack of subject matter in the schools, and Bruner, who set forth the idea that the methodology of a discipline could be taught at any level in the development of a child, led to increased attention to subject matter both in curriculum development and in teacher training. There was a burgeoning of curricula in mathematics, the sciences, English and the arts and humanities, and social studies. There was a spate of summer institutes, experienced-teacher fellowship programs, and preservice training programs, all of which focused on the subject matter of the disciplines. Concurrently as a result of the work of such men as Smith, Bellack, and Gage there came to be a great deal of research and curriculum development related to the science of teaching. The thrust of this work was curiously abetted by the writings of the "romantic critics" of education--Kohl, Kozol, and others-- who saw the importance of teacher attitude and student-teacher relationships in promoting learning, and who preached an "art" of teaching.

Toward the end of the 1960's these two thrusts could well have produced a wider gap between the subject matter disciplines and the schools of pedagogy than had existed before the beginning of the decade, were it not for the emergence of some programs like that for the training of teacher-trainers (TTT), a program specifically designed to bring subject matter and pedagogy together. In many of the projects sponsored under TTT, the fusion of subject matter and pedagogy has had enormous effect on the university departments involved and, even more spectacularly, on the students in the schools.

The effect of the TTT program has yet to be fully
felt, however, and, as those responsible for teacher education plan ahead, it would seem important for that effect
not to be lost. While the titles of the five activities
might indicate that each could be entirely pedagogically
oriented, the contribution of the disciplines is crucial to
the success of the activities in achieving their goals.
Each of the five activities is addressed separately below.

Protocol Materials

These materials are intended to be examples of "real"
behavior of people in the various roles they play in education (as student, teacher, administrator, parent,
citizen, and so forth), presented to allow prospective
teachers to see operating in that behavior certain specified
concepts might be related to pedagogy, social psychology, to the
various subject matters have existed for a long time; they
are the base from which the disciplines have emerged. The
concepts of language have emerged from analysis and interpretation of what people have said or written; those of
literature from examination of literary texts; those of
physics from examination of certain natural phenomena; and
those of history from examination of the actions of individuals and of nations. The need for new protocol materials in the disciplines is limited save in a few areas.
There needs to be some material which allows prospective
teachers to develop the ability to analyze and interpret
the behaviors that we have come to call "critical" or
"scientific" or "historical" or the like as those behaviors
are manifested in children. Prospective teachers see
adults--their teachers--behaving like physicists, but
they seldom see when children are behaving similarly. They
need to learn how to do so.

This role of subject matter in the development of protocol materials is important, but less crucial than the role
subject matter can play in the development of protocol
materials in pedagogy and the social sciences related to
pedagogy. In those materials, the behavior manifested is
usually that of a teacher teaching students. More often than
not, there is a lesson in some content area (for example,
reading, mathematics, or social studies). Since these
materials present the behavior through film or video tape,
there is a high degree of verisimilitude that engages the
attention of the viewer. The viewer is asked not to react
emotionally or evaluatively, but analytically and dis-
passionately; and he is asked to focus his attention on the
form, that is to say the teaching behavior, in the material.
By consciously paying little attention to the <u>content</u> of the
teaching, the viewer may well tend to assume that the
content is acceptable. In many protocol materials such may
not be the case. Similarly, in those protocol materials
that seek to provide data for analysis of behavior in the
content areas, the teaching strategy may be unacceptable
and neglected in the analysis.

If this is the case, it is crucial that any protocol material be rigidly scrutinized for the conceptual adequacy of the <u>content</u> of the lesson by a subject matter specialist, and the <u>form and technique</u> of the lesson by a specialist in psychology and pedagogy. Not to do so is to run the risk that the materials intended for analysis may inadvertantly act as the wrong model for future behavior.

Training Materials

What has been said above applies even more importantly to those materials that are specifically designed to show students what to do when they teach. Teaching should not be analyzed and defined in a fashion that abstracts teaching from the thing taught. Even training material that isolates a particular form of teacher-student interaction will show a teacher and a student interacting <u>about</u> some content. The presentation of that content must be intellectually sound according to the best thinking of the discipline that treats it as subject matter. A training film may portray a beautiful relationship between student and teacher, one that seems to illustrate the best facilitation of learning. The whole thrust of the training film is vitiated if one sees the student learning that there was no black culture before 1954. Such an example is blatant, of course, but subtler errors, misapplications of theory, or discarded notions are even more pernicious than such a blatant falsehood. It is to prevent those subtle errors that provision for subject matter specialists to help conceive and review the training materials seems hardly a luxury, but a necessity.

Teacher-Training Complexes

As the term "complex" implies, these new institutions would bring together the schools, the colleges of education, the communities, and the subject matter discipline in a new confederation in order to make the training of prospective teachers more adequate to the situations they will face once th are actively engaged in their profession. It goes without saying that there is an important place for the disciplines in these complexes, but to let the matter drop there is to perpetuate a problem that has long plagued the teacher trainer. It is true that there is subject matter in the schools and in the arts and sciences colleges of the universities. However, to infer that the two aspects of subject matter are the same can be risky. Literature in the schools might be said to be the object of critical attention; in the universities, of historical attention. Or to take grammar as an example, an important function of the schools is to insure that children employ the grammatical richness of the language in communicating in speech or in writing with other people. In the university the emphasis might better be placed on the analysis of grammar and language systems as a disciplined form of inquiry. The function of that analysis might well be to enable the teacher in the school to understand better what his students are doing.

The difference in function and approach to subject matter that separates general from special education may also separate scholarly from pedagogical education. It may be useful for certain kinds of students to be able to perform the functions of the textual editor or the descriptive bibliographer; it would seem more useful for the prospective teacher to be able to perform a content analysis of textbooks in order to discern critical biases.

All of the disciplines are so wide and complexly structured that it is necessary for the establishers of a training complex to determine what aspects of each discipline are most useful to the prospective teacher. In English, for example, it would seem that psycholinguistics and sociolinguistics are more useful than is philology. Further, it would seem that courses dealing in analysis of the concepts and procedures of the disciplines are of greater use to the prospective teacher than are courses which simply present the results of those procedures and the scattered details with which those concepts deal. To this end the disciplines must contribute in the planning of the program of the complex, but must, in turn, be required to examine their premises, procedures, and conceptual bases.

As a result of such examination, there should emerge a program for prospective teachers which will provide a sense of the conceptual bases of the discipline, the power and limitation of that discipline as a means of knowing, the basic procedures of that discipline, and, finally, how that discipline might be made available to children of various ages. In literature, for example, we might say that three of the basic concepts of the literary work are voice, metaphor, and form. These concepts tell a great deal about the aesthetics of a work, but little about the human significance of the work. Critics operate through language to lay forth these three concepts as they operate in specific literary works. These concepts may be made apparent to young children through such devices as role playing, word games, and examination of the formal elements of comic strips and children's stories.

It is essential, therefore, that scholars in the disciplines, particularly those scholars who have a commitment to general education and therefore to teacher training, be a part of the curriculum planning process in a training complex. These scholars must, however, be asked to confront people from the pedagogical fields and from the schools, and particularly people from the community, in order to assure that their conceptions will meet the real needs of schoolchildren and society. They must be asked to justify the discipline and the selection of concepts in the discipline in terms of the real world. Once they have held themselves accountable in this way, then, and only then, should they proceed to planning the training of teachers.

Elementary Models

The models proposed seek to create a structure for the total education of elementary school teachers. From the summaries [1] it would seem that the models are formal arrangements of the components of a teacher education program, and are concerned with the relationships of the various parts of a program to each other, whether those relationships be structural or sequential. An obvious feature of these models is the specification of goals of the program and clarification of the roles of the various decision-making groups.

As a member of one of these decision-making groups, one is impressed by the artfulness and clarity of many of the models, but remains wary of the series of empty boxes on the various organizational charts, boxes labelled "subject matter instruction," or "educational objectives." The models are beautiful buildings, but at this point no one seems to inhabit them. As they become inhabited, there must be close to scrutiny of the content to insure conceptual adequacy and efficacy. As with the teacher training complexes, these models must be scrutinized not only for the interrelation of structural components but also the content that is being taught. In the basic subjects--language arts, mathematics, social sciences, natural sciences, and arts-- the elementary years are crucial to the future development of the individual. The teachers that these models produce must know what they are doing in each of those basic subjects when they are presenting them to children or facilitating the development of the children's skills in each of the areas. It is urgent that the content of these models be as elaborately worked out as the organization.

Performance-Based Certification of Teachers

This last activity seems to be the one that sums up the other four activities. It represents a call to make professional training of teachers comparable to the professional training of doctors, dentists, and architects. The qualifications of an individual will depend upon what he does as judged by other members of his profession, not simply upon whether or not he has been in a certain number of classrooms. The elementary models, the training complex, the protocol and training materials all provide ways to enable prospective teachers to gain and demonstrate their professional competence.

---

[1] Klatt, J. and LeBaron, W. A Short Summary of Ten Model Teacher Education Programs. Washington: National Center for Educational Research and Development, Office of Education, 1969; and the articles comprising Volume 3, Number 3 (Spring, 1970), Journal of Research and Development in Education.

The import of this activity is to force the teacher trainer, whether in the traditional disciplines or in the pedagogical fields, to think--or rather to rethink--what it is that he has been doing. It forces him to focus not merely on the history or taxonomy of his field, but also on the skills, concepts, and procedures a person must master if he is to be certified as a teacher. This is a radical rethinking of the disciplines and a rethinking that is long overdue.

To say this is not to overlook the many pitfalls that await the person who devises performance criteria. To think of a discipline in terms of performance is to relate behaviors to specific aspects of the subject matter, aspects which occur in a context. "A student demonstrates his understanding of irony in a column by Art Buchwald." Such a statement forms an infinitesimal part of the language arts, and one could generate objectives like this in the billions. There must be both a grouping of these objectives into some conceptual scheme, and a selecting of those groups that are most pertinent to the teaching situation and most respectful of the conceptual framework of the discipline.

In English, such action already been undertaken by the Illinois Statewide Curriculum for the Preparation of English Teachers (ISCPET). The performance objectives in the report of that project are a base for the development of any performance based criteria for the certification of secondary English teachers. It may be that they should be modified; certainly they need to be expanded and made more specific, but they represent an important start, one undertaken by the joint efforts of those in English and those in pedagogy. It would seem important that similar steps be undertaken in other disiciplines.

The second major pitfall is that related to evaluation. Just as the selection of objectives runs the risk of trivialization of the discipline, the demand for certain kinds of quantification can reduce the evaluators to thinking only in terms of standard test scores and the like. In setting forth criteria, the representatives of the disciplines and the evaluation staffs must strain their imaginations to the utmost to develop observational techniques, questionnaires, attitude scales, and other measures perhaps not yet conceived to certify that the objectives have been met. The recent trends in evaluation give hope that such can be done; there must be full partnership between the disciplines and the evaluation staffs.

Summary

Two threads are apparent throughout all of these comments, partnership and performance. There must, it seems, be a partnership of the subject matter disciplines and the pedagogical disciplines; neither can effect the training of teachers alone. Such a partnership means that the subject matter component and the pedagogical component cannot be related to consecutive parts of the students' training

236

(e.g., a fifth year in pedagogy or a fifth year in subject matter). There must be integration throughout the whole of preprofessional training. Whether it be in the planning of models of training, setting forth of criteria, or development of materials for analysis or training, the two components must inform, test, and harmonize with each other.

To do this, both must look at what they do and what they want the trainee to do. They must examine the performance of professionals and determine the concepts underlying that performance. They must look at the behavior of people in the real world so as to influence the training of teachers for the real world. Performance has a form, how one does things, and a content, what one does. For a purpose of analysis form and content can be separated, but in performance they cannot. Performance must be analyzed so that the performer can be trained, and the performer must learn about both form and content. Performance in education deals with people teaching or learning something. The disciplines tell us about the something; pedagogy and psychology tell us about teaching and learning; both must help the student become a performing teacher.

Appendix D

SUMMARY OF THE REVIEW OF COMMITTEE PAPERS

Carol C. Tittle

Additional perspective on the program proposals developed by Committee members was provided by a group of
external reviewers. Abstracts of the proposed programs
were sent on May 20, 1971, to a number of individuals
knowledgeable about and concerned with the problems of
teacher education. A copy of the abstracts is presented
at the end of this summary section (see Appendix 1).

The group of reviewers was assembled from names
suggested by Committee members, as well as by staff of the
Bureau of Educational Personnel Development. The group of
reviewers represented community groups, school administrators
and teachers, critics of teacher education, associations for
professional groups in education, and university faculty
and administrators--both in education and the liberal arts.
The distribution in Table 1 shows the groups represented. A
total of 70 abstracts were mailed, and 38 individuals responded (54% returned comments).

Table 1. Distribution of External Reviewers

Group	Number Mailed	Number Returned
Institutions of Higher Education		
Education Deans/Faculty	27	14
Liberal Arts	7	1
State Education Departments	3	3
School Superintendents	10	7
Teachers/Professional Associations	4	2
Teacher Education Associations	6	4
Community Organizations/Critics	8	2
Other Education Groups (R&D		
Centers, Regional Laboratories)	5	5
Total	70	38

Three sets of comments were received: (1) ratings of a
number of ideas in the Committee papers; (2) comments on the
most useful and least useful aspects of each proposed program;
and (3) suggestions for ideas which reviewers felt were overlooked in the Committee's papers. It should be noted that
these comments were based on abstracts of the papers as they

had been developed by the middle of May. Individual
Committee members have revised or developed new papers since
that date. The comments served, therefore, to guide the
revisions of preliminary papers and to provide a partial
framework by which to assess the recommendations contained
in the final report.

The summary below takes into account the revisions, or
new papers, prepared by Committee members and is intended
to represent the pros and cons of the main ideas reflected
in the papers which are presented in the appendices to the
final report.

1. Ratings of Major Ideas

A number of items were rated for their potential
utility in the redesign of teacher education programs. The
raters were to take into account the usefulness of the items
as they related to a major goal of the Office of Education:
to improve the quality of education for disadvantaged
minority, racial, and ethnic groups. Items were rated on a
scale from one (critical item; must be taken into account in
designing teacher education programs) to five (of little or
no interest for redesigning teacher education). The ratings
for each item are given in Table 2 at the end of this paper.

Items which were rated as critical (given a rating of
one or two by 80% of the group responding were:

    #3   Establish performance-based teacher education
         programs
    #9   Develop measuring "instruments"--knowledge/
         skills/observation of teaching behavior
    #23 Personalize or individualize teacher training
         program.

The high ratings for two of the items, performance-based
teacher education and development of measuring "instruments,"
are emphasized in the Committee recommendations for a program
of competency-based teacher education and a project proposed to develop instruments for competency-based teacher
education and certification. The emphasis on personaliza-
tion/individualization is a general goal for education, and
is well discussed in two Committee papers. (See chapters
4 and 6 by M. Vere DeVault and H. Del Schalock.)

A second group of items were rated as critical by at
least 60% of the individuals responding:

    #1   Establish a parity group for policy making
    #5   Use training materials
    #8   Develop a data-based feedback system for per-
         formance following training
    #10 Establish training complexes, consortium train-
         ing centers, parity based teacher centers
    #22 Recruit students and adults from minority
         groups.

Two of these items are reflected specifically in the
Committee recommendations: training materials and organizational structures for teacher training. A third, the
data-based feedback system, is encompassed in the provision
for recording trainee performance and evaluation by teacher
trainers, in the development of instruments for use in
classroom and simulated practice settings, and in the
evaluation program for the centers for teacher training.
The concept of a parity group for policy making is not
specifically mentioned in Committee recommendations, but is
discussed in the chapters by Benjamin Rosner and H. Del
Schalock. "Parity" is a policy issue which could be included in guidelines for project funding. Recruitment from
minority groups is not discussed directly, but is also a
general policy which could be given priority in most inservice or preservice teacher education programs, and implemented through project guidelines.

The remainder of the items were given ratings of _one_
or _two_ by fewer than 60% of the group. One item, "Establish
extra-legal certification systems, " was rated as critical
by less than 40% of the group, and yet is one of the
Committee recommendations. The rationale for extending the
career line of teachers through Educational Specialty Boards,
working outside a state framework, is given in the text of
the final report and in the paper by Myron Lieberman
(Appendix B).

2.   Comments on Proposals

Reviewers were asked to comment on the aspects of each
proposal which they thought most useful for reform, and on
the elements in each which they found less desirable. The
main points mentioned for each abstract are summarized
below.

A.   A Five-Year Goal for Training Complexes

A major feature of this proposal was the use of the
concept of "neutral ground" to mean interdependence; reviewers favored the concept of essentially "forcing" the
necessary partnership or closer integration of schools and
universities, and the involvement of community and industry.
When narrowly interpreted as building new institutions, many
reviewers were skeptical of the possibility, and preferred to
change the present institutions involved in teacher education. The sequential exposure of students to the education professions and the gradual induction to teaching were
considered strong features.

Another set of comments considered the separation of the
theoretical (university) and practical learning experiences
of students to be a weakness. The concept of the Educational
Service District was considered premature, in view of the
present stage of knowledge in teacher training, and the ESD
was seen as potentially bureaucratic in character. The
number of training complexes proposed for development in a
five-year period was seen as unrealistic; competent

personnel would not be available to staff the training complexes.

B. A Master Program for Reform In Teacher Education

Strong features of the program were the emphasis on teacher competencies and the development of protocol and training materials. The capacity for schools to identify the performance they seek in teachers and the option for students in the program to identify the types of competency they wanted to develop were considered positive features of the program. The research potentiality of the system and the idea of a dynamic, continuously evolving and evaluated model were also identified as strong features of the program.

The reliance on a systems approach was received positively by some reviewers and less favorably by others. Some reviewers questioned the suggestion of a central policy committee, and suggested a stronger emphasis on local needs. A weakness of committees was noted as the amount of time members would have, and a strong staff was suggested as a necessary condition for program development.

C. Levers for Change in Teacher Education

The description of sources of power for improvement of teacher education was seen as a valuable analysis. Cooperation between school and university staff in training and curriculum efforts, the concept of parity-based governance, and transcripts with competency profiles were seen as useful aspects of the proposal. There was considerable agreement that changes in teacher education must be accompanied by other changes, such as curricula in the schools.

The proposed split of university faculty into two groups--foundations at the university and clinical in training schools--was regarded as undesirable by a number of reviewers. It was suggested that the two groups must work together throughout the teacher education program. The idea of two entry points into the profession--paraprofessional and undergraduate--was considered unnecessarily restrictive. The "extra-legal" certification of teachers trainers to extend the career line for teachers received both positive and negative comments. Several reviewers suggested that this certification should be done within the "legal" (state) framework. Some reviewers commented that the proposed rotation of faculty to develop training schools was unrealistic.

D. BEPD, NCERD, and Teacher Education That Makes a
    Difference

The statement of basic guidelines for educational personnel development programs was endorsed by many reviewers. The statement included a field centered, personalized, and performance-based teacher education program; a broad base for decision-making; evaluation data; and a research orientation. Some reviewers questioned certification at the "product" level, i.e., teacher behaviors must result in specified learning outcomes for children.

The idea of a statewide network of centers, established on a cost-sharing basis, received both positive and negative comments. Some reviewers noted that state boundaries were limiting, but others commented that the state was too large a unit with which to start. Centers for the Preparation of Educational Personnel (CPEP) integrated the training complex and Elementary Models ideas satisfactorily for some reviewers.

E. Programmatic Themes and Mechanisms

Among the major ideas stated in this plan were levels of criteria, the levels at which performance-based teacher education and certification could occur. Reviewers found this a very useful clarification of the concept of "performance." The focus on the criterion levels as they related to various phases of preservice and inservice teacher education programs and the idea of curricular intervention were identified as strong aspects of the paper. The criterion levels were seen as providing a strong emphasis on accountability, although the concept of a National Confirmatory System was considered unworkable and unnecessary by a number of reviewers.

Curricular intervention through instructional modules based on protocol and training materials was endorsed by a number of reviewers, as was the idea of university and field based laboratory experiences. The funding plan (concentration in one site, then funds moved to a new site) was questioned; some reviewers indicated institutions might not be able to sustain programs under this type of funding plan.

3. Additional Suggestions

This section summarizes many of the ideas which reviewers suggested were overlooked in the abstracts of Committee papers. The decision to circulate abstracts rather than full papers was taken in view of the length of the original papers. The brief abstracts, however, could not adequately represent the more considered discussion given to a number of issues in the original papers. As a result, some of the ideas summarized below will have been discussed in individual papers, but are presented here to emphasize the suggestions of the reviewers. The suggestions have been grouped under headings for clarity of presentation.

A. Teacher Education: General Structure

Both school and university staffs should be effective teacher trainers.

School districts should be encouraged to see teacher education as an integral part of their responsibilities and programs.

A longer continuum is needed for teacher preparation, with guided, supervised induction.

One alternative is the use of the BA as the entry level for teachers, except for paraprofessionals, with all formal preservice teacher education placed in state supported units in existing school organizations, and provision for increased inservice and postgraduate training in the university.

Both the career concept for teachers and the schooling system are outdated; a human and social development model is needed, not a school context.

B. Teacher Education: Content

More attention should be given to the affective aspects of the teacher's behavior.

Teacher education needs to be less standardized and less traditional in emphasis.

Teacher training institutions as we know them should not have a monopoly on teacher training, and, similarly, teacher education programs should be more open and outside existing structures.

A better integration of theory and practice is needed.

There should be more emphasis on differentiated staffing, and realistic levels of expectation for teacher performance roles.

C. Career Factors

There should be some consideration of the problem of retraining those teachers who have left teaching and then want to return.

With high dropout rates for new teachers, perhaps there should be a briefer training for these teachers and more thorough training for career teachers.

The joint problems of recruitment and selection, in a society which gives few rewards to this profession, are not considered.

D. Performance Base

The push to performance-based preparatory programs runs the danger of re-inventing the two-year normal school to train teachers.

Lack of knowledge of the performance-based area should be fully recognized.

We do not have the know-how to prepare fully professionally trained people in performance-based settings.

It must be recognized that competence for teachers exists in a context.

There is the problem of context in developing the performance-based certification at Criterion Levels 1, 2, and 3.

The role of the state department offices of teacher education and certification should be given more attention.

E. Accountability

A greater emphasis on accountability is needed so that teacher preparation institutions will validate their efforts.

The university faculty must be held accountable.

Teacher education is accountable to the universities and to the teaching profession, and, broadly, to the public. There is a distinction between accountability and responsiveness to other agencies (schools, etc.)

There appears to be a confusion between student performance objectives and teacher education objectives (training in behavior shaping).

F. Other Factors

Increased capital investment in instructional systems for schools is needed.

More attention should be given to strategies to improve the schools themselves.

Teacher education cannot be reformed without a direction for change in public education.

Training of administrators: a discussion is needed of the role, objectives, and evaluation of school administrators.

Increase research on the educative process.

G. Planning

Mechanisms are needed to establish community educational needs, then state, regional, and national goals, in terms of student performance objectives.

Any plan for teacher education should seek to encourage the development of the profession.

Teachers should share in decision making. Teachers should have a role in planning the teacher education program, and planning should be more open.

H. OE Goals and Sitting of Projects

There is a lack of attention to USOE goal of improving the quality of education for depressed and minority groups.

It seems that most funding will go to where salaries are already high and where there are good working conditions, rather than to core city areas.

Special attention should be given to problems of large urban school systems that are heavily black.

More emphasis is needed on pupil and societal priorities; priority in sitting should be given for disadvantaged minority, social and ethnic groups.

There ia a problem in how to handle the poor, small teacher education institutions--which are continually left out of funding efforts.

I. Technical Support and Program Development

Strong Federal motivation is needed, but also as much decentralization as possible.

Cooperative work should be done with NIE, NCERD, and NIH.

More attention should be given to diffusion and installation strategies.

Long term funding should be used to develop self-supporting mechnisms.

Careful technical assistance should be lent to project sites before starting programs.

Realistic strategies for organizational development are needed.

Organizational and other models should be "tested" before implementing on a large scale.

The number of centers should be smaller in order to permit careful data-dependent monitoring, and some training centers should train researchers.

More attention should be given to research and confirmation methods so that training centers and training procedures do not develop a "truth" of their own.

Training materials must be data-dependent for modification.

Successful practices should be collected and disseminated.

In summary, it can be noted that many of the comments made by reviewers suggest difference in the views of individuals concerned with teacher education. There appears to be considerable uncertainty about the appropriate criteria for accountability in teacher training. On the one hand, some reviewers would equate the accountability of the schools with accountability in teacher education, i.e., pupil growth is the only valid criterion for teacher education. On the other hand, some reviewers would limit the accountability of teacher education to the preparation of competent teachers, recognizing the criterion of pupil growth as a research variable to guide the selection of content for teacher training curricula.

More basic differences tend to center on a concern over the use of technology, more detailed definitions of skills and competencies, and possible standardization in teacher education, versus the concern that teacher education reflect a "humanistic" and open approach to the education of teachers and pupils. The reconciliation and accommodation of these basic views seem to be necessary conditions for the broad acceptance of any new program proposals and the improvement of teacher education.

Table 2. Ratings of Items

After reading the program descriptions included in the set
of materials, rate each of the following items for their
potential utility in the redesign of teacher education programs, in line with OE objectives, e.g., to improve the
quality of education for disadvantaged minority, racial,
and ethnic groups.

>   1--critical item; must be taken into account
>   in designing teacher education programs
>   2--
>   3--important item, but not as high in priority
>   4--
>   5--of little or no interest for redesigning
>   teacher education

ITEM	Frequency of Ratings Given Each Item					
	1	2	3	4	5	NR*
1. Establish a parity group for policy making	16	10	7	2	2	1
2. Apply systems design to teacher education programs	15	7	12	4	-	-
3. Establish performance-based teacher education programs	23	8	4	-	1	2
4. Use protocol materials	7	13	12	4	1	1
5. Use training materials	10	14	9	3	2	-
6. Use the Models for Elementary Teacher Education	7	10	13	4	4	-
7. Develop Education Service Districts	4	4	15	8	4	3
8. Develop a data-based feedback system for performance follow-ing training (Micro Confir-matory Systems)	9	14	8	5	2	-
9. Develop measuring "instruments" knowledge/skills/observation of teaching behaviors	27	6	3	1	1	-
10. Establish training complexes, Consortium training centers, Parity-based teacher centers	18	7	5	4	2	2

* No Response

247

ITEM		Frequency of Ratings Given Each Item					
		1	2	3	4	5	NR*
11.	Establish extra-legal certification systems	6	7	10	8	4	3
12.	Develop standardized exercises to assess degree of skill in performing classroom tasks	12	6	9	5	5	1
13.	Institute state regulated performance-based certification	12	6	13	3	2	2
14.	Integrate academic disciplines in teacher education programs	10	6	12	4	5	1
15.	Establish state networks of Centers for Preparation of Educational Personnel	7	7	8	11	2	3
16.	Develop national confirmatory feedback system	6	10	5	12	4	1
17.	Establish "facilitating groups" to provide direction/technical assistance for ideas such as performance-based certification	8	14	10	2	2	2
18.	Establish Institutional Training Centers	8	8	9	7	2	4
19.	Establish Competency-Based Program Centers	8	9	11	5	3	2
20.	Establish national committee for policy recommendations in training educational personnel	9	9	12	4	3	1
21.	Modify college/university transcript to reflect profile of teacher competencies	10	12	5	6	3	2
22.	Recruit students and adults from minority groups	17	7	7	3	3	1
23.	Personalize or individualize teacher training program	26	5	4	1	1	1

Total Number of Responses = 38

Appendix 1

Abstracts Circulated by the
Committee on National Program Priorities in Teacher Education
May 17, 1971

A FIVE-YEAR GOAL FOR TRAINING COMPLEXES: PROPOSAL A

The concept of a Training Complex has for its objectives the development of an entity sufficiently independent of existing institutions to take responsibility
for the training of the classroom teacher, and also establish
a system that will interact and be interrelated with those
institutions that are concerned with teacher preparation on
a continuing basis. The training regimen offered by the
Training Complex follows the sequence of teacher preparation in higher education, either undergraduate or the
combination of undergraduate and graduate, and precedes the
inservice preparation that the schools continually provide
the teacher. "Neutral ground," as a concept upon which the
Training Complex is built, therefore, does not mean isolation
but rather interdependence. "Neutral ground" is suggested as
a functional technique for involving both higher education and
the schools, and to a certain extent the community and industry,
rather than as a means of ignoring them or allowing them to
disengage from the teacher training process.

The Training Complex would be staffed by school teachers
and college faculties, supplemented by part-time faculty
from industry and from the community. The pupils would be
youngsters from the schoolroom and school dropouts, adults
without schooling, and others for specialized purposes.
Starting with small groups, eventually, the trainee would
take on full school classes. At the end of from half a year
to a year in the Training Complex, the trainee would enter
the school system as an intern, the internship to cover the
first year as a teacher and under direct control of the school.

College teacher preparation would abandon student internship and would concentrate on the theoretical aspects of
learning, on subject matter specialization and on career
development. The Training Complex could perform a direct
function in this preservice phase by conducting career interest workshops for college students interested in teaching.
Starting at the freshman and sophomore years, these workshops could serve to identify those students most interested
in and suited to teaching careers, then sequentially expose
the student to elementary and secondary education, education
of the handicapped, etc. In the junior and senior years,
workshops could be developed along specialized interest lines
and include work in the schools as teaching aides and tutors.

The Complex would also serve as the core for another
kind of institutional framework, the Educational Service

249

District.[1] Such districts are conceived as comprehensive agencies which would include the country's more than 20,000 public school districts and 3,000 higher education institutions and link the schools, universities, community, and industry. The role of the Districts would include placement, paraprofessional recruitment and programming, diffusion of protocol and training materials, curriculum innovation, serving as a locus for community social action programs, and research services.

The development schedule for Training Complexes over a five-year period calls for 100 Training Complexes in Year 1 to 3,000 in operation in Year 5. The cost per Training Complex is estimated at $1.5 million; total cost in Year 5 would be $4.5 billion, and annually thereafter.

A NATIONAL MODEL FOR REFORM IN TEACHER EDUCATION: PROPOSAL B

The central theme of the Model is the potential of systems design in education, and the National Model is based on a systems design. A system which establishes controls by providing a knowledge about the nature of change and its impact on learners delivers a continual flow of information useful in determining the future course of the various alternatives. Through the operating systems design, the National Model for teacher education serves as a major research instrumentality--to direct continuing reform in teacher education. Reform in teacher education will result from the National Model through the dissemination of both its products and processes (use of systems management, procedures for faculty training, etc.).

Three specific types of activities are required if the National Model is to function effectively. These include: (1) policy making and coordination, (2) implementation of operating instructional programs, and (3) the development and regeneration of protocol and training materials.

It is recommended that policy leadership be provided through a strong national committee in the area of competency-based teacher education. The competency-based teacher education is at the level of the assessment of the performance of the teacher, that the teacher can perform in stated and specified ways. The National Committee functions: to identify continuing national needs; to monitor and disseminate information concerning the effectiveness of competency-based programs as they evolve; to coordinate, through subcommittees, local Competency-Based Program(CBP) Centers; and to make regular reports and recommendations to OE.

The operating instructional programs of the National

---

[1]See Smith, B.O. (Ed.) Teachers for the Real World, Washington, D.C.: AACTE, 1968. p. 104.

Model take place within the CBP Centers (see Figure 1). These Centers include the operating elements of both the Training Complex and the Experimental [2] Models Program. The Experimental Models Program functions within the Training Complex in that the latter is responsible for the interinstitutional cooperation which gives major impetus to operating instructional programs. The Training Complex assumes certain management functions, faculty training within the schools, and final certification of teachers. The option is presented to teachers in preparation to identify the sets of criteria by which their own performance is to be judged and ultimately certified. Schools will be in a position to identify the kinds of performance they want in the teacher they seek. Certification is then a verification of the fact that the teacher can perform as indicated in the records available--that the teacher can perform in stated and specified ways.

Within each CBP Center the Models Program assumes responsibility for teaching/learning activities, management of resources and learners, faculty training on campus, student recruitment and placement, and assessment and research activities.

Each of the CBP Centers is served by the National Program for Protocol and Training Materials. It is recommended that these instructional materials be developed with balance between the need for program variety among CBP Centers and the need to reduce to a minimum duplication of materials which could be equally effective for instructional programs in more than a single center.

LEVERS FOR CHANGE IN TEACHER EDUCATION: PROPOSAL C

The levers or mechanisms by which reform in teacher education can be attained come from four sources of power: the school, the community, the university, and professional associations. Reform based solely on the power of any single source is inadequate. The identification of mechanisms which focus the power of all sources on a common objective will be most effective in institutionalizing change.

Analysis of the policies and practices of the sources of power suggests that changes in teacher education must be accompanied by changes in governance, certification, school and university curricula, school and university curriculum evaluation, and university admissions and school employment practices. Specifically, the levers may be defined as: parity control (governance), legal and extra-legal certification, performance-based teacher education (curricula), a confirmatory mechanism (curriculum evaluation), and recruitment (admissions and employment). These levers are

---

[2] The term Experimental implies models in both elementary and secondary education.

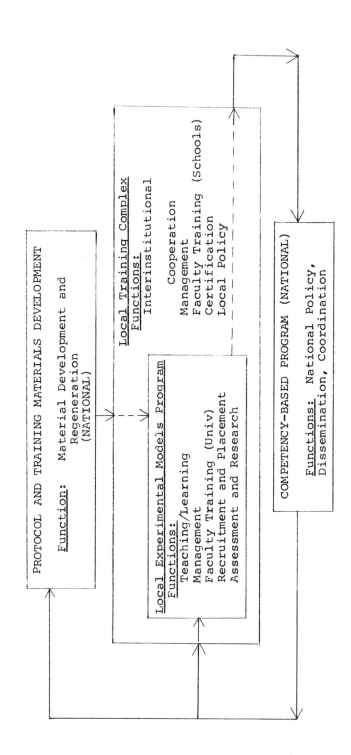

Functions of the Present BEPD Programs
Within a Competency-Based Program Center

Figure 1

inserted in the Parity-Based Teacher Education Program model, although they could be employed in a variety of teacher training contexts.

The Parity-Based Teacher Education Program is a school-university model. The governance of the teacher education program, both the university and school components, is conducted by a parity group. Each aspect of the training program is involved in the confirmatory system, as indicated in Figure 2. The model serves to prepare school personnel to assume the field-based training responsibilities typically associated with methods and curriculum faculty in the university. In addition to training personnel, the role of the education faculty includes that of change or dissemination agent.

The model assumes that curriculum reform in the schools is an indispensable aspect of teacher training, since the training school must be an effective example of quality. The model also assumes that the school based training component must be defined and concretized by specific, standardized exercises or School-Based Tasks. These tasks form part of the confirmatory mechanism, along with a change in the university transcript to a profile of competencies (Figure 3).

The model assumes that there are two entry points for preparation as teachers; the school route appropriate to the paraprofessional and the university route appropriate to the high school graduate. The program attempts to design the preparation of school-based teacher trainers by using the lever of extra-legal certification as a teacher trainer, extending the career line of teachers.

The university faculty would be divided into two groups: One group would be based primarily at the university and concerned with the foundations of education, research relevant to teaching and learning, and monitoring a confirmatory system. The second group, concerned with methods of instruction and curriculum, would be reassigned and housed in specific schools designated as training schools. The major responsibility of this latter group would be the training of selected numbers of cooperating teachers to train pre-service teachers and paraprofessionals, and induct new teachers over a two-to-three-year period. The cooperating teachers, or teacher trainers, would be expected to take over the training responsibility of the school within a three-to-four-year period. Then the education faculty would be transferred to a new school to be designated as a training school, but would provide continuing support and dissemination of new training and curricula materials to the teacher trainers in the developed training school. It is this rotation of education faculty which is the strategy for reforming schools on a systematic basis.

BEPD, NCERD, AND TEACHER EDUCATION THAT MAKES A
DEMONSTRABLE DIFFERENCE: PROPOSAL D

To be effective instruments of educational reform,

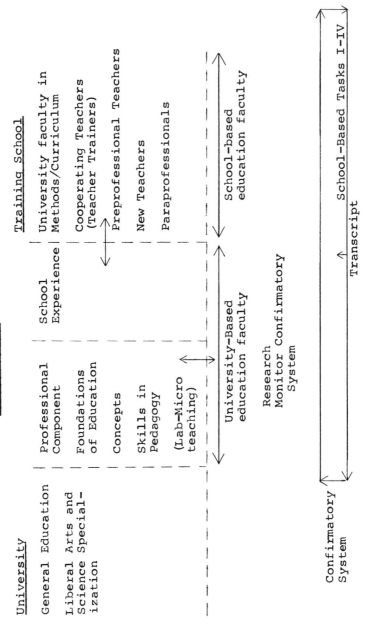

Figure 2. Parity-Based Teacher Education Program

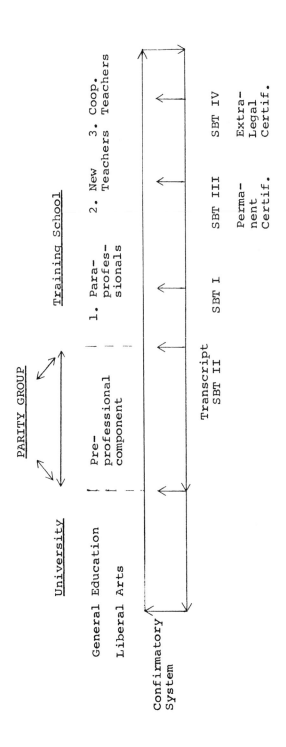

Figure 3.   Levers for Reform

255

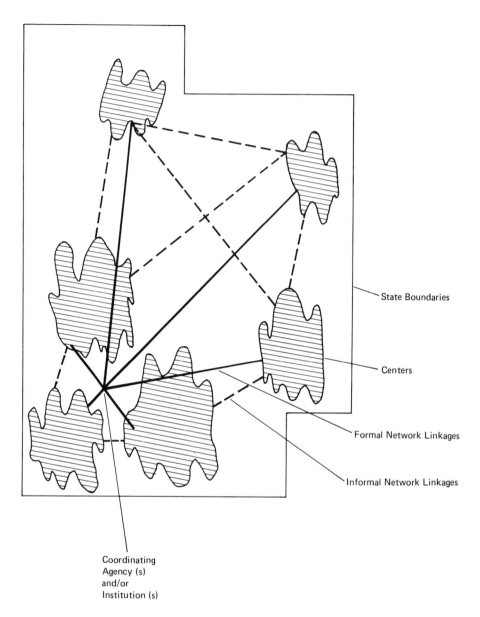

State Boundaries

Centers

Formal Network Linkages

Informal Network Linkages

Coordinating
Agency (s)
and/or
Institution (s)

Figure 4.   A schematic illustration of a state-wide
network of Centers for the Preparation of
Educational Personnel, and the formal and
informal linkage mechanisms that would be
necessary for it to function effectively.

Educational Personnel Development Programs must do the following: (1) Shift from the current emphasis on providing opportunities to experience, to a performance base. The outcomes of the program must be specified in terms of knowledge, skills, attitudes, sensitivities, competencies, and so on. (2) Shift from a primary focus upon knowledge and skill mastery to one of product development. The production of tangible products involves, for example, the completion of instructional tasks resulting in specified learning outcomes in children and the completion of instructional support tasks resulting in products such as a "unit" of instruction, an examination, a curriculum guide, a course evaluation plan. (3) Shift from a data-free to a data-dependent mode of operation--the collection of data on teacher mastery of skills, knowledges, effictiveness, and relation of these data to the teacher preparation program. (4) Shift from a training function to a research, development, and training function. (5) Shift from an impersonal, instructor oriented environment to one that is personalized and student oriented. (6) Shift from a college or university centered program to a field centered program. (7) Shift from a narrow decision-making base to one that is broader--comprising schools, university, students, community, and professional groups.

The proposal would establish on a cost-sharing basis illustrative state-wide networks (see Figure 4) of Centers for the Preparation of Educational Personnel (CPEP). Each Center would have the organizational characteristics of a Training Complex and the operational characteristics of one or more of the Elementary Models. The Training Complex provides the context within which skills and competencies can be developed and demonstrated. The design of the CPEP should keep in mind that the Center is seen as an integral part of all teacher education programs within a state and not simply a demonstration program; that it is a context within which only selected aspects of any given teacher education program will be conducted; and that it will be developed around exemplary elementary-secondary programs. Centers would identify competencies to be demonstrated at the product level, carry out assessment techniques, and provide training leading to the demonstration of specified competencies. The Center would use protocol, training, and integrating materials that are available and sonconant with the program. It follows that in order for a state to adopt a competency-based plan of certification at the product level, the state must first establish a network of Centers where competency can be demonstrated.

The state is proposed as the primary unit of organization for the network, with regional linkages: certification is a state responsibility and legislation, funding sources, and many institutions may be primarily defined by state boundaries. The rationale for cost-sharing between state and federal governments rests on the importance of education nationally, and a need to demonstrate commitment at both levels.

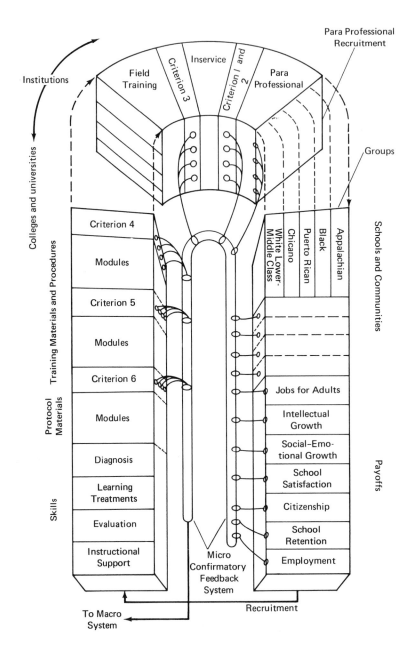

Figure 5. Micro Confirmatory-Feedback System

Each state-wide network initially funded could serve
as a "pilot" state in relation to a region, and assume
responsibility for establishing regional linkages, and
perhaps establish demonstration programs within other
states. Within each state, one or more of the Centers
would have the functions of research, development, evaluation, and diffusion. (other branches of OE could
support the research and evaluation functions.) Each
network of Centers would link to industry for assistance
in the design and development of its instructional and
support systems so materials, etc., can be produced and
marketed. It is also proposed that diffusion networks be
established.

PROGRAMMATIC THEMES AND MECHANISMS: PROPOSAL E

The contention in this paper is that successful reform
in teacher education should focus on two themes: the development of a nation-wide system for confirmation of the
outcomes of teacher education; and the development of
curriculum intervention strategies to increase the power of
teacher education programs.

The nation-wide system for confirmation arises from
the idea of performance-based teacher education and certification, and can be clearly spelled out in six criterion
levels. At Criterion Level 1 observation of teacher performance are linked to pupil outcomes, sampled over a two-year
period; at the lowest level, teachers in preparation would
demonstrate understanding of concepts and principles. It
is proposed that for teacher education programs Criterion
Levels 6 through 3 be operationalized. For a Micro
Confirmatory-Feedback System, the criterion levels can be
related to training as shown in Figure 5.

Figure 5 shows "Payoff Categories--Skills" in the lower
left-hand corner (increased skill in diagnosing pupil status
and learning difficulties, giving learning treatments,
evaluating, and the instructional support domain). Inter-
secting the training at various points are three levels of
performance criteria--Levels 6,5, and 4. Criterion data at
each level are fed into the Micro Confirmatory-Feedback
System. Following the teacher preparatory phase, the
prospective teacher would enter a training school or
center for specific field training (assessed at Criterion
Level 3). After entering regular teaching, and engaging
in inservice work, permanent certification could rest on
performance criteria at Levels 1 or 2. The final block in
Figure 5 represents schools and their communities. At the
end are the main items which are payoffs from the entire
micro-system, including the number of persons from the
poverty community trained as paraprofessionals, pupils'
school achievement and social-emotional growth, satisfaction
with the schools, school retention rates, rate and type of
employment after school, etc. The Micro Confirmatory-
Feedback System functions to confirm performance, to return
information at each phase of the training system, and as an

259

information flow to the macro-system, the National Confirmatory System.

In curriculum intervention, it is proposed that the teacher education curriculum be developed around instructional modules and incorporate two types of laboratory instruction. Many of the modules would lend themselves best to instruction under laboratory conditions: those which require the interpretation of behavior shown on film or video tape and those which require the student to examine, produce, acquire, or exhibit a skill. Each teacher education program should be characterized by a large, in-house component of laboratory-based instruction in which problems in the interpretation of behavior are solved and in which teaching skills are practiced. In the later portions of the curriculum, the student should move from the in-house laboratory to a field-based laboratory. The development of modules would be tied to the protocol and training materials development programs.

To institute curriculum reform, a concentration strategy is proposed. NSF funded the support of computers and their utilization on college campuses until the computer utilization was sufficiently established to eliminate external support (and funds were then rotated to new institutions). Sufficient funds could be made available to selected institutions to permit them to reorganize their curriculum to incorporate all of the developments--modular construction, protocol and training materials and laboratory-based instruction, as well as participation in some type of field-based training center. External funds would then be withdrawn and placed elsewhere.